A BRITISH BOY IN FASCIST ITALY

PETER GHIRINGHELLI

The
History
Press

Cover illustrations. Front, top, left: Benito Mussolini (*London Illustrated News*); *top, right*: flag of the RSI; *middle*: author's ID card photo, 1944; *bottom*: author in Hong Kong, 1952. *Back*: Italian immigrants from Manchester and Leeds, 1910.

First published 2010

The History Press
The Mill, Brimscombe Port
Stroud, Gloucestershire, GL5 2QG
www.thehistorypress.co.uk

British Library Cataloguing in Publication Data.
A catalogue record for this book is available from the British Library.

ISBN 978 0 7524 5343 9

Typesetting and origination by The History Press
Printed in Great Britain
Manufacturing managed by Jellyfish Print Solutions Ltd

Contents

Abbreviations

British

ARP	Air Raid Precautions
HMS	His Majesty's Ship
ILH-KR	Imperial Light Horse and Kimberley Regiment
Lt-Cdr	Lieutenant Commander
SS	Steamship (as prefix to ships' names)

Italian

Anti-fascist:

CLN	Comitato di Liberazione Nazionale (Committee for National Liberation)
CLNAI	Comitato di Liberazione Nazionale per l'Alta Italia (Committee for National Liberation for Northern Italy)
GAP	Gruppi di Azione Patriotica (Patriotic Action Groups)
PSI	Partito Socialista Italiana (Italian Socialist Party)

Fascist:

ENR	Esercito Nazionale Republicano (National Republican Army)
GIL	Gioventù Italiana del Littorio (Italian Fascist Youth Movement)
GNR	Guardia Nazionale Republicana (Republican National Guard)
MVSN	Milizia Volontaria per la Sicurezza Nazionale (National Militia for National Security)
ONB	Opera Nazionale Balilla (Italian Fascist Youth Movement)
RSI	Republica Sociale Italiana (Italian Social Republic)

X-MAS   Decima Flottiglia Motoscafi Antisommergibili (Tenth Anti-
             Submarine Torpedo Boats Squadron)

rastrellamento Literally 'a raking', but used to describe anti-partisan operations
             and searches carried out by Republican Fascist and German
             forces

German

KdS	Kommandure Sipo-SD
	(SD Regional Command)
SD	Sicherheitsdienst (Security Service)
SS	Schutzstaffel (Elite Guard)
SS–Aussenposten	SS Forward Commands
SS–Oberstgruppenführer	SS Colonel-General
SS–Gruppenführer	SS Lieutenant-General
SS–Hauptsturmführer	SS Captain
SS–Sturmbannführer	SS Major
SS–Scharführer	SS Sergeant
SS–Rottenführer	SS Corporal

INTRODUCTION

More than an introduction, I think a word of explanation is required. Between June 2003 and January 2006, the BBC asked the public to contribute their stories of World War Two to a website called 'WW2 People's War'. The submitted material, amounting to 47,000 articles and 15,000 images, is now permanently archived.

In November 2003, after several prompts from my wife Margaret, I decided to submit my story under the title *A Childhood in Nazi-occupied Italy*. The limit for submitted contributions was 2,000 words and I condensed my story to fit that limit. Then in late 2008 Sophie Bradshaw, a commissioning editor for The History Press, having read my account, contacted me and suggested that I should expand it for publication. This book is the result.

I kept no diaries in Italy, nor did I subsequently write anything down, so all is based on my memory. The problem, of course, is that human memory is fallible. I wrote my story for 'WW2 People's War' exactly as I remembered it, but afterwards when I came to consult others, especially those in Italy, I found that I had often been mistaken in dating events. Unfortunately, it is not possible now to access my original BBC account to correct it. Wherever there is a discrepancy between the two versions, the one given here, based on detailed research, is the more accurate.

Throughout the book, *Fascist* (spelt with a capital F) refers to members of the Italian Fascist Party, and *Partisan* (with a capital P) refers to a member of an Italian Partisan Group, otherwise I have used lowercase. Where *fascist* and *partisan* appear in cited official documents, I have retained the original lowercase.

I should like to thank my dear friend Clara Fortunelli in Vicenza for track-ing down obscure books in Vicenza's public library and scanning pages for me; also Roberto Rivolta, a boyhood friend, now living in Luino on Lake Maggiore, for reminding me of events and shared experiences and sending me photos; and Pancrazio De Micheli in Porto Valtravaglia for giving me per-mission to publish photos of years gone by, which have appeared in a series of yearly calendars of the Valtravaglia, for which he is the co-ordinator; and finally Margaret, my wife, who has been a great help in patiently reading and correcting the manuscript.

I

Pre-war Days in Leeds

For many decades after the Second World War, those who had lived through the war divided time and their lives into two distinct periods, always known as 'before the war' and 'after the war'. 'Before the war' is a half-forgotten age, a different world, a dim and distant past. Leeds before the war was a black city, literally; all its stone buildings were black with decades of grime and soot, typical of a northern industrial city, before the post-war Clean Air Act was introduced and the many splendid Victorian municipal buildings sand-blasted clean. Gas lamps were everywhere and gas lamp lighters still made their rounds carrying lamp-post ladders; known as 'knocker-uppers', they also knocked on bedroom windows to wake people up for work in the mills and factories. There were no pedestrianised areas or one-way traffic systems then; it was a city of clanking trams, solid-tyred lorries, many cars, but even more bicycles and horse-drawn carts, and the roads had many water troughs for horses to drink from. Order started to be made of the traffic chaos in 1934 with the introduction of the Transport Secretary Leslie Hore-Belisha's pedestrian crossings, with glass orange lights which inevitably became known as Belisha Beacons, the forerunners of post-war zebra crossings. Life in Leeds seemed to be regulated by factory whistles and sirens, especially at five and six o'clock, when thousands of factory workers poured out onto the streets on foot and on bicycles, and long queues formed at tram stops.

But my father wasn't a factory worker; he was a knife grinder, an Italian immigrant who had arrived in Leeds in 1920 at the age of 16. He came to work for Peter Maturi, an uncle by marriage, a cutler who had emigrated to Leeds in the late 1890s. My father didn't look like the stereotypical olive-skinned Italian; he had fair hair and grey-blue eyes, probably inherited from his mother, Mathilde Skenk, of Austrian descent who was from the South Tyrol; my paternal grandfather, who I never met, was also a fair-complexioned northern Italian. My father had a flair for languages and was already fluent in French as well as Italian (most Italians then spoke regional dialects and not Italian), and he quickly learned English both spoken and written.

My mother, Elena Granelli, on the other hand, despite her Italian name, neither spoke nor understood any language other than English. She was born in Leeds in February 1905. Her parents, Ferdinando and Maria (*née* Molinari), were initially ice cream makers who had also settled in Leeds in the late nineteenth century. My mother, in her late teens, sold ice cream from a cart in Leeds City Market, and that is where she met my father. He worked nearby in George Street and used to pass her as he came into the market on Fridays with a large basket to collect knives and cleavers for sharpening from the butchers' stalls. Friday was a traditional fish day and was the best day for butchers to have their knives, cleavers and saws sharpened.

Elena, always known as Nellie, was the eldest of five children; the others were Rosa, Millie, Louis and John. Rosa was taken to Italy while still an infant because the fogs and industrial smoke-polluted air of Leeds gave her severe respiratory problems, and her parents thought that she would stand a better chance of surviving babyhood in the fresh mountain air of the Apennines, where they both originated from. Rosa never returned to England; she was brought up in Pianlavagnolo, a tiny hamlet high above Santa Maria del Taro in the region of Emilia, my grandfather's home village, and she eventually married and settled there.

My parents married in Leeds in 1928 and I was born in June 1930 in Lady Lane. The rooms they rented are now long demolished and replaced by an office block. However, my earliest recollection is of our rented semi-detached house in Longroyd Street, in the Hunslet district of Leeds. Then recently built, and most unusual for those days, it had a bathroom with separate toilet, hot and cold water, and a front garden. My father was forever trying to invent things. He would dismantle old clocks and crystal wireless sets and experiment with them and reassemble them. A couple of years after the GPO introduced the black Bakelite Type 232 combined telephone set in 1934, my father brought home about twenty old candlestick Type 150 telephones and dismantled them. From the parts he tried to make a perpetual motion machine and was forever tinkering and adjusting it, convinced that it could be done. I need hardly add that perpetual motion is impossible, but my father was entirely self-taught and, not knowing that perpetual motion would violate both the first and second laws of thermodynamics, he just kept tinkering away.

His inventiveness did pay off in another way and by the mid-1930s my father was making a good living. This came about because he had constructed a mobile grinding contraption out of spare car parts and a motorcycle he had owned when courting my mother. He had adapted the engine to drive the grindstone through the modified gearbox, which also drove the two motor-bike wheels at walking pace, giving it full mobility. It attracted much attention and was photographed and featured in a local paper. As well as doing his rounds, he still worked in George Street, especially on Fridays when hundreds of girls in scarves and shawls, workers in the many clothiers and tailors, brought in their scissors and shears to be sharpened, some with dozens of scissors from their co-workers.

We lived well and, again, most unusually for those days, by 1937 my mother had a Hoover vacuum cleaner, an automatic washing machine and an electric iron; this at a time when many Leeds houses didn't have electricity and women used a pair of flat irons, made of solid cast iron, with one on a gas ring heating while ironing with the other. No one, of course, had refrigerators. I have good cause to remember the washing machine. After the wash, the water was discharged from the machine via a flexible pipe which terminated in an aluminium u-bend hooked onto a sink; but the only way to get the water flowing was to create a vacuum by sucking briefly on the pipe. I had watched my mother do this many times and one day, while she was away from the washing machine, I picked up the discharge pipe and sucked hard and long, filling my mouth with very hot water and caustic soda, almost instantly burning my throat and then drenching me. I tried to shout but all that came out was a strangled cry. Fortunately, my mother came quickly to my rescue. Those were the days long before Health & Safety regulations were even dreamt of!

We also had a five-valve wireless set and my dad put up a long wire antenna in the back garden so that he could listen to Italian long-wave radio transmissions. Of course, by then all the Italian news was fascist propaganda. In the late 1920s my father joined the Italian *Fascisti all'Estero* (Fascists Abroad) association led from Rome by Giuseppe Bastianini[1] through Italian consulates abroad. Meetings were held in the Italian consulate office in Bradford and we used to travel there by tram, changing to Bradford trams at the Leeds terminus. These were social occasions and there was always an Italian buffet and a dance to Italian records.

Until 1935 I hadn't realised that I was different from the other boys in the street, but in that year, with the Italian aggressive invasion of Abyssinia (modern-day Ethiopia), all that changed quite dramatically for me. I started to be bullied at the Protestant primary school I attended at the top of Longroyd Street. I started school at an early age because I could read from the age of 3 or 4. I cannot remember how this came about, but my mother used to sit me on her knee and read to me and gradually I associated the words she spoke with the letters on the page and soon I was reading whole sentences. None of this helped me in the schoolyard at playtime, however. Two incidents in particular stay in my mind. In one incident I was violently pushed in the locker room and cut the back of my head on the low coat hooks. The other happened in the playground when a group of boys, calling me a dirty 'eyetie', held me down on the ground and, with my mouth covered, made me inhale continually from a bottle of smelling salts. It was the worst pain I had ever experienced, and when they released me I was unable to get up for a few minutes. When we got back into class I tried to tell the teacher what had happened, but I got little sympathy from her and she gave me a short lecture about not going behind people's backs telling tales. I went back to my desk and sat in a daze; later I was asked a question but I didn't hear it and couldn't answer even when it was repeated, so I was hauled out and made to stand in a corner wearing a dunce's cap, a tall cone of white paper marked with a capital D which was used for this purpose. I went to school the next day but this time, at playtime, I squeezed through a gap in the bent iron railings and went home and told my mother that I didn't want to go back, but without explaining why. She took me back to school, of course, but at the weekend my father finally got out of me what had happened. This resulted in him explaining to me what Italy, Italians and 'Eyeties' were, and showing me drawings of the Italian Tricolour and the Union Jack, demonstrating which was which; all very confusing for a boy of 5.

In October 1935, in response to the Italian invasion of Abyssinia, the League of Nations imposed limited and ineffectual sanctions on Italy, and in a theatrical response Mussolini called on all Italian wives to donate their wedding rings, together with any other gold, silver or bronze trinkets or copper artefacts they might have. This culminated on 18 December 1935, which was declared *La giornata della fede* (Wedding Ring Day). In exchange for their wedding rings, donors were given a steel ring with XIV ANNO FASCISTA – ORO ALLA PATRIA (14th year of the Fascist Era – Gold to the Fatherland) inscribed either externally or internally, as preferred, in a mock-leather presentation case.

The collection was also made in Britain, and for this memorable occasion the Italian Ambassador, Dino Grandi,[2] came up from London to the consulate in Bradford to preside over the ceremony. I can remember my mother giving up her gold wedding ring there. To applause, all the married women walked up to a basket before him and placed their gold wedding rings in it as 'a gift' to Il Duce, and in return Grandi gave them their steel wedding rings (*fede d'acciao*). My mother had absolutely no interest in politics then or subsequently, but she was a very devout Catholic, as were most Italian women. In Catholicism marriage is regarded as a holy sacrament and the blessed wedding ring is part of that sacrament. But in this case the political stunt was sanctioned by the Church. Setting an example in Italy, in a blaze of publicity, the Archbishop of Bologna, Nasalli Rocca, donated his gold pastoral cross, and Queen Elena gave her wedding ring. The Bishop of Civita Castellana went further: on 8 December 1935 he sent his pastoral cross to Mussolini, saying: 'I thank Almighty God for permitting me to see these days of epic grandeur.'[3] And in October 1935 the Archbishop of Milan, Cardinal Idelfonso Schuster, celebrated a double event in his cathedral which was given maximum publicity: a *Te Deum* for the anniversary of the Fascist March on Rome, together with a blessing of pennants of Fascist units; in his words, 'of the army of men engaged in carrying the light of civilization to Abyssinia'.

'The Italian flag,' he said, 'is at the moment bringing in triumph the Cross of Christ in Ethiopia, to free the road for the emancipation of the slaves, opening it at the same time to our missionary propaganda.'[4] With such examples, any religious qualms my mother and other wives might have had were swept away. However, my grandmother was not convinced, and what happened to the gold is anybody's guess!

Following this I was sent to a Catholic school, St Joseph's, where I wasn't bullied. Most of the kids were sons of Irish immigrants and the rest were English Catholics. But it was a long daily walk to school across Hunslet Moor, nothing unusual in those days, and no boy, heaven forbid, ever went to school accompanied by his mother.

For me, the big event of 1935 was the birth of my sister Gloria Maria. She was born at home, as was usual in those days, and about a week before she was born I went to stay with a kind English Protestant couple, the grandparents of my best friend Peter who lived a couple of doors away. His grandparents lived a few miles away, but closer to my new school, my own grandparents being too far away. I have a vivid recollection of this, particularly of their hissing gas lights in the living room and bedrooms, and having to go to the outside privy with a candle. I also recall being given sweet rice pudding and lettuce without olive oil and vinegar dressing. My mother had strongly advised me never to mention that we put olive oil on salad. In those days English working and middle classes were not as cosmopolitan as they are now in their diet, and olive oil was only sold in small bottles in chemist shops for medicinal purposes, chiefly for earache. My father bought olive oil in 5-litre cans from an Italian merchant in Leeds market, where we also got our spaghetti and rice, among other things. Peter's grandparents also very kindly gave me Heinz tinned spaghetti and I think they were somewhat surprised when I didn't recognise it as being anything like proper food. I was glad to get home and meet my new sister a few days after her arrival on 20 September.

My father was an excellent cook; indeed, he was far better than my mother. She prepared our daily meals, but if it was a special event, such as Christmas or Easter, or a dinner with friends, he did all the cooking. I remember those meals as very festive occasions; there would be salami, olives and *prosciutto* (now known as Parma ham) for an antipasto, followed by clear chicken soup (made from the giblets, skin and neck of the chicken). Then there would be risotto made from the chicken stock, always with saffron and dried *porcini* mushrooms, collected by my father in local woods and served with chicken topped with freshly grated Parmesan cheese; and the meal ended with fresh fruit and cheese, liqueurs and a small cup of black, concentrated, freshly ground coffee. At those meals we had wine, nearly always 2-litre straw-covered flasks of Chianti, and from about the age of 5 I too had a glass of wine mixed with water. It is hard to imagine now, but chicken, especially a capon, was an infrequent delicacy in those days. Poultry was all open farm reared and bought fully feathered, to be plucked and cleaned at home; the battery hen system hadn't been thought of then. I especially remember Hunslet Feast, as the annual fair on Hunslet Moor was called; among the coconut shies, freak shows and steam-driven shamrock swings and roundabouts, there was Chicken Joe's stall always doing a roaring trade with a crowd around him listening to his patter. My dad always bought a plump capon from him for a treat the following Sunday.

Another pre-war event which stuck clearly in my mind was the sight of the German Zeppelin airship *Hindenburg*,[5] flying very slowly over Leeds at a very low height on a clear sunny afternoon in the summer of 1936. It was so low that it gave the impression that it was about to land. This was at a time when even seeing an aeroplane in the sky was a most unusual sight. It was also the first time I had seen the swastika other than as a small drawing; there were two large ones on the rear fins of the airship. An MP for Leeds raised the matter in the Commons with the Under-Secretary of State for Air, Sir Phillip Sassoon, asking him if he was aware that on 30 June the German airship *Hindenburg* flew for the second time within a few weeks at a low altitude over Leeds. That this was a photographic mapping mission seems pretty obvious now, but at the time the government flippantly dismissed the suggestion.[6]

Shortly after this I caught scarlet fever. Today it is not considered to be a serious disease and has been practically eradicated in Britain. With a short course of antibiotics it is now easily cured, but this was far from being the case then. I was taken to Seacroft Isolation Hospital and put in an isolation room. A few days later my parents were allowed to visit me, but I hardly recognised them in long white gowns, white bonnets and face masks. A few days after this I was given a wrong injection which left me paralysed down my left side. My pillows were taken away and I was flat on my back for several weeks. At frequent intervals I had nosebleeds, and to stem these long strands of cotton wool were stuffed up my nose. On two occasions I pulled the cotton wool out as I could hardly breathe, but after the second incident my hands were put into cotton mittens day and night, and only taken off when the nurse washed me. I was fed on liquids from a pot container with a spout. On a couple of occasions, having called for the nurse several times for a urinal glass without getting a response, I wet my bed. A clean urinal glass was kept in my bedside locker but, unable to move, I couldn't get to it. The result was a real ticking off and an uncomfortable rubber sheet being placed under me. I was told that it would not be removed until I learnt not to wet the bed. All trivial, but the injustice of it still rankles with me.

Eventually, after what seemed to me like months, I was discharged and moved to a children's convalescent home in Roundhay, on the then outskirts of Leeds. After a few weeks there, on the spur of the moment, one evening I absconded. I walked to Roundhay Park tram terminus and took the tram to Leeds city centre and made my way to George Street, where I knew my father would be. The next day I was taken back to the convalescent home to apologise and collect my things, and that was the end of that. I went back to St Joseph's school, although now I was supposed to have a weak heart and I wasn't allowed to run or take part in games at school.

Meanwhile, my mother's parents had prospered and now ran a sweetshop and tobacconists in Meadow Lane, Holbeck, adjacent to the Palace picture

house. I used to love being taken to visit my grandparents, almost weekly, by
my mother. My grandmother baked all her own bread and made marvellous
Yorkshire pudding. One day, shortly after my recovery, we visited my grandmother's only to discover that my mother's youngest brother, my Uncle John,
had run away from home. He was only eight years older than me, so he was
about 16 or 17 at the time. None of us had private telephones then, so it was a
few days after the event that my mother found out. In fact, he had joined the
Argyll and Sutherland Highlanders, and after his initial training in Scotland
he appeared home on leave in full Highland dress, complete with busby, kilt,
sporran and white spats. To me he looked magnificent and I was awestruck.
However, as he was not yet 18 my grandmother promptly bought him out of
the army and he became an apprentice engineer. Johnny, as he was known,
was a great character and had a lasting influence on me. When war broke
out he volunteered as a fighter pilot in the RAF along with his school friend
Charlie 'Chuck' Coltate, but he failed the stringent medical examination with
a perforated ear drum and was rejected, whereupon Chuck withdrew his
own volunteer application. Later, when Italy entered the war, as the son of an
enemy alien the only options open for John to serve his country were either
the Pioneer Corps or the Merchant Navy; he volunteered for the latter, as
did Chuck. Both served as engineering officers on the same ships. Their first
ship was torpedoed and sunk in the Atlantic. The ship had been at the front of
a large convoy and they and other survivors remained in the water until the
last ship fortuitously picked them up. It had been a close call; other ships had
sailed by as convoy vessels were not allowed to stop.

They then both served on the SS *Sacramento*, which sailed from Hull to New
York throughout the rest of the war. Shortly after the war, Johnny married
Margaret Callaghan, who had served as a Land Army girl, and they emigrated
to Canada in the 1950s and settled in Manitoba. Johnny never spoke about
the war and I only heard about his ordeal from Margaret many years later,
although she now cannot remember the name of the ship.

In 1938 we moved from Longroyd Street, 'flitted' was the term then used,
to a new detached house at the top end of Dewsbury Road, within walking
distance of the newly opened Rex cinema. In pre-war Leeds there were
dozens of cinemas, all well attended, and it was a regular thing to see long
queues in the evening for the latest films. It was called 'going to the pictures';
no one ever called them 'films' or 'movies', and cinemas were called 'picture
houses'; the shows were continuous and you could stay in as long as you
wished. Even the smallest picture houses had a uniformed 'commissionaire',

usually a retired army warrant officer, with a peaked cap and white gloves. When business was slack he would stand outside and bellow 'Seats in all parts!', or if there were queues he would decide how many went in at a time. The format was always the same: a short topical feature; a cartoon; the B film; the news and next week's trailers; then the main feature film, followed by *God Save the King*, at which everybody stood up.

The main picture houses in the centre of Leeds, among others, were the Assembly Rooms, the Paramount, the Gaumont, the Majestic, the Ritz and the Scala. These were all sumptuous picture palaces, some with electric organs which rose out of the floor during the intervals. At the Paramount there was community singing with the entire audience singing along to the lyrics projected on the screen, with a white dot bouncing along the words in time to the organ music. At the Queen's Theatre in Meadow Lane around 1934 or 1935, possibly one of the first times I had been to a picture house, there were still live variety acts on stage between films, such as jugglers and ventriloquists. The Queen's was one of the very last cinemas to do this. I used to go to the pictures regularly and often, like other kids my age, alone. If it was an 'A' film, where kids under 16 had to be in the company of an adult, you would ask any couple or single woman to take you in, always on the strict understanding that you wouldn't sit with them or pester them once you got your ticket. I got in this way to see Richard Tauber in *Heart's Desire* by mistake; I had thought the main film was *King Kong*, which I eventually saw the following week. This was at a picture house on my way to St Joseph's school (the name of which I forget, possibly the Parkfield in Jack Lane); it was a second-rate cinema so it must have been long after both films were released.

For my eighth birthday I had a special treat in town when my mother took me to the Scala to see *Snow White and the Seven Dwarfs*, which had just been released. Another treat that year was *The Adventures of Robin Hood* in brilliant Technicolor, and in late 1939 *The Hunchback of Notre Dame* starring Charles Laughton. The very last major film I remember seeing just after the war broke out was *The Four Feathers*, also in Technicolor, at the Pavilion in Dewsbury Road, along with a short film on air-raid precautions, what to do with incendiary bombs and how to cope in a gas attack. We really should have worn gas masks in picture houses for you could hardly breathe for cigarette smoke, and clouds of it could always be seen billowing in the film projection beam.

It's a wonder, too, that we all survived without our feet dropping off. In the mid-1930s it became a craze for all the best shoe shops to have a shoe-fitting x-ray machine. Often these contraptions, known as pedoscopes, were placed in the shop entrance to attract customers. Like lots of children, I often used to put my foot in to see the bones of my foot, complete with the eyelets and nails of my footwear, blissfully unaware of the potential danger. In those days not even physicists had any inkling how lethal x-ray radiation is. I also had a kit of moulds for lead soldiers and farm animals. The idea was that you melted down your broken lead figures over a gas ring, or by burning old paint in a tin, and then poured the molten lead into the moulds. I used to make lead paperweights. But most sought-after of all the metals was mercury; if anyone had some he would proudly bring it to school in silver paper to show off.

At the time of the Munich crisis, in September 1938, we were all issued with gas masks. They were kept in a cardboard box with string to sling over your shoulder and were carried at all times. Everyone was under the impression that there was a legal requirement to do so, but although there wasn't, the effect was the same, with people getting sacked from their employment for turning up to work without their gas mask, and accused of putting themselves and others at risk in the event of a gas attack, for it was widely believed that the war would start with bombing and deadly poison gas.

Very quickly shops began to sell leather and cloth covers for the government-issue cardboard boxes and alternative containers for gas masks, and I remember that I had a brown canvas cover for mine. At first we got into trouble for always trying them on, but the novelty soon wore off and we got to hate gas drill at school as the masks smelt of rubber and quickly fogged up. Rubbing a sliced raw potato on the inside of the visor was supposed to prevent this but it never seemed to work.

In early 1939 we got our Anderson air-raid shelter. I think it must have been February or early March as I remember that the frozen ground was still too hard for my father to dig, and the curved corrugated steel sections of the shelter lay in the garden for weeks before he dug the required deep hole and fitted it in. Contrary to what many thought, protection came from the thick layer of earth that was placed over it, and the instructions were that the excavated earth should be used for this purpose, but you still saw many with the bare shelter only partly dug in. These shelters were only issued to houses with gardens, of course, and my grandfather's house and shop didn't have one, so they had to use a public air-raid shelter. At first these shelters were little more than trenches dug in public parks; they had started to appear during the Munich crisis, as had huge round open tanks of water for fire-fighting.

From time to time my dad hired a car for trips to the seaside. The last time he did so was in the early summer of 1939 when we all went to Scarborough for the day. I don't remember anything of that day except the return journey, during which, to the consternation of my mother, my dad put his foot down on a straight stretch and triumphantly announced: 'We're doing sixty!' This was the fastest I had ever travelled, other than on a train, and it seemed to me as if we were flying. It never occurred to me that this would be the last time I would be in a car for the next six years.

2

THE PHONEY WAR

The prospect of war in 1939 seemed very exciting. Already we were beginning to see searchlights criss-crossing the sky at night, spectacularly lighting up the undersides of clouds. Right next door to the Crescent cinema, at the top of Dewsbury Road, there was a toyshop which specialised in lead soldiers. Up until then these had been primarily cowboys and Indians, along with cavalry troopers and red-coated infantrymen, but a new range appeared from about 1938. These were small lead soldiers in khaki and black berets, mostly in a seated position, with a peg on their undersides which slotted into location holes in the seats of model half-tracks, lorries (as trucks were then called), and anti-aircraft guns and searchlights; others were standing in various positions. The model tanks had realistic-looking chain tracks and cost as much as 2s 6d, a small fortune for someone on 6d weekly pocket money. I saved up and bought an anti-aircraft gun, for about 9d I think, to start my collection. I use the word loosely, for my entire collection eventually consisted of that single gun and a 15cwt truck with three soldiers in the back. But at the time I was far more interested in the daring deeds of Desperate Dan in the *Dandy* than I was of an impending war. I had the comic on order at the newsagents since the first issue on Friday 4 December 1937, and also the *Beano* which first came out in July 1938. Had I kept them they would have been a cracking investment; there are now only twelve known copies of the first edition of the *Beano*, and in 2004 one sold for £12,400; a first edition of the *Dandy* went for £20,350 that same year! My mum paid 2d each for mine, along with her *Picture Post* and *Radio Times*.

All boys I knew collected cigarette cards which we generally played for either by flicking them at a wall or by playing marbles, taws as we called them, and I ended up with a large collection of cards held by elastic bands. In 1938 Will's Cigarettes issued an ARP (Air-Raid Precautions) series and we were all wised up on the use of the stirrup pump and how to deal with an incendiary bomb with a bucket of sand, with instructions on how to nail a wet carpet to a door in the event of a gas attack; clearly the cigarette manufacturers believed that adults couldn't be trusted in these matters.

Meanwhile, Leeds was being transformed: public buildings were now almost hidden behind barricades of sandbags, leaving only narrow corridors through to their entrances, and public air-raid trenches continued to extend. And so we all drifted serenely into war.

On Sunday 3 September at eleven o'clock, Chamberlain's announcement of the declaration of war on Germany, following their attack on Poland, almost came as an anticlimax; we had been told since early morning to stand by for an important broadcast. I remember it principally because almost as soon as he had finished telling us that we were at war there was an air-raid warning, which turned out to be a false alarm. I remember it also because shortly afterwards that same morning, the BBC announcer said, in his plummy accent, that with immediate effect all theatres and cinemas would be permanently closed. I was more upset over this than by the actual declaration of war, especially when it was explained to me that cinemas were picture houses. It made no difference that day because no cinemas opened on a Sunday back then, but the prospect of not seeing Laurel and Hardy or Will Hay again filled me with dismay; the seriousness of war was beginning to sink in. The banning of bonfires was also a blow to me. The last one I saw was on Guy Fawkes' Night on Holbeck Moor, memorable because the pile of old planks, crates and boxes was truly colossal and, with several Leeds civic dignitaries in attendance, it was lit by Amy Johnson.[1] Huge crowds turned out to see her on that unforgettable night.

In compensation, things immediately got exciting with the introduction of the blackout, and Leeds at night was plunged into total darkness. People now have little idea what a blackout is, especially when there was a new moon or on a cloudy night, from October to March; the nearest you can get to imagining it is by closing your eyes. All advertising lights, shop windows, street lighting of any kind and outdoor house lights were switched off, resulting in pitch blackness; cars would suddenly loom up out of the darkness with a dim light shining from small slits on their covered headlights. Tram windows had some sort of netting with slits to see where you were, which was fine in daylight but useless at night; they drove along clanking their bells every few yards as they had done for years in fog. Not a chink of light was permitted from houses, and for the first few days until the blackout was perfected there were constant yells of 'Put that light out!' from the patrolling air-raid wardens.

After about a fortnight things eased off; cinemas and theatres were allowed to re-open and people were permitted to use torches, providing they were shone downwards. There was a rush on torchlight batteries and heavy material for curtaining, and for white and luminous paint for kerbs and pathways. Actually, the blackout was imposed a few days before war was declared and initially there was much grumbling about it. The problem was that the blackout couldn't be turned on at a moment's notice like just drawing a curtain; it had to be laboriously put in place and usually involved brown paper on a wooden frame, blankets, blinds and finally the heavy material curtains, with a trip outside in all weather to inspect for chinks of light. All this meant that you had to start putting up 'the blackout', as it was called, well before it got dark, and then you had to take it all down and stow it away in the morning. On top of this, we used shaded lights with bulbs of low wattage. After a few weeks we didn't bother too much with the bedroom windows other than using simple blackout curtains and candles. I used a torch to read in bed, sometimes reading under the bedclothes when I had been told to switch it off and stop wasting the battery.

I found it all exhilarating until one day I went to the Palace picture house next door to my grandparents' shop and saw *The Face at the Window*, a film about a series of murders blamed on a wolf-man whose face loomed up at the window terrifying his victims. Up until that point I hadn't had a care in the world, but on coming out of the picture house into the blackout I developed an instantaneous and irrational fear of the dark; it was a stupid phobia which made my life a misery. I told no one, certainly not my mates, and to combat it I used to force myself to blow out my candle upstairs before getting into bed. This phobia, always fuelled by the ghostly face at the window, persisted, but the blackout and being afraid of the dark was not the best mix, and I used to dread my mother asking me to go outside and check if any light was showing from our windows, making lame excuses to put it off as long as possible. By an odd coincidence, a few months after I returned to England after the war, *The Face at the Window* was at the same cinema and I saw it again. It turned out to have a silly plot, more ridiculous than horrifying, and any remaining traces of my fear of the dark vanished there and then.

Newsreels suddenly became very exciting for boys like me, with their reports of daring deeds and dastardly acts at sea, but undoubtedly they were very worrying for adults. On the first day of the war the British passenger liner SS *Athenia* was torpedoed without warning south of Rockall Bank in the North Atlantic, with the loss of 118 lives.[2] She was sunk by U-boat *U-30*, commanded by Lt Fritz-Julius Lemp, who had mistaken her for an auxiliary cruiser. Those drowned included women, children and twenty-eight American citizens. The German command first learned of the sinking from the BBC news. Fully realising the implications, Hitler ordered that the matter be flatly denied. But Goebbels, the Nazi propaganda minister, went further and absurdly claimed that the British Admiralty had deliberately ordered the sinking of the *Athenia* to gain favour with neutral states and to bring the USA into the war.

Many merchant ships were sunk by mines and torpedoes almost daily throughout the war with barely a mention in the press, but the *Athenia* made headlines and was extensively covered in cinema newsreels in the following weeks because the incident came within hours of Chamberlain's BBC announcement of war.

Then came the evacuation, and many children were taken by train to live in the country, away from the cities which were expected to be heavily bombed. There was a real mass exodus and I rather envied all these children, reported in the newspapers as crowding the railway stations and cheerfully waving goodbye. Judging from the newsreels they all seemed to be going on holiday.

Because so few of us remained, many schools closed down and pupils were gathered at fewer locations. St Joseph's school was closed and I was allocated to St Francis' Catholic school in Holbeck, the school to which my mother and her sister and brothers had gone. It had a very good reputation and my mother always had fond memories of it, and I was looking forward to going. But I don't think I learned anything there except to keep my mouth shut. I learnt that lesson on the second or third day when we had the inevitable gas mask drill during morning assembly. For this the Mother Superior blew a whistle, the shrill old type with a pea in it such as football referees use, whereupon we all smartly opened our gas mask cases at the ready; she then blew her whistle again and we put our masks on. There followed an interminable ARP talk on the dangers of gas; she went on and on and my gas mask visor began to fog up. Since it was blindingly obvious that this was an exercise with no gas, even to me as a child, I put a finger between my cheek and the rubber of the mask to let some air in to clear the visor. The whistle blew again and we took the masks off. She then called out three boys' names whom she had seen doing what I had done – obviously for the same reason. We got a lecture on how bad this was and how wicked these particular boys were. To set an example for us all to remember, she hit all three with a cane so thick that I had initially mistaken it for her walking stick. They got six whacks each on both hands: three on their palms and three on their knuckles. I thought this was a bit harsh and I was glad she hadn't spotted me. But she proceeded to ask us if anyone else had let air into their masks and, getting no response, lectured us on the goodness of honesty and of the perils of eternal damnation for the dishonest.

She asked again if anyone else had tampered with their mask and I put my hand up. I was called out to the front, thinking I was going to be praised for my honesty and, blushing crimson, I hoped this wouldn't go down too badly with my new classmates. I need not have worried about that, for instead I was told to hold out both hands and I got the same three whacks, front and back. Lesson learned. My schoolmates probably thought I was an idiot. Unfortunately, a caning wasn't the only unwelcome thing I was given at St Francis'; shortly before leaving that overcrowded school for Lisbon I caught head lice, with unfortunate results later on in Italy.

But apart from that, the war seemed to us lads a big disappointment. There were no cavalry or bayonet charges across no-man's-land or gas attacks as in the last war. Instead we got songs such as *We're Going to Hang out the Washing on the Siegfried Line* and *Run, Rabbit, Run Rabbit, Run, Run, Run*, and month after month went by with nothing happening. The French Maginot Line, we were assured, was impregnable.

There was some excitement when one of the many anti-aircraft balloons went adrift and dragged its steel mooring cable over some house roofs, damaging some slates. But that was about it.

Lord Haw-Haw[3] was not to be missed in the evenings with his *This is Chairmany cawling, Chairmany cawling*. It was illegal to listen to him but nearly everyone did. His propaganda quickly backfired and he became a figure of fun.

All that changed dramatically in May 1940 with the German invasion of Belgium and Holland, and their rapid advance through France, bypassing the famous impregnable line. On 10 May we heard on the wireless and from newsboys shouting 'Extra! Extra!' that Chamberlain had resigned and Winston Churchill was the new Prime Minister. In the following days the newsreels were harrowing, showing French roads blocked with seemingly endless streams of civilian refugees on foot, on carts and in cars, intermittently strafed by Stuka dive-bombers, their engines screaming to cause maximum panic. Worse was to follow at Dunkirk, with the evacuation of the British army and the remnants of some French units.

At the time it didn't strike me as odd, but we might have been watching a cartoon before the news came on with these distressing scenes, followed by trailers for next week's show, then the 'big picture', such as a George Formby comic film – the audience howling with laughter.

Apart from all this, life went on as usual. Late one afternoon, sometime in May 1940, I was out playing with a few lads with a tricycle which I still had. Our street branched off from a steep road that ended on Dewsbury Road; beyond Dewsbury Road the ground dropped steeply to open ground with municipal allotments. That afternoon we were using the tricycle as some sort of toboggan on wheels to freewheel down the hill. I stood on the pedals and steered it, with another lad seated on the saddle and a third standing on the back axle. Aside from the exhilarating ride, there was the added thrill of trying to stop before it ran into traffic at the T-junction of Dewsbury Road. We had started with a short trial run, but by the third time we had gone right to the top of the hill to gather more speed. On the fourth or fifth run we came unstuck in spectacular fashion.

We always ran on the pavement rather than in the road because the flag-stones were smoother and without drainage grates. We had almost reached the bottom when we saw two old ladies coming up the hill blocking our path. I remember grabbing hard on the brakes but they had no effect and we careered on, heading straight for them. At this point I steered us off the pavement to avoid a collision but the tricycle tipped over, sending us sprawling onto the road. I remember putting my hands out as we hit the road, with the other two landing on top of me – fortunately there was no traffic. My left arm felt very numb and my ribs ached, but other than that we had the usual grazed knees and I thought I was okay. The worst to suffer seemed to me to be the tricycle, and I was wondering what excuse I could think up to explain the mess it was in since it was being kept for my sister Gloria; I hardly heard a word of what the two angry women were saying to us, I was more concerned about my dad's reaction than I was of theirs.

I got home late dragging the wretched tricycle. My father was already home from work and my mother and sister were still at my grandad's. Sure enough my dad hit the roof, my hands and knees were dirtier than usual and he finally told me to go and get washed. I remember putting the plug in the sink and turning the tap on but I couldn't lift my left arm. I was washing my face with my right hand when my father came in demanding to know why I was taking so long. I tried again to lift my arm to speed things up, but suddenly it seemed that I had two elbows and my left forearm folded in the middle, hurting dreadfully. My dad's attitude immediately changed and he swept me up in his arms. He scribbled a note for my mother and, holding me in a blanket, we caught a tram into town and he carried me all the way to Leeds Infirmary.

The next thing I remember is being strapped down on an operating table, a mask being placed over my face and being told to breathe deeply; in those days the only anaesthetic was gas. When I came round, which seemed to me a second later, my arm was in a plaster of Paris cast. I had snapped both bones of the forearm, the radius and the ulna. I was told I had a double fracture, but to me the word 'fracture' was new and at the time I didn't realise it meant 'break'. We got one of the very last evening service trams home, well after 11 p.m; I had been in the operating theatre a lot longer than the second I had supposed. We were seated on the tram near the conductor's platform; I wasn't in any pain but suddenly a great feeling of nausea swept over me as the tram rocked and I vomited. My dad explained to the conductor what had happened and I remember him being very kind and concerned and telling my father not to worry. Little did I know then, but it was to be many weeks before that plaster came off and when it did I would be on a ship sailing from Portugal to Italy.

3

ITALY DECLARES WAR

*C*ombattenti di terra, di mare e dell'aria! Camicie nere della rivoluzione e delle legioni! Uomini e donne d'Italia, dell'Impero e del regno d'Albania! Ascoltate! 'Fighters on land, sea, and air! Blackshirts of the revolution and the legions. Men and women of Italy, of the Empire and of the Kingdom of Albania. Listen to me!'

With these opening words, at 6 p.m. on 10 June 1940, from the balcony of Palazzo Venezia in Rome, Mussolini pompously declared war on Britain and France. At about 10 p.m. that same day there was a knock on our door and my father was arrested. I was asleep in bed when two plainclothes men arrived, but, awakened by the commotion, I went downstairs. My sister too was soon up. On the sideboard in our living room we had two framed photographs, one of Mussolini and the other of the king of Italy. This seemed to be proof that my father was a dangerous character. The photo of Mussolini was smashed, whether accidentally or not I don't know; both photographs, or what was left of them, were confiscated. I think the police may also have been puzzled and suspicious of the boxes of old telephone parts my father had, as these were taken away. My father was escorted to a car and driven off. I remember my mother on her knees after they had left, tearfully picking up the shards of broken glass. It was around 2 or 3 a.m. before my sister and I finally got to bed again; I don't think my mother went to bed at all that night. Early the next morning we hurried to my grandparents' house, only to discover that my grandfather had also been arrested. Gradually it emerged that all Italians, whether Fascists or not, had been rounded up in compliance with Churchill's drastic Collar the Lot order.

Sir John Anderson, the Home Secretary, and the Home Office in general were opposed, in principle, to the mass arrest of all Italians, and after much discussion and argument with MI5 and the Foreign Office, at meetings on 30 and 31 May, it was agreed that: 1) 1,500 'desperate characters' (defined as members of the *fascio*) were to be arrested at once and interned or deported; 2) other Italian males between 18 and 60 were to be interned at some later date; 3) British and Italian diplomats were to be exchanged.

But as soon as Mussolini declared war, dismissing what the Cabinet had agonised over, Churchill issued his terse order and the police snapped into action at once.[1]

While arrests were being made, anti-Italian demonstrations erupted. At the time I wasn't aware of any animosity or violence against Italians, but these are the facts as I now know them, partly based on the well-researched accounts of Peter and Leni Gillman, Juliet Gardiner and, above all, Lucio Sponza, and partly on my family's experience. On the night that Italy declared war, while all Italian adult males were being arrested, mobs ransacked Italian property far and wide all over Britain.

The worst mob violence was in Scotland, particularly in Glasgow, Clydebank and in Edinburgh, where there was smashing of windows, looting and arson. A Scottish newspaper, *The Scotsman*, reported the wrecking of property and looting in Leith, along with arson attacks – the crowds jeering and singing patriotic songs. Many Italians were taken to hospital with head injuries. The *Daily Express* reported that an Italian was pushed to the ground by half a dozen 'hooligans' and had his face kicked in brutally. Mobs of thousands in Port Glasgow, Renfrew, wrecked and looted dozens of Italian-owned shops. In the Paisley Road district of Glasgow, at about midnight, a swelling crowd moved along smashing the windows and looting the contents of every Italian shop they came to. Restaurants and shops were ransacked and stripped bare, with tables and chairs stolen and even light fittings ripped out. The police charged the mob with truncheons on several occasions and there were many arrests, but the police were greatly outnumbered. As is usual with mobs, 'the wrecking activities seemed to be led by a comparatively small number of young men' – mindless yobbos as we would call them now. No account was taken of who the owners really were; one prominent Italian restaurant owner who had his premises ransacked was a British subject and had served in the First World War in a Scottish infantry regiment. Another man, the press reported, had two sons in the Black Watch.

In London, in what the press sensationally dubbed the 'Battle of Soho', there were pitched fights between Italians and Greeks, which seems to have been triggered by personal animosities and grudges, since Greece and Italy were not at war in June 1940. And even for many Londoners who took part in these riots, the attacks were more to do with rampant xenophobia than they were to do with the war. Described as 'a capable middle-aged working woman' by Mass Observation investigators, who had been sent to Soho to investigate, one woman commented: 'After they have cleared out the Italians, they'll clear out the Jews. You'll see – and a good job too. I ask you, why should these foreigners be here, why should they be employed at lower rates, and so many English out of work?'² There clearly was confusion, at least in this lady's mind, as to why Italians were being arrested and their premises attacked.

Of the disturbances in many cities, the worst in England was in Liverpool, where crowds thousands strong threw bricks and stones through the windows of shops run by Italians before invading them and stripping them bare, with terrified Italians barricading themselves in inner rooms. It was reportedly particularly bad in Great Homer Street, in the Kirkdale district, where the windows of two Italian shops were smashed and a crowd numbering nearly 4,000 threw stones and bricks over the heads of the police at the upper windows, where they thought the shop owners had taken refuge. In Wales the worst was in Newport, Cardiff and Swansea, where the police had to make baton charges to disperse looting mobs. And then on the following night, in many places, it all flared up again; particularly in Edinburgh, with the mob systematically targeting and looting any Italian premises that had been missed the night before.

This was not misguided patriotism or even anti-fascism, but rather bigoted, ignorant xenophobia. Gardiner concludes: 'The entry of Italy into the war seems to have been the excuse for some, mainly young, men to vent their xenophobia, frustration at unemployment (the incidents were most serious in areas of high youth unemployment) and, in Scotland in particular, anti-Catholicism.' Probably because of this, and contrary to what might have been expected, there were no demonstrations at the Italian Embassy in Grosvenor Square in London, and crowds of Italians took refuge there, hoping to be repatriated to Italy.

The final directive of the Aliens Department at the Home Office to police forces was that all Italian males between 16 and 70 years of age who had been resident in Britain for less than twenty years, and all Italian males who were on the MI5 suspect list, were to be immediately arrested and interned. But police forces largely ignored these instructions. For example, my grandfather, in his sixties, who had been in England for over forty years, had no political affiliations whatsoever and was a devout Catholic, was also interned. In fact, as with all national groups, the Italians in Britain were a mixed lot: most were patriotic; some, like my father, supported Mussolini; others simply used the Italian Fascist Club as a social club; while others were anti-fascists. But MI5 and Special Branch made no distinctions and seemed to have little idea of these gradations. They took the slogan 'Collar the Lot' quite literally.

I have in my possession a copy of a letter from my grandfather's parish priest, Reverend John Lucey, dated 18 October 1940, to the Officer-in-Command, Metropole Internment Camp, Isle of Man. He wrote:

> I write in the interests of Mr F. GRANELLI, 39608, HOUSE N 3. For close on thirty years I have known him and his family. My people speak in the highest terms of the man in question and I have always found him to be a most loyal subject, quiet and unassuming in manner and character … From years of very intimate observation of the people of South Leeds I'm confident all would rejoice at his return home to his dear wife who is in poor health. Let me assure you, that, had I not known the circumstances of this case to the extent to which I do, I would not have approached you in this matter. In the interests of all concerned I sincerely hope the Authority will give immediate consideration to this petition.

Sadly his petition fell on deaf ears.

Arrest and internment generally followed the same pattern: two or more police officers, either plainclothes Special Branch or uniformed officers, would call and make the arrest and arrange conveyance to a local police station, followed by finger-printing and a couple or more nights in a police station cell. Special tribunals would decide what category the arrested person fell into: 'A' – high security risk; 'B' – doubtful cases; and 'C' – no security risk. But tribunals differed widely in their interpretation of this. Manchester and Croydon seemed to favour 'C', while in Leeds you were lucky to be classified 'B', with hardly anyone deserving a 'C'. The prisoners were then transferred to various collecting points after which most were sent to Warth Mills, a large disused cotton mill near Bury in Lancashire, used as a transit camp. This was the worst part as they were ill-prepared and there was minimal sanitation – some sixty buckets in the yard and eighteen cold water taps for 2,000 men of all ages. There was no electricity or adequate bedding, most sleeping on the floor. From there they were transported to the Isle of Man, where accommodation was considerably better. Afterwards, on the whole, treatment was humane (with, as always, exceptions).

Much of the anti-alien hysteria was inflamed by the press, the foremost being the *Daily Mail*. They even printed a letter from a retired brigadier suggesting that all aliens, presumably the families of internees, should be made to wear armbands clearly stating their country of origin – hardly an original idea: shades of the Nazi yellow Star of David armbands here? Pondering on all of this later, it made me better understand what Jews have had to endure for 2,000 years, and how quickly normal, sane people can be whipped up into a baying, mindless mob.

Four days later, mid-morning on Friday 14 June, without any warning, my father appeared on our doorstep. He had been released under escort for repatriation to Italy. My mother, sister and I were British citizens, but we could accompany him if my mother so chose. She had no hesitation in deciding to do so and within minutes we were frantically packing. We were allowed one suitcase each, and I remember our dash to my grandmother's house to get two large suitcases.

It meant leaving all my books – I had quite a collection by then. My mother allowed me to select three; I chose a *Natural History of the World*, Odham's *The New Pictorial Atlas of the World* and another that I valued most of all but unfortunately now can neither remember the subject nor title. I also grabbed my stamp collection album. While my father remained at home, we returned to my grandmother's to say our tearful farewells; the parting hit my mother particularly hard. United once more back home, we made our way to Leeds City station to await our special train to an unknown port.

Unknown to us, on 4 June the Italian Minister for Foreign Affairs, Count Galeazzo Ciano[3] – Mussolini's son-in-law – and the British Ambassador in Rome, Sir Percy Lorraine, had agreed that should war be declared there would be an orderly exchange and repatriation of their respective nationals. Details were arranged in London on 6 June, when the Italian First Secretary, Cristoforo Fracassi, and another senior diplomat, Egidio Ortona,[4] went to the Foreign Office to discuss a suggestion made a few days earlier by Fracassi that, given the impossibility of crossing embattled France, embassy staff should travel by sea and the exchange made in neutral Lisbon.[5]

Regarding who was to be exchanged, first were the staff of both countries' embassies and consulates, with additional names to be recommended by each Ambassador to fill the ships' spare capacity, but subject to security clearance for those without diplomatic immunity. The list of Italians in the UK was drawn up by the Italian Ambassador, Giuseppe Bastianini (who had taken over from Dino Grandi in September 1939), and he submitted 730 names to the Foreign Office. However, the arrests had been carried out so fast and without proper supervision that many on the list were missing and could not be located; even some diplomatic staff had been arrested and no one had any idea of where they were detained. Bastianini appealed to the Foreign Office; they tried to sort things out but found that the War Office, who had control of the detainees, was 'either unable or unwilling to say where they were or to whom orders for their release should be addressed'.

Eventually, forty-nine were traced and released from the Oratory School in Brompton Park, London, while others, like the Italian consuls of Liverpool and Cardiff, were eventually found in police cells, as was my father. The Foreign Office now discovered that MI5 refused to release about forty Italians on the agreed list who were members of the London *fascio* on security grounds. A few others asked to be taken off the list, either because they were anti-fascists or because they decided to remain with their families, opting for internment. This brought the number down from 730 to 629. Hundreds more desperately sought to be included, but no one was allowed to be added to the list, even to make it up again to 730.[6]

My father was on Bastianini's list and when he was located he was given about thirty minutes to make up his mind. He opted to return to Italy, and my mother decided to go with him. Whatever the outcome, my parents were adamant that we should all, if possible, remain together. But whether we were included on the Ambassador's final list of 629, or simply added to it in Leeds, I do not know.

The special train that picked us up in Leeds was sealed; once on no one was allowed off. It had started in London from Euston Station the previous evening, 13 June, at about 10 p.m., stopping at various cities to pick up Italians. So far as I can remember we were the only ones to board the train in Leeds. The train came steaming in to the segregated platform where we were standing. It stopped, all the doors opened, and to my surprise a kilted soldier in a tin hat came out of each door and stood facing it armed with rifle and fixed bayonet. As the train pulled out of the station we stood in the train corridor among the soldiers; however, a man got up and offered his seat to my mother who sat with my sister Gloria on her knee. After a while, a friendly soldier let me sit on his kitbag. I thought it strange that we were travelling on what appeared to me to be a troop train; it never occurred to me that they were guarding us. As soon as we got on we discovered that no one knew where they were. Probably the soldiers didn't know where they were either, since all road and station signs had been removed to confuse the enemy should there be an invasion, which in June 1940 seemed imminent. We knew that our destination was Glasgow, but we didn't go to the city station; instead the train continued along to the docks at Greenock on the Clyde, stopping right alongside a towering ocean liner.

4

MONARCH OF BERMUDA

The ship we were alongside was the SS *Monarch of Bermuda*, weighing 22,424 gross tons. I subsequently discovered that the ship had been used for three-week cruises to Bermuda for the Furness–Bermuda line, running between New York and Bermuda from its launch in 1931. But on 17 December 1939 it arrived in Greenock with the first Canadian soldiers to come to Britain, having been converted to a troopship in November 1939. When we saw the ship it had recently returned from the British forces' Narvik landings in Norway, in April 1940. Gone were the pre-war red and black of the three funnels and the ship's white superstructure; all was now painted a drab battleship grey. For us, even the portholes had been painted over and the ship's sides had the single word 'Diplomat' painted on them in huge white letters.

On the platform between the train and the ship was a long row of trestle tables with immigration and customs officers at each one, and behind the tables were large wicker crates. We were called forward with our suitcases, forming long queues at the tables. Searches were carried out very speedily, with everything tipped out on the tabletops and many items, other than clothing, were thrown into the wicker baskets. All were forbidden to take any sterling. Those who had been at the Italian Embassy, both staff and Italians to be repatriated from London, knew of this. Bastianini had got round this by letting everyone put their money in envelopes, signed and sealed. These were placed in an embassy suitcase, which had diplomatic immunity, where they would remain until arrival in Italy. But those who joined the train en route to Glasgow, like us, were unaware of this. Any money found at Glasgow was confiscated before we boarded.

My father noticed what was happening at these tables and quickly took some pound notes out of his wallet and pushed them under the plaster of Paris still on my arm, leaving just a small amount in his pocket. I do not remember anything being confiscated from us, other than the remainder of my father's money and two of my three books, my then favourite one and my atlas.[1] My stamp album with my entire stamp collection also went winging into the basket. Why I was allowed to take the book on natural history I do not know; maybe the officer took pity on my distressed look. Whatever the reason, this was the only English book I had throughout the rest of the war and it remained with me until my departure from Italy in 1946. Meanwhile, my parents were hurriedly repacking our four suitcases and trying to get the lids closed on the partly folded contents which now seemed twice as bulky.

There was a commotion, and the dockers and baggage handlers downed tools and refused to carry on loading the ship 'for the enemy'. We seemed to be stuck for quite some time while discussions went on, the baggage handlers claiming that they were not on strike but were having an overdue tea break. But the 'tea-break' showed no sign of ending and eventually we had to struggle up the gangplank with our luggage ourselves. For single adults this wasn't a problem, as they only had one suitcase, but families with children had more – four in our case. Finally, it was suggested by the embassy staff that each adult male should take two suitcases on board and they would be sorted out on the ship. The embassy's heavy trunks were a particular problem as the dockers would not allow their lifting gear to be used, so they had to be manhandled up the narrow passenger gangplank. It was pretty chaotic on deck trying to sort out the luggage of over 600 passengers.

All I remember of our accommodation onboard is that it was some sort of small storeroom; there were two two-tier bunks for us with little space between them, and a rack with a large number of life jackets of the old cork variety. Then came another shock. We had boarded the ship on 14 June and expected to sail on the next high tide; instead we were still there the next day, and the next. Day after day came and went but still we remained cooped up and not allowed on deck. It was hot and claustrophobic. The reason for the unexpected delay was that all belligerents had to give advance clearance and allow our safe passage. We finally left Glasgow on 20 June.

Early that morning I awoke to the pleasant throbbing of the engines, indicating that we were under way. Though we were unable to see out, it became obvious that we had left the Clyde when the ship began to gently roll. It was nice to know that lifebelts were to hand for there was a real

danger that we might have to use them. In 1940 Britain was surrounded
by minefields with designated clear shipping lanes through them. However,
every time there was a storm there was a danger of the mines coming adrift
from their moorings and floating freely into the 'safe' lanes. Consequently,
a sharp lookout had to be maintained at all times. But the main danger was
from free-floating magnetic mines dropped from enemy aircraft. In June 1940
alone, five British ships were sunk by mines: on the 6th, SS *Harcalo*; on the 8th,
SS *Hardingham*; on the 12th, SS *Baron Saltoun*; on the 13th, SS *British Inventor*, a
tanker; and on the 18th, SS *Niagara*. Losses for 1940 were 728 vessels, including
416 neutral ships.

Despite the fact that the ship was fully lit and Germany informed of
the ship's route, we maintained a zigzag course to avoid any trigger-happy
U-boats. Because of this, progress was slow and it took us twelve days to reach
Lisbon, a journey which normally could be comfortably done in three at
most. Comfort on the *Monarch of Bermuda* was decidedly lacking. My father
had to queue at the galley for our food and we ate all our meals in the small
storeroom where we slept. No one was allowed on deck except for a couple
of lifeboat drills, and these were both long and tiring, particularly the last
one which was a precautionary lifeboat-stations drill when a loose mine was
sighted. When the alarm sounded, life jackets were handed out from the rack
in our small cabin by a soldier and then returned afterwards, so we were disrupted more than the others with this procedure. Gloria, my 4-year-old sister,
couldn't grasp what was going on and was usually crying loudly, especially
when the lifebelts were taken, and my mother was upset trying to placate
her. We didn't see many people at these boat drills as we all stood under the
lifeboat allocated to us. In fact, we were not allowed to communicate with
anyone on the ship, and were under armed guard at all times; probably by the
same Scottish soldiers who were on the train, which would explain why they
had their kitbags with them.

Crossing the Bay of Biscay there was a storm with heavy seas. Giuseppe
Bastianini's son, Lucio, also records that we were stopped in the Bay of Biscay
by a U-boat which insisted on checking his father's identity and to ensure he
really was on board.[2] Presumably all went satisfactorily for both sides, since we
were not torpedoed, but I cannot myself recall this event. He also mentions
that even his family and the diplomatic staff were under armed guard and
forbidden to communicate with other Italians, just as we were. Our arrival at
Lisbon and transfer to the *Conte Rosso* on 26 June came as a great relief. I have
always enjoyed sea travel but not that memorable, claustrophobic journey.

5

CONTE ROSSO

We were quickly transferred to the SS *Conte Rosso*, a prestigious first-class ocean liner of the Lloyd Triestino Line. She had sailed from Pescara with the British Ambassador, Sir Percy Lorraine, together with his diplomatic and consular staff and other British citizens living in Italy, who were conveyed to the *Monarch of Bermuda* for their return to Britain. The *Conte Rosso* really was a beautiful ship, and was still in her peacetime livery. Here is how the *New York Times* of 27 May 1922 enthused about the ship when she arrived in New York on her maiden voyage, under a banner headline:

The new Lloyd Sabaudo liner *Conte Rosso*, described as the largest ship flying the Italian flag, arrived yesterday, having made her maiden voyage from Genoa and Naples in nine days and eight hours. Officials of the line went down the bay to escort the vessel to the foot of West Fifty-fifth Street.

Built at the yards of William Beardmore at Dalmuir, Scotland, the *Conte Rosso* is 590 feet long, has a width of 74 feet and a displacement of 21,000 tons. She has accommodation for 200 first cabin, 250 second cabin, and 1,500 steerage passengers. She is fitted as an oil and coal burner.

The liner is thoroughly modern in conveniences. She made a favourable impression on those who inspected her. Leading artists of Italy contributed their talents in decorating the saloons. The decorative work alone cost $400,000, it was said. The grand halls are panelled in mahogany and oak, with wood sculptures and inlaid work. The dining hall and lounge are in the style of the fifteenth century. French mirrors, antique vases, stained glass windows and rich tapestry beautify the music and dance salons.

Each room on three of the decks has one or two beds. An open air restaurant on the forward part of the main deck is among the innovations …

The Lloyd Sabaudo Line and other Italian shipping companies amalga-
mated and formed the Lloyd Triestino Line in 1932, at the height of the
Great Depression. Thus the *Conte Rosso* began serving the Trieste–Bombay–
Shanghai route, one of the major escape routes for European Jews. Up to
20,000 Jewish refugees, from Germany and Austria mainly, were able to find
refuge in Shanghai, China. No visa was required to get there as late as 1939,
when most, if not all countries in the world were closing their doors to them.
It was called 'the Port of Last Resort'.[1]

Everything on the *Conte Rosso* was sumptuous, and the thick carpets and
sweeping staircases reminded me very much of the luxurious Paramount
cinema in Leeds. As a family unit with young children, we were allocated
a cabin, but I cannot now remember whether it was first or second class.
Whatever it was, it was a huge improvement on the small storage space we
had occupied on the *Monarch of Bermuda*. The other thing that was immediately apparent was that there were no soldiers on board, so clearly the British
passengers who had travelled from Livorno to meet us in Lisbon had not been
under armed guard.

We had the complete run of the ship, except for a few restricted areas.
After dropping off our four suitcases we went on deck for a breath of cool
fresh air. It was late evening and Lisbon was a blaze of light; it seemed such an
amazing sight after months of the blackout. On one of the decks, as we lay at
anchor, a loading door was open; it was a sunny day, the sea calm, and below
the open door were a number of bum-boats laden with fruit. The bare-footed
Portuguese trinket and fruit sellers would throw up a thin cord with a weight
at the end attached to a thicker rope and basket. You pulled up the basket of
fruit, or whatever, and then lowered the money to them. The fruit was very
cheap, for just a few coins we bought some delicious fresh figs. This was the
first time I had ever seen figs, let alone eaten them.

But the most memorable moments of our stay on the *Conte Rosso* were
the meals. We each had an allocated number for meal sittings and table places,
always using the same table. The service was first class, and for years my mother
kept one of the printed menus as a souvenir. Stewards served us at every meal.
When we asked our steward where our British counterparts had eaten he
seemed surprised at the question: food was only served in the dining rooms
and the ship's restaurant, he said. He also added ('hint, hint', as my father said)

that they had tipped well on leaving the ship. I also hadn't realised how many children there were with us, and soon I was running around the ship with a number of boys and girls of my age and older.

At either our first or second meal, Giuseppe Bastianini appeared in the dining room in full Fascist uniform: black shirt, black fez, jackboots, the full panoply – an impressive figure, although at the time I didn't realise how theatrical it all was. A number of his senior diplomats, some also in the official Fascist full-dress black Saharan uniform, were with him. He gave a short speech that was loudly applauded, then went from table to table, stopping to say a few words; his entourage broke away and did likewise. After a while it seemed he was about to leave but as he passed our table with two of his colleagues he caught sight of me and stopped. He looked directly at me then came over. He spoke in Italian to my father, but, on learning that neither my mother nor Gloria nor I understood it, he switched to English.

It transpired that what had caught his eye was my arm, which was still in plaster in a sling. By now it was several weeks since my fracture had been set and the plaster looked distinctly grubby. My parents told him that it should have been removed some time ago, at which the Ambassador sent for the ship's medical officer there and then. For the few minutes while we were awaiting his arrival he sat down beside me and chatted, though all I can remember now is that he laughed when I told him how I had broken it, and again when I said that the full plate of salami before us for our first course made it seem like Christmas. I was relaxed with him simply because I had no real idea who he was, and I certainly didn't realise that he was one of Mussolini's close associates. The upshot of this was that the very next morning I was called to the medical bay and my plaster was cut open and removed, much to my great relief. The last time I recall seeing Bastianini was a few days later on deck; he came over and said: 'Ah, Peter, the flying cyclist!' and asked me how my arm was.

Flying was the right word. One balmy evening, after we had gone through the Strait of Gibraltar into the Mediterranean, I was playing with some boys and girls. There was a swimming pool on the *Conte Rosso* which had been drained but left uncovered, although well lit. We were variously standing and sitting on the edge at the deep end. One of the boys jumped in at the shallow end and then another at a deeper section. In a moment of madness, and purely to impress the girls, I jumped in at the deep end. At the moment I jumped, the ship must have pitched upwards slightly because I landed on the tiled bottom some 7ft below, flat on my feet, with my weight mainly on my heels, and felt excruciating pain in both ankles and pain in my groin. I winced and came out on my tiptoes, pretending that nothing had happened. Nor did I say a word to my parents about my sprained ankles and how I had got them, having already had umpteen lectures following the tricycle debacle. Somehow I managed to cover up what had happened by walking around mostly on tiptoe.

For the next few days, apart from trips to the dining room, I lay on my bunk taking a keen interest in my book of nature, reading about dolphins instead of going up on deck to watch them sporting around the ship as I had done before my farcical stunt. By the time I was feeling fit enough to venture on deck we were in the Tyrrhenian Sea, within sight of the western tip of Sicily. Possibly for safety reasons, we came very close to the north-west tip of the island, near Trapani, sailing eastwards along the entire north coast, close enough to distinguish individual houses, before turning south into the Strait of Messina. We docked in Messina and I was sorry to leave the *Conte Rosso*, as I am sure were many others. It had been like a holiday cruise and the crew had been very good to us all. As a souvenir my mother was given a red silk sash with *Conte Rosso* embroidered on it in gold thread. My sister Gloria still has that sash.

As for the *Conte Rosso*, on 12 December 1940 she was converted to a troopship, after which she made four successful trips to Tripoli in convoy, taking troops to North Africa and bringing back Italian refugees. On her fifth trip, ten months after we left her, the *Conte Rosso* ran out of luck. On 24 May 1941 she was in a convoy with two other converted passenger ships, *Esperia* and *Marco Polo*, all three carrying troops from Naples bound for Tripoli. Close escort for the convoy was provided by two destroyers (*Camicia Nera* and *Freccia*) and three torpedo boats (*Procione*, *Orsa* and *Pegaso*), and by an outlying escort of the cruisers *Bolzano* and *Trieste* and the destroyers *Corazziere* and *Lanciere*. East of Sicily, a British U-class submarine, HMS *Upholder*, daringly penetrated the convoy's strong protective shields and hit the *Conte Rosso* with two torpedoes.

This sinking is now listed as the fifteenth most notable disaster to merchant shipping of the Second World War; including the crew, 1,212 perished.[2] The commander of the submarine, Lt-Cdr Malcolm David Wanklyn, was awarded the Victoria Cross for his action.[3] By a strange twist of fate on 13 April 1942, HMS *Upholder*, the most decorated submarine in the Royal Navy, was sunk in an almost identical attack on another Italian convoy off Djerba, by the Orsa-class torpedo boat *Pegaso*, commanded by Lt-Cdr Francesco Acton; *Pegaso* was the same torpedo boat that had escorted the ill-fated *Conte Rosso*. Lt-Cdr Wanklyn VC lost his life on this occasion and the Italian convoy reached Tripoli intact. My mother was very upset when she read of the loss of the *Conte Rosso*, but that lay in the future.

At the time, the treatment we had received on the *Monarch of Bermuda*, compared with the *Conte Rosso*, seemed unduly harsh. But with hindsight one can take a more balanced view, and things would certainly have been different on the *Conte Rosso* had she already undergone her conversion to a troopship as the *Monarch of Bermuda* had. Another factor was that Italy had only been in the war a few days and the crew of the Italian ship had yet to experience the hardship and dangers of it, whereas Britain had been fighting for nearly a year and, with the fall of France, stood alone, with invasion expected almost hourly. As for the armed guards, we had been described as 'desperate characters' and there appears to have been a fear at Cabinet level that we might mutiny and seize the ship.[4]

Not everyone has bad memories of the *Monarch of Bermuda*. Egidio Cavalli, a respected and successful London restaurateur, was arrested on 10 June and interned, and although he wasn't a member of the Fascist Party, inexplicably he was not released for repatriation. However, his Italian wife, Lina Adorni, was sent back to Italy along with us. This must have been very distressing for her as she did not know where her husband was and she was travelling with her three young children: Mario, aged 10; Algerio, aged 9; and Giulia, a baby only 6 months old – all three British born. Algerio, who like me survived the war, distinctly remembers that they were treated kindly and sympathetically on the *Monarch of Bermuda*, and recalls his mother being very grateful to the crew.[5]

Not all sea crossings with Italian internees went as smoothly or as safely as ours. The *Arandora Star*, on which my father almost certainly would have been embarked had he not opted to return to Italy, sailed from Liverpool at 4 a.m. on 1 July, bound for Canada. It was torpedoed at midnight the same day, 75 miles north-west of Donegal, and sank in the early hours of 2 July with great loss of life. The first reports were alarming: two-thirds of the Italians and about a third of German internees on board had drowned, while casualties among the crew and the accompanying guards were inexplicably comparatively light: 42 out of 174 crew members, and 37 army guards out of 200. The British press soon found an explanation for the high number of Italians drowned, with *The Herald* proclaiming 'Aliens Fight Each Other in Wild Panic' and the *Daily Express* reporting that the crew and guards had told of the stampede among the aliens when they realised the ship was going down, with Germans fighting Italians in a mad scramble for lifeboats. One of the guards claimed, it was reported, that they had to restrain the cowardly lot forcibly, with the whole mob thinking of their own skins first. A seaman said that the rush for the boats was sickening, with Germans punching and kicking their way past Italians, who reportedly were just as bad. And so on.

The Shipping Minister, Mr Ronald Cross, took a similar line in the House of Commons by stating: 'Lifeboats and life rafts more than sufficient to accommodate all passengers and crew were provided' – the implication being that the passengers were entirely to blame for not using them, with one MP, concerned about the reported behaviour of the aliens, asking if he would see to it 'that any minority British crew is afforded the protection they will deem necessary'.[6]

The truth emerged slowly, and was rather different. The total number on board the *Arandora Star* was 1,673. This was made up of 734 Italian civilian internees; 565 Germans (including Nazis, anti-Nazis, Austrian refugees, Jews, and the officers and crew of the scuttled *Adolph Woermann*, and 86 POWs); in addition there were the 174 officers and crew and the 200 guards already mentioned. For these there were fourteen lifeboats (with a total capacity of about 1,000) and a number of life rafts. To make matters even worse, of the fourteen lifeboats, only ten could be successfully lowered. One lifeboat was destroyed in the initial explosion, one could not be lowered off its winches, another capsized as it was being lowered because it had damaged davits, and a fourth was swamped and lost. Strangely, at least four of the remaining ten lifeboats were launched more than half empty.

Of the rafts, about twenty were thrown overboard; three large ones quickly filled up but the remainder were small and found to be quite useless. There was no fighting on board and very little panic, and, as the Gillmans point out, it was rather odd that the allegations of panic came from the armed guard, the group with the highest survival rate of the lot. It seems that the majority of the Italians drowned because they were mainly middle-aged and elderly and were confined to the lower decks, and when the torpedo struck all the lights went out. By the time many Italians finally got to the open upper deck, the lifeboats had already pulled away. Most of those who went down with the ship were doomed from the very start. The final death toll was 805 (470 Italians, 243 Germans, 55 officers and crew, and 37 guards).[7]

One of the internees on the *Arandora Star* was Piero M. Salerni, a brilliant Italian engineer; he had a British wife and had spent most of his life in Britain. His case illustrates how chaotic and draconian the Collar the Lot policy had been. Salerni, an anti-fascist, was arrested on the night of 10 June. The first his employers learnt of this was when he didn't turn up for work and couldn't be contacted. In fact, he was engaged on secret war-work for the Ministry of Aircraft Production, headed by Lord Beaverbrook, and Salerni had invented a new transmission device which, under his guidance, was being developed by a British company in conjunction with the Ministry. On 27 June, having discovered that he was interned and unable to secure his release, the Ministry of Aircraft Production asked the Home Office if he could at least carry out his work in his internment camp, and that Aircraft Production Ministry officials be permitted to visit him there. It was essential that he stay in England, and the Ministry of Aircraft Production's letter concluded: 'I understand that you anticipate success in preventing his shipment to Canada which would otherwise take place in the very near future. I hope there is no possibility of a snag arising on this point.' But snags there must have been aplenty, for Piero Salerni was one of the 470 drowned Italians.[8] My father was indeed very lucky and had undoubtedly made the right choice.

6

ARRIVAL IN ITALY

After disembarking at Messina we caught the ferry to mainland Italy, a short hop to Reggio di Calabria. On arrival a group of teenage lads with bare feet were waiting to carry baggage from the ferry to the nearby railway station. In Leeds I had seen many poor kids without shoes, but they were walking on smooth pavements; here they were carrying heavy loads over stony ground. My father hired one of them; we expected him to take two of our four cases and my father to carry the other two, but instead he slipped a leather belt through the handles of the two larger cases and put them on his shoulder, then he picked up the other two, one in each hand, and almost jogged along to the station with all four cases. I also saw *carabinieri* (Italian policemen) for the first time; in those days they still wore plumed, black, cocked hats, looking much like Spanish matadors, and with their capes and blue trousers, with a broad red stripe, they looked as if they had just stepped out of the early nineteenth century. Now they wear peaked caps and their uniforms are thoroughly modern, though they have still retained the red stripe.

At Reggio we got on the train to Rome. Ciano records in his diary that Bastianini was in Rome, 'back from London', on 4 July, so I assume that this was the date we arrived in Messina. I remember little of the train journey to Rome except stopping for about ten minutes at Naples station, where many of our party got off. The station was bustling with life, and young boys and girls were selling lunch boxes, fruit and drinks. We let down the window and bought some food boxes. I still remember how tasty they were: each contained two freshly baked crisp bread rolls with salami and lettuce, an orange, fresh figs and a small bottle of red wine.

On arrival in Rome we booked into a *pensione* (bed and breakfast accommodation) and spent the rest of the day sightseeing. I was impressed with the
Colosseum and the Vatican, but what also caught my eye was the profusion
of flags and fascist uniforms. The *fascio* emblem seemed to be everywhere,
as did slogans such as *Mussolini ha sempre ragione!* (Mussolini is always right!)
and *Credere! Ubbedire! Combattere!* (Believe! Obey! Fight!) There were flags
everywhere. Nowadays very few people have ever seen a city bedecked with
flags, but in the 1930s it was a common sight, even in Britain, especially for
grand events such as royal visits or national occasions, such as the Jubilee of
George V or the coronation of George VI in 1937.

But in Rome it was just a normal day. Indeed, I discovered later that it
was very unwise not to display the *tricolore* (the national flag) on special com-
memorative days, such as the Fascist March on Rome on 28 October[1] – the
date on which the Fascist year began, counting from 1922 (this Fascist dating,
always written in Roman numerals, was made compulsory on all documents,
from school essays to all printed matter, from 29 October 1927; thus 1940 was
year XVIII 'of the Fascist Era'). If you didn't display a flag you were likely to be
taken to a police station to explain your lack of 'patriotism' or, worse still, put
under surveillance. But on that day I knew nothing of this. It was all very col-
ourful and strange. The country seemed to be at peace; there wasn't a sandbag
to be seen nor were windows criss-crossed with protective tape as in Britain.

Next morning we caught the train to Genoa, en route for Chiavari, 45km
south of Genoa. We were on our way to my mother's sister Rosa's family to stay
with them until my father's parents' house in Musadino, on Lake Maggiore,
was ready for us. My Aunt Rosa lived in Pianlavagnolo, a very remote hamlet
high in the Apennines. Although Pianlavagnolo is in the province of Parma, in
the Emilia-Romagna region, it was then more easily accessed from Chiavari
on the Ligurian coast. I remember nothing of the long train ride up the leg of
Italy, but I do still have a vivid recollection of the final section of our journey
because it was so different. We took the one and only daily bus from Chiavari
to Santa Maria del Taro. The bus also carried goods and I think we were the
only passengers that day. The road went via Currasco into the Sturla Valley,
and at Borzonasca a road diverged, snaking back and forth up to a gap in
the mountains, Passo del Bocco, at 953m; then a long winding road brought
us down to Santa Maria del Taro at 713m, under the impressive rock face of
towering Monte Penna. As the crow flies, the distance from Chiavari to Santa
Maria del Taro is only about 20km, but by road at that time it was nearer 100;
now there is an *autostrada*, and it is a car journey of about fifty minutes.

The bus only took us as far as Santa Maria because from there my aunt's hamlet was only accessible on foot; so with a guide and our cases on a hired mule, we set off on the long climb to Pianlavagnolo. Santa Maria was small enough, but Pianlavagnolo was just a cluster of a few houses. My Aunt Rosa was married to Luigi Granelli. Somehow they found room for us, but with their five children it was a tight squeeze. My cousins were Angela 9, Anna 6, Zita 4, Maria 2 and Giovanni, born on 2 July while we were still at sea approaching Sicily.

Unlike Rome and other Italian cities, up in the Apennines there wasn't a sign of fascism nor indeed of flags; the villagers were all profoundly religious and every Sunday they would all make the long trek to Santa Maria del Taro to attend Mass, and take foodstuffs to be sold in the market held every Sunday. Life was hard there but the people were happy. Our shoes were unsuitable for the mountains and on our first return to Santa Maria we were measured for new footwear; boots for my father and me, and shoes for my mother. Handmade, they were ready in a few days and fitted like slippers as soon as we put them on. They were probably the best boots I have ever had, but unfortunately I quickly grew out of them.

As remote as Pianlavagnolo was, it did have electricity, as did all the surrounding villages. My Aunt Rosa's house had electric lighting in the house and in their attached cowshed, which was partly built into the hillside. My father noticed that on early dark mornings and late at night my uncle went to the cowshed with a lantern. It transpired that the switch in the shed had been placed well inside and was difficult to find in the dark. At first my father simply offered to move it nearer to the door, but in the end he devised it so that the light came on when the door was opened and went out when it was closed (as it later did in fridges and cars), with an internal switch to override this when working inside and the door was closed. I remember the villagers being amazed and standing inside the shed as the door was closed before they would believe that the light really went out.

My mother had thought she had got rid of my head infestation with a fine-tooth comb while aboard the *Monarch of Bermuda*, but now it was found to be worse than ever and I had passed the lice on to my sister. To solve this we had our heads shaved. It was not the fashion as it is now, and if you had a shaved head (called *rapato* from *rapa*, meaning turnip) then everyone knew why. My sister Gloria was utterly devastated by the loss of her hair. My mother crocheted a cap for her that she wore constantly and would not take off, even in bed.

It got even worse for her. One day we were in a field as the hay was being mown, watching the men swinging their scythes as they cut the meadow grass, when suddenly Gloria screamed. She was clearly in pain and her dress was taken off to reveal a scorpion which had stung her back. She was carried back to the village feverish, her eyes twitching, and it was several days before she fully recovered.

Pianlavagnolo wasn't as isolated as first appeared. All around Santa Maria and under the towering rock face of Monte Penna there were other similar clusters of houses: people from Grondana, Morballo, Pianozzo, Casoni, Campeggi, and many more from the Alta Valle del Taro, would all meet in Santa Maria, bringing their wares to market. Nearly everyone brought mushrooms, the succulent *porcini*, either dried or fresh, to sell to dealers from Chiavari and Parma. My Aunt Rosa dried them in the sun on a sheet laid on a low hut rooftop. All this area was later subject to savage German and Republican Fascist reprisals, with villages burnt to the ground, as I shall recount later.

7

MUSADINO

In late summer we left Pianlavagnolo for the final leg of our journey, retracing our steps to Chiavari and then by train back along the south coast to La Spezia; there we caught a train to Parma, and changed trains again for Milan. All I remember of this part of our journey are the many tunnels we went through along this mountainous route, criss-crossing the Apennines and the Taro Valley.

We arrived in Milan to another profusion of flags and Fascist uniforms, and it was in Milan that I was bought my Balilla uniform. All Italian children, practically from birth, became members of the *Opera Nazionale Balilla* (National Balilla Organisation), and membership for all schoolchildren was obligatory. The Balilla uniform was quite striking: *grigioverde* (military grey-green, the Italian equivalent of khaki) shorts, black shirt, a blue neckerchief and a black fez with a tassel bearing a badge of a Roman eagle grasping a horizontal fasces in its talons (a later variant badge was a simple fasces, and the badge of the *figli della lupa* was the Roman she-wolf). The uniform was completed with a pair of knee-length 'stockings' made of *cafioc*, a synthetic cotton, dyed *grigioverde*, with two black bands at the top. But these were a sham in that they had no feet; they ended in a loop of elastic at the ankle end which went under the foot. You were expected to fit these over your socks. To make matters worse, they were kept up with a band of weak elastic which wasn't quite up to the job, with the result that thousands of Balilla paraded around with one or both of their mock stockings concertinaed around their ankles.

Balilla was a mythical boy, who, by throwing a stone at the occupying Austrians in 1776 in Genoa, sparked off a rebellion which led to their expulsion.

The rebellion and Austrian expulsion are true enough, but the boy Balilla is probably a historical fiction like the Angel of Mons – a legend tailor-made for the Fascists, except that they pepped it up a little by inventing a sequel in the twentieth century. Balilla groups were supposedly founded in 1921, when another mythical 11-year-old boy, with 'flashing eyes' and fired by 'prodigious enthusiasm', presented himself at a *Fascio di Combattimento* (Fighting Group) and asked permission to form a Fascist fighting squad, complete with black shirts and banners, for the sons of fascists to unite themselves against attacks from 'the sons of socialist subversives'. Fascist legends aside, the ONB (*Opera Nazionale Balilla*) was formed in 1926, becoming in 1937 the *Gioventù italiana del Littorio* (GIL, Italian Youth of the Lictor's Emblem) and expanded to include all children.

The GIL was subdivided into the following age and gender groups:

Boys
Figli della lupa (Sons of the She-wolf – added in 1933), ages 6–7
Balilla, ages 8–10
Balilla moschettieri (Musketeers), ages 11–12
Avanguardisti (Avant-guards), ages 13–14
Avanguardisti moschettieri (Avant-guard Musketeers), ages 15–17
Giovani Fascisti (Young Fascists), ages 18–21

Girls
Figlie della lupa (Daughters of the She-wolf – added in 1933), ages 6–7
Piccole Italiane (Little Italian Girls), ages 8–14
Giovani Italiane (Young Italian Girls), ages 15–17
Giovani Fasciste (Young Fascist Girls), ages 18–21

From 1936, children were enrolled automatically in the *Figli della lupa* when they started elementary school; then from 27 October 1937, when the GIL was founded, all Italian children were technically enrolled when their births were registered. As might be expected, the boys wore black shirts, but contrary to this, all the girls' groups, from 6 to 21, wore white blouses; indeed, this was their distinguishing feature. Officially, member-ship of the GIL was obligatory, but in practice never more than 50 per cent in each category were actively enrolled and my later experience bears this out. Not that that mattered to me then; I felt very proud and included wearing the Balilla uniform.

We spent the day in Milan sightseeing. As we left Milan on the train for Porto Valtravaglia, little did I think that the next time I would see the city it would be practically in ruins. Laden with our suitcases, with the addition of some pots and pans we had been given and bought, we trudged up from Porto Valtravaglia to my father's village of Musadino.

It may help at this point to explain the topography of the area where we were to spend the rest of the war. In 1940 Porto Valtravaglia, on the east bank of Lake Maggiore, was little more than a large village of just over 2,000 inhabitants. It was a prosperous place with a large glass factory dating back to the eighteenth century and most of Porto's men worked there; the rest were mainly fishermen. Much of the glass blowing was done at night, and the fishermen cast their nets at night, so Porto was known in Valtravaglia dialect as *el paes dei mèzaràt* (the town of bats), and the inhabitants *i mèzaràt* (the Bats). Porto was and is a *comune* (municipality), and the *frazioni* (dependent hamlets) in its administrative area were Domo, Ligurno, Muceno, Musadino, Ticinallo, Torre and the few houses of San Michele. These *frazioni* were scattered on the surrounding hills and mountains and their inhabitants had nicknames; those of Musadino were called *i rebelìtt* (the Rebels).

If you look at a map of the area now, or visit the location, none of this will be apparent. Places like Domo, Musadino and Muceno are almost conjoined by a spreading Porto Valtravaglia as more and more tourist villas and houses are built. Roads are now broader and tarmacked, gradients are less steep, and, as tourism increased in the 1960s, Porto's commercial fishing shrank and the glass factory closed down. But in 1940 Musadino was a small village of about twenty houses. As in all these small villages at that time, there was no street lighting or pavements, just stone cobbled narrow roads between the houses. These houses were all stone built with ancient red-brick roof tiles. Very few had rain gutters, and in heavy downpours water just cascaded noisily along the streets, which doubled as water channels, as it had done for centuries.

Invariably, in houses dating back to earlier centuries, all ground-level windows were heavily barred with interior wooden shutters, harking back to a violent past. Villas of more modern design, often built by villagers who had returned from America and other countries to retire, were scattered around the periphery. At the northern end of Musadino, on the very outskirts of the village, there was a small, old chapel – San Pietro – first mentioned in twelfth-century records but probably already old by then. This chapel was only opened at Easter and on 29 June, the feast day of Saints Peter and Paul.

For the rest of the year the women and children of Musadino, and a few devout men, attended church at nearby Domo.

The Milan Archdiocese, in which we were, still used the ancient Ambrosian Rite, named after St Ambrose, the powerful fourth-century bishop of Milan, instead of the Roman or Gregorian Rite from which it differed in several respects. Unlike in Leeds, the sexes were segregated in church. The women and girls, all veiled, sat on the left, and the men and boys on the right. The result of this was that at Mass, and particularly at evening Benediction, the left pews were always crowded while those on the right were conspicuously half empty.

The mountain directly behind Porto (as Porto Valtravaglia is known locally) is Pian Nave (1,057m) and to its right, looking from Porto and Musadino, are Monte Colonna (1,202m) and Monte Nudo, the highest local peak at 1,235m. Directly behind Monte Colonna is Monte San Martino, rising to 1,088m. Musadino itself is at 346m, a steep climb from Porto and the lake at 190m. The hills, known as the *pre-Alpi*, are wooded and rugged, and it was then very easy for strangers to become disorientated in woodland scrub, but after a year of going up almost daily you got to know every path and landmark like the back of your hand, venturing further and further as you became familiar with the tracks and shortcuts. You also learnt where the spring sources of fresh water were, often little more than a piece of bark acting as a channel shoved in the hillside, where you could replenish a flask; I got to know these springs so well I never needed to carry a flask. The main watershed from Pian Nave is the Rià, which starts just below the San Michele military road as a stream, and in summer is often just a trickle all the way to Porto, forking into several streams. Over the centuries the Rià bed became very wide, especially from Musadino downwards, and after even moderate rain the streams merge, becoming a raging torrent with swift flowing water filling the entire width of the bed, and you can actually hear heavy boulders being rolled along by the water. There are many such deceptive watercourses in the mountainous areas of Italy and they are known as *torrenti*.

The entire area is in the province of Varese, known as *il Varesotto*. Varese itself is on the far side of the mountain chain and was then more easily accessible by road or tram from the small town of Luino, 8km up the coast north of Porto, or from Laveno to the south of Porto. Luino gives its name to a large section of the province known as *il Luinese*; it comprises sixteen municipalities, nine on Lake Maggiore's shore, stretching from the Swiss border down to Castelveccana. The *Luinese* thus includes Porto Valtravaglia and the village of

Musadino. Across the lake, which is about 4km wide at Porto Valtravaglia, is Piedmont with range upon range of mountains, culminating in the perennially snow-covered Italian Alps about 60km away. And a few kilometres north of Luino is the Swiss border, the Canton of Ticino and the lofty wall of the Swiss Alps. The highest Alpine peak visible across the lake from Musadino is Monte Rosa, the second highest peak in Europe at 4,634m, 65km away in the Valle D'Aosta. The military road I mentioned, above the source of the torrent, was built during the First World War. Starting about a kilometre north of Muceno, it zigzags back and forth up the mountain, so that the gradient is suitable for horse-drawn traffic; it rises to 866m then drops slowly down to San Michele, at 820m, and continues down the other side of the mountain to Brissago.

We arrived at Porto Valtravaglia and walked to Muceno along what was known in dialect as the *stradung* (the 'big road'), the main carriageway to Muceno, and from there to Musadino. I think my father chose this longer route to avoid the steep ascent on the direct route. As we walked along the road we were caught up by a lad somewhat older than me. He introduced himself as René from Musadino and when we told him who we were he insisted on taking two of the suitcases and chatted as we went along. By now I could understand some Italian and one phrase of his in particular: 'If we win this war we'll all be riding around like milords, but if we lose it we'll all be in rags begging.' 'Milord' was a word used to describe any English person who, in the pre-war days before mass travel when only the wealthy upper classes went abroad, were all assumed to be rich. Quite a few of the villagers in those early days, probably judging us by our clothes, thought that my father had returned with pots of money.

As for clothes, the early 1940s were the last years that European national dress still lingered on in remote areas among poorer people; in urban areas it had all but disappeared since the end of the Great War and the advent of the cinema. Nearly all the men in Musadino wore wide, rough corduroy trousers, *alla zuava*, fastened below the knee like plus-fours, shirts with no collar and Alpine-style hats. These hats were often from serving in the *Alpini* and bore an eagle feather. All wore broad leather belts with a metal clasp at the back, on which hung a *falcetto* (a machete with a curved end), always kept very sharp, and well-studded boots of natural-coloured leather. Old women wore black dresses, and young and old went in bare feet in *zoccoli* (wooden-soled sandals with just a strip of leather over the toes). Nearly all the women carried a *sciuèra* on their shoulders, a large conical basket with twisted cane shoulder straps.

I remember that on that morning, as we walked along with René, I was proudly wearing my Balilla uniform, which attracted some surprised stares when we entered Musadino. In fact, I don't recall any of the boys in Musadino having uniforms of any kind. It turned out that René was the son of Valdo Albinati, a man about ten years older than my father but who was our next-door neighbour, and he put us up for a couple of days as our own house wasn't quite ready. So once again we were crowded into a single room. But crowded as it was, their house seemed like an enchanted place to me. They lived on the first floor, the rooms all branching off a wide balcony that was completely covered with two large vines which formed a shady canopy, and when we arrived the balcony was festooned with succulent bunches of red and white grapes. The Albinatis were a family of four: Valdo, his wife Maria, his son René and daughter Anna, a young woman of about 18; they had lived for many years in France, hence René's French name rather than the Italian Renato.

Finally, after a few more days, all was ready and we moved into the house where my father was born: No 1 Via San Pietro. Valdo's house was attached to ours at right angles, but separated from our courtyard by a wall. Built in the mid-eighteenth century, access was through a door built into the right side of a huge double coach door, leading down to a courtyard. Our house was on three floors; the original living room was on the ground floor but we used it only for storage. Our actual living room and main bedroom were on the first floor; on the second floor was another bedroom. Like many village houses of that time, there were no internal stairs. From the ground floor you took a double flight of stone steps which brought you to the first-floor balcony, and from there a steep flight of wooden stairs took you up to the second floor. The living room and adjoining bedroom were more or less level with the road, and the two bedroom windows that faced the road were heavily barred. There was no rain guttering or down pipes, so when it rained the water just noisily dripped off the traditional red roofing tiles.

Both the ground-floor room and the living room had a very large fireplace, but there was neither gas nor any running water in the house. The living room had a shallow stone sink which discharged directly into the courtyard below, but all water for drinking, cooking and washing had to be fetched from a public tap outside our house, and we were constantly filling our two buckets. Directly opposite the tap there was a shrine dedicated to the Madonna, in which there was, and still is, a fine painted copy of Michelangelo's *Pietà*, and I never tired of looking at this replica of great Renaissance art. Less inspirational was our latrine in the courtyard: it was simply a hole above a large cesspit, the contents of which had to be emptied manually every couple of years. For this there was a special cart in the form of a very long oval barrel on wheels pulled by oxen, which sprayed the contents, by then well rotted, directly onto fields as a valuable source of nitrogen. There was also a specially adapted wheelbarrow with a larger watertight box which served a similar purpose.

Almost as soon as we arrived in Musadino my father was called up, leaving my mother to cope as best she could. I was enrolled in school. In Fascist Italy school for all was from 5 to 10 years of age; *asilo* (kindergarten) was from 5 to 6, then five years of elementary school. After that was *scuola media* (middle school) but only on recommendation of a teacher, followed by an entrance examination and parental agreement. School in Italy was a totally different experience from the schools I had attended in England. At primary school in Leeds we had never been given homework, nor did we take any work home for revision, whereas in Italy it was normal to be given homework right from the first year. In Italy all children went to school with a *cartella* (a small briefcase). Each child was given state-issue school books, the reading and history ones being heavily biased towards fascism and patriotism.

Both schoolwork and homework was done in *quaderni* (exercise books). These, always of thirty-six pages, were of two kinds: *quaderno a righe* and *quaderno a quadretti* (lined or with squares for arithmetic). The *quaderno a righe* differed in style for each class. For the first three years they had guide lines for lower-case letters and for capitals; and in the second and third years three guide lines for each line of writing which got progressively smaller. In the fourth and fifth classes the exercise book was lined normally, without guide lines, for the height of letters and each came with a sheet of blotting paper. From the very start, emphasis was placed on good calligraphy. The covers of these exercise books were brightly illustrated with a variety of images, but they were always based around heroic military deeds or fascist themes. In your *cartella* you also carried your *astuccio* (pen and pencil case) with writing instruments, a mandatory rubber in two sections for pencil and ink, and a selection of spare pen nibs; fountain pens were absolutely forbidden.

The standard of education was surprisingly high in Fascist Italy. I had learnt precious little at the primary schools, or 'junior schools' as they were then called, that I had attended in Leeds. The term *scuola elementare* (from ages 6 to 10) was roughly equivalent to the English infant school (from 5 to 7 or 8) and junior school (from 7 or 8 to 11 plus). In my schooling in England there seemed to be a lot of emphasis on reading and writing, with a lot of dictation, and simple arithmetic, with a particular stress on learning the multiplication tables by rote. But I cannot remember being taught anything about history or geography, other than episodic events such as the Battle of Hastings and the Gunpowder Plot, and that London was the largest city in the world and the hub of the empire.

In Italy, from classes 3 to 5, we started with pre-history (the Iron Age and the early lake settlements), progressing to Roman history (the foundation, the early Roman kings, the Republic, with coverage of the three Punic wars, then the Empire). We also covered much medieval history, the Renaissance, and, in greater detail, Italy's *Risorgimento* through to independence in 1861; then the Great War, and the 'iniquity', in Fascist eyes, of the Treaty of Versailles. All this with a strong Fascist emphasis, as if the royal house of Savoy and Fascism were an inevitable progression from Julius Caesar and the Emperor Augustus that was divinely mandated. In arithmetic the emphasis was on the metric system, with the relationship between units of length, area and volume thoroughly explained. The multiplication tables had also to be memorised, as in England, but only from 1 to 10, thus falling short of the 1 to 12 times tables deemed necessary in Britain to cope with inches to the foot, and the old pounds, shillings and pence currency system.

The reason that I probably learned more in primary school in Musadino, and later in Porto Valtravaglia, is that the class sizes were very small – something like a dozen village kids at most – and we had personal attention from excellent dedicated teachers. Compared with this, classes in Leeds were large. I have no idea what class sizes were like in Italian cities, but clearly they would be more comparable with Leeds than Musadino. The other big difference between the two systems was that in Italian schools there was no corporal punishment; the cane was simply unheard of.

In 1940, however, there was still much entrenched illiteracy in Italy, particularly in the south, and mainly in adults who would have been of school age before Mussolini took power and made elementary school attendance compulsory. This began to take effect in the late 1920s when school attendance in rural areas rose impressively from 41,771 in 1928–29 to 265,915 in 1936–37.[1] As for adults in Musadino and the surrounding villages, I do not recall any who were illiterate.

The schoolhouse for Musadino and Domo was midway between the two villages. It included the *asilo* and the first three elementary classes. For the last two classes, *quarta* and *quinta*, we went to the municipal school in Porto. Both boys and girls attending the *asilo* and first-year elementary wore an identical black smock with a large bib-like stiff white collar. Because I could neither read nor write Italian I was initially placed in the lowest class; all were 6 year olds, except for one boy of 7 who had failed to reach the required standard to move up to Class II and was repeating his first year. So although 10 years old, older than anyone in that school, I had to wear this girlish smock. It wasn't too bad sitting down in class, but I hated walking to and from school wearing it; I partly coped with this by tucking it in my trousers like a shirt and pulling it out somewhat crumpled when I got to school. Worst of all was playtime, when all three elementary classes joined for the break. Almost from day one I became a figure of fun, with my frock-like smock and shaved head. Inevitably, after the third or fourth day I ended up having a fight with one of my tormentors, a boy from Domo. We were rolling around on the ground, with a group around us urging us on, when the boy I was fighting suddenly whipped out a large safety pin, pulled it straight and tried to stab me with it muttering that I was an English pig – rather an odd choice of words as he was quite plump. Others took up this refrain and the noise attracted a teacher who broke us up. The upshot was that, much to my relief, I was no longer required to wear the dreaded smock.

But it didn't end there. After Sunday Mass the new parish priest, Don Carlo Agazzi Rota, ran a playgroup for the children of the parish, which included those of Domo and Musadino. This was in Domo, the location of the parish church of Santa Maria Assunta. Don Carlo was a kindly 36-year-old priest who had arrived at Domo in February 1941 on the death of his predecessor, Don Carlo Biella. About the second or third time I went to his playgroup there were some stilts he had had made for us, but there weren't quite enough for all so we had to wait our turn, and there was a bit of an argument when it came to my turn. This passed off for a while but flared up again after the playgroup closed. First one or two started chanting 'Inglese, Inglese', then more joined in until I was chased under a hail of stones all the way back to Musadino. Not a single stone hit me, but I felt both angry and deeply humiliated. I seemed to belong nowhere. In England I had been taunted as an 'Eyetie' and here I was in Italy being stoned as an 'inglese'. Of course, what had happened in Italy and in England was just a case of kids bullying a stranger, but it stemmed from the bigoted nationalism of adults. It cured me for life of all nationalisms. I never went back to the playgroup, but I missed the stilts. My mother, nevertheless, despite being short of cash, had a pair made for me by the village carpenter for my eleventh birthday.

Along with skipping the playgroup, I had stopped going to school. I would leave the house with my *cartella* and a kiss from my mother, then bunk off, walking in fields and woods until I saw the school closed. The worst thing was the bitter cold, but I kept moving to keep warm. Then one day, after about a week or so, I got overconfident and misjudged things. I was walking along the top of a wall near the school when one of the teachers came by and called me to her. I was wearing *zoccoli* but in bare feet; there was still snow about and over the days I had found that if I left my socks on they soon got wet and made my feet freeze, so I would take them off while they were still dry, stuff them in my *cartella*, and put them on before returning home. I thought that the teacher was going to start shouting at me, but instead she took me by the hand and led me into the school. Rather than taking me to my class she took me to a room and gave me a hot drink. She asked me why I had not been to school, and because she had been so kind to me I told her about the smock and also that I was bored of repeatedly writing out the alphabet and reading out simple words. She asked me to come back to school, and although she couldn't officially place me in Class III straight away, she would let me sit in with them for the rest of the year and put me in the third grade the following year. She also asked me about my family life and finally she gave me a note for my mother and a sealed letter to take to a lady in Muceno.

The lady in Muceno turned out to be from Milan, from where she and her children had been evacuated. She was extremely kind to us and gave me about half a dozen thick warm socks and some shirts. Her son also gave me his old Class III textbooks. Oddly enough, it was while wearing a pair of these warm socks and my handmade boots that my feet nearly did freeze. This was on a particular saint's day and I was attending Mass at the nearby village of Sarigo. The temperature had really plummeted to about −20°C. About halfway through the service my toes began to hurt with cold. The sermon, about how God sees everything and cares for us, seemed endless and for the first time I began to lose my faith. After the service my feet were so frozen I could hardly walk home. When I eventually got home my mother massaged them until I could bear to put them in warm water.

These must have been extremely worrying days for my mother. She was alone with two young children, hardly spoke or understood Italian and had practically no money. What's more, food was in short supply. Surprisingly, food wasn't rationed when we first arrived in Italy; it was introduced around the time we arrived at Musadino, but there was little food in the shops and we barely had any money for the little there was. However, Giacomo Isabella (always known as Mino), the village baker and grocer, let my mother have all her groceries on credit. And, helpfully, some of the village women showed her which wild herbs to collect to make soup. For weeks we lived on a very watery soup; it always seemed to have lots of midges floating around in it which had to be skimmed off with our spoons. For breakfast we had chocolate and bread; my mother thought that the chocolate would be nutritionally beneficial for us. But while that may have been true of genuine chocolate, the *ersatz* 'chocolate' then made in Italy had no cocoa in it; all my mother was doing was running up a bigger and bigger bill. We also used rejected skimmed milk which was given away free at the Musadino dairy works. This wasn't the healthy skimmed milk now recommended, but milk from which all dairy fats had been totally removed and was given away to very poor people or to feed pigs – it was little more than grey-coloured water but was better than nothing.

I stopped getting weekly pocket money, but my mother always found a few *centesimi* (cents) to buy me *Topolino* (Mickey Mouse), a weekly comic. This had been produced since Christmas 1932 by the publisher Arnaldo Mondadori in association with Walt Disney. Like the *Dandy* and *Beano* in Britain, it carried wartime propaganda. The back always had a comic strip of the misadventures of *Ciurcillone e Re Giorgetto* (Big Fat Churchill and little King George), with Churchill always getting the gullible king in a pickle and them both ending up being chased by Italian and German soldiers. Later I often wondered if this was all tongue in cheek, because *Ciurcillone*, aside from the trademark cigar, looked remarkably like Mussolini, and King Emmanuel III of Italy was only of very diminutive stature; he was never photographed standing beside average-sized men, but always on horseback, in very tall plumed hats or seated. Surprisingly, this American comic continued to be published in Italy until 27 January 1942.

Around this time my foolish jump into the swimming pool on the *Conte Rosso* came back to haunt me. My heels were fine but increasingly, every time I jumped, even from low-lying walls, I felt a stabbing pain in my groin. Eventually it got so bad that I had to tell my mother. I was taken to the doctor in Porto and from there to the hospital in Luino by train to be operated on for a double hernia. As I was being strapped down on the operating table, the rubber gas inhaler cup was placed over my mouth and I was told to count to ten. As I did so I made the sign of the cross with my left hand, and as I started to breathe in the gas I heard a nurse say: 'How strange, they must cross themselves with their left hands in England.' I stopped counting and tried to tell her that I had used my left hand because my right hand was already strapped down, but all that came out was an indistinct mumble as I drifted off into unconsciousness. It seemed like a split second later that someone was patting my cheek and I came round to find myself in a nice warm bed.

Later that day my mother and father arrived. My father was in uniform. His regiment was in the *Lupi di Toscana* (Wolves of Tuscany) infantry division and was about to embark for Spalato (modern-day Split), which Italian troops entered on 14 April 1941; but of course he didn't know where he was going when he came to visit me on compassionate leave. Nowadays most hernias are routinely dealt with under a local anaesthetic, rarely requiring an overnight stay in hospital, but in the early 1940s all operations generally meant a fairly long hospitalisation, at least until the stitches were removed. There were no children's wards, just general male and female wards. I passed the time memorising all Italian irregular verbs and points of grammar from the Class III textbook I had been given. One day a film projector was brought in and we had Charlie Chaplin shorts. In Italy he was known as *Charlot*. I was literally in stitches laughing at him, and I had to stuff my handkerchief in my mouth to stop myself shaking, as each jolt of my body was painfully straining my stitches. It was a great relief to me when the stitches were finally taken out, but I was very reluctant to leave hospital, where I had been warm and very well fed.

8

AN INTERLUDE AT THE SEASIDE

A week or so after my discharge from hospital I was sent to a *colonia marina*, a seaside summer camp for children of poor workers. These *colonie* were run at state expense under the auspices of the GIL, the Italian Fascist Youth Movement. The one used by the province of Varese was in Loano, and that is where I was sent. My mother accompanied me on the train from Porto to Luino, and from there we went on the electric tram which connected Luino to Varese. At Varese I said goodbye to her and joined a small group of children bound for the summer camp. As the train came steaming in I saw that it had a large brass *Fascio littorio* on the front – something that I now realised all Italian railway engines, both steam and electric, carried.

On the journey south we passed very close to a prisoner-of-war camp and I could clearly see British soldiers in khaki uniforms in the barbed-wire compound. Some waved and I waved back; I thought they were waving to me, but it was probably to the young women on the train. At Genoa, and along the coast west of the city, I saw war damage for the first time. The train travelled very slowly over damaged bridges and past scores of ruins. The devastation was the result of a daring raid on 9 February 1941, when ships of the British Gibraltar force, the battleships HMS *Renown* and HMS *Malaya*, together with the cruiser HMS *Sheffield*, had extensively shelled Genoa and the Ligurian coast, virtually with impunity, firing 275 rounds of 15-inch, 782 of 6-inch and 400 of 4.5-inch shells, causing severe damage in the city, with 144 dead.[1]

Many of the children at the state-run holiday camp were from families repatriated from the Italian colony of Libya. They had arrived in Italy a few months after I had, many for the first time. They too had been brought to Italy on the *Conte Rosso*, so we had much in common. I was also at the holiday camp when news came through that the *Conte Rosso* had been torpedoed, and we all realised how lucky we were to have made it safely to Italy. At the camp the boys dressed in Balilla uniform and the girls, as *Piccole Italiane*, in white blouses. I have a clear memory of the black *mantelline* (cloaks) we wore on colder days on our daily walks. I thought the long cloaks were fantastic and they reminded me of the swashbuckling heroes I had seen in films. Not that we had many really cold days because Loano has a very mild climate with lots of palm trees growing along the waterfront.

Life in the camp followed a very rigid routine. It began with a salute to the flag at half-past seven in the morning, then half an hour of exercises before breakfast at eight. After breakfast we had a free hour; then we were marched to the beach where, in the shade, we practised deep breathing with sunbathing for one hour, followed by paddling and immersion in the sea. Lunch was at one o'clock, followed by a siesta. After our siesta we were either marched to the beach again or taken for a walk. Then more exercise, supper and in bed for nine o'clock.

It was at the seaside camp that I first experienced a Fascist totalitarian state in action. During our 'free' period we listened to *Radiorurale*, which was broadcast to those primary schools fortunate enough to have a radio (it was claimed that 3,768 schools had them).[2] It was broadcast for thirty minutes every morning. These educational programmes had a strong patriotic or Fascist bias, with broadcasts such as *The Founding of Rome* or *The Red Terror in Spain*. In addition to the school programmes, we also had several news bulletins a day. We had to listen to two of them, the newscast at breakfast and another at lunchtime, broadcast over the dining room loudspeakers. As soon as the martial music began, which preceded all newscasts, we all had to rise and stand to attention in silence until the news ended. Then, following a teacher's cry of '*A chi la vittoria?*' (To whom victory?), we all responded with '*A noi!*' (To us!), and we at last sat down to our meal. The news was generally about Italian victories, unprecedented heroism acknowledged by the enemy and victorious strategic retreats in the North African desert to ensnare the foe. At the time I believed all this. Much later I learnt the full extent of the defeats suffered by the ill-equipped and badly led Italian army in North Africa. Aside from this, however, we were very well treated and the teachers, mostly young women, were very kind to us.

Shortly after I had settled in at the camp I developed a schoolboy crush on a girl of my age of mixed race – Arab and Italian; her name was Lina. I never actually spoke to her but I used to gaze at her from a distance, and it never went further than that. Then one day to my horror I found I had lice again. I knew that if my hair was shorn off it would ruin my chances with Lina for good, so I tried to conceal my lice infestation and actually got through one cursory health check without them being discovered. Nevertheless, I came unstuck when I had my first haircut, and yet again I had my head shaved. This time my humiliation was worse in that my dormitory bed was stripped and changed and I had to wear a woollen bonnet stuffed with camphor, even in bed at night, for about a week. The bonnet full of camphor didn't quite go with the image of a Fascist Balilla, so I was forbidden from wearing the uniform. Next morning, after the teacher explained to the class that there was absolutely nothing wrong with me, Lina and all the other girls avoided me, and that was the end of that. Fortunately, this drastic treatment rid me of lice once and for all, and getting on the train back to Musadino came as a great relief.

9

RETURN TO MUSADINO

When I returned to Musadino I found that we had an influx of women and children, evacuees from Milan mainly but also from other Lombardy cities. Special trains were laid on for employed men and women to commute daily to their work in Milan. These 'commuter' trains were rather exceptional in that they consisted of cattle trucks and freight vans fitted with benches. The crowded trains left Porto around 5 a.m. and the last train got back around 10 p.m. There had been only a few evacuees before I left for the seaside. Milan then, as now, was a highly industrialised city and it had been bombed by the RAF as early as June 1940 from a French airfield near Salon, and a further four times in the same year from England. But a truly devastating attack came on 24 October 1942, when eighty-eight Lancaster bombers of 5 Group, Bomber Command, attacked the Pirelli factory in broad daylight. The raid only lasted fifteen minutes, during which 135 tons of bombs were dropped, destroying 441 homes with 173 people killed. This bombing raid came as a complete surprise and the alarm sounded after the first bomb had already exploded. Thirty-nine bombers returned to Milan that very night as fires were still raging. Like all Italian cities, Milan had insufficient public air-raid shelters and no effective anti-aircraft defence, and so presented an open target. Lurid photos of children lying dead in rubble were published in every newspaper in an attempt to make the public hate the British. But this approach completely backfired in that it simply showed how effective the bombing raids were and how ill-prepared Italy was for modern warfare.[1]

The influx of Milanese evacuees had a direct effect on my fortunes. By now I spoke both dialect and Italian reasonably well, and on my return I was accepted by all the village boys as one of them, a *rebelìtt*; it was now the turn of the poor Milanese boys to become the object of our scorn and taunts. We would jeer at them in dialect with *Milanaiz, spetascez, mangian scerez, a deëz a deëz* (*Milanesi, spetezzatori, mangiano ciliegie dieci alla volta* – Milanese farters eat cherries ten at a time), probably a reference to city children not being used to seeing fruit growing on trees. But this attitude soon passed, and they in turn came to be accepted by us. Much of this was due to our parish priest, Don Carlo, organising excursions for all of us.

I particularly remember with pleasure the first outing I went on with the group to San Michele. San Michele was just a tiny hamlet, a clutch of small houses and cowsheds, much like Pianlavagnolo near Santa Maria; the big difference was that no one lived in San Michele in the winter. Cattle and flocks of sheep and goats were driven up to San Michele in the spring for summer pasture, left to roam freely, and then brought down again at the end of September before the winter snow. It was also a tourist attraction for Milanese on *villeggiatura in montagna* (on holiday in the mountains) in pre-war Italy, and there was a small *trattoria* serving meals and drinks (in which I was later to work) and a small tenth-century chapel dedicated to Saint Michael, from which the hamlet got its name. It was on this excursion that I first heard the unaccompanied harmony singing of north Italian mountain folk. One of the adults suddenly broke out into song with *Quel mazzolin di fiori* … (That bunch of flowers …) at which several joined in, singing low … *Che vien dalla montagna* (… that comes from the mountains); then all, high and low, in harmony … *e bada ben che non si bagna, che lo voglio regalar* (… be careful that it doesn't get soaked, for I wish to give it as a gift). Nearly all the young men of the Valtravaglia were capable of singing like this, with a large repertoire of traditional songs for three voices.

Another very enjoyable excursion with Don Carlo was to Cannóbio; we travelled there by ferry from Porto, back and forth across the calm lake, to Oggebbio and Cannero, recrossing to Luino and Maccagno and finally to Cannóbio. The primary purpose of our priest taking us there was to see a painting of the Pietà, which had miraculously shed tears of blood in 1522, and which had been held in great veneration by the faithful ever since. We also visited Cannóbio's justly famous grottos – deep caverns with crystal-clear blue water accessed by rowing boat – which I found much more interesting.

I made friends with several boys from Milan; two of them remain firmly in my mind: Amleto and Dino. Amleto was a teenager and one day he was waiting for me as I came out of school. He asked me if it was true that I spoke English, and when I said it was he took out a small English book and asked me to read a line. He then asked me if I would give him some English lessons and perhaps correct his pronunciation. Then he asked me if I could play chess, and when I told him I couldn't he offered to teach me in exchange for the English lessons. So we struck a deal. He brought a chessboard and a set of chessmen with him to my house about once a week, and after I had listened to him reading from my nature book we would play chess, at which he invariably beat me. But Amleto also gave me a lifelong love of astronomy. He didn't have a telescope, but on summer evenings if there was a clear sky we would lie on a grass bank looking at the stars. In those days, in the clear mountain air and with no road lighting, one could see thousands of stars, and the Milky Way stood out as bright as the moon. These were enchanting evenings, with the starry sky above and bushes around us pulsating with the light of myriads of glow worms and fireflies.

Dino was more interested in girls than chess and astronomy, but he was great fun to be with. He and Amatore, a local lad, and I formed an almost inseparable trio, particularly in our regular summer forays to relieve local farmers of their fruit. Once or twice we nearly got caught. On one occasion a farmer chased us and, running at full pelt, I went to duck under a vine but failed to see the bottom strand of wire supporting it; my forehead hit the taut wire and I was bounced back into the long grass, knocking myself out for a few minutes. By sheer luck the farmer went running on past me in pursuit of Dino and Amatore. When I came to he was well in front of me, all three heading for the horizon; so I waited until they had all disappeared into the distance, then I got up and went home. On another occasion, in Dino's absence, Amatore took me to where his uncle stored his maturing wine in an outhouse in one of his fields. We managed to get the small door open and took two bottles of an early vintage. We had just managed to dig the corks out with our penknives and had savoured a few mouthfuls when we spotted his uncle approaching with his shotgun. It was quite normal in those days for farmers to load their guns with rock salt and there was never any fuss made if a boy, on very rare occasions, got his backside salted. We dropped the bottles and ran off, with Amatore's uncle after us; we ran and ran but he simply wouldn't give up. Finally, nearing Porto, we split up. I made a large detour and returned to Musadino, while Amatore made a similar detour in the opposite direction to where he lived. When he finally got home his sister Anita told him that he had missed all the fun. She said their uncle had chased away a gang of robbers, three or four dangerous brutes, who had tried to steal his best vintage wines.

Amatore and Anita lived with their mother in Prè, a few kilometres north of Porto on the main road to Muceno. Their father had died a few months before Amatore was born, the result of a bad beating and a dose of castor oil he had received from the Fascists a few years before his death. Such beatings and resulting deaths were not uncommon.

Benito Mussolini had founded his *Fasci di Combattimento*, paramilitary groups, in 1919 in Milan on a decidedly left-wing programme. Mussolini shot to prominence at the outbreak of the Libyan war in 1911, when he was sentenced to twelve months for trying to organise a general strike against the colonial venture. His sentence reduced on appeal, he was released from prison on 12 March 1912 to a clamorous welcome (it was at a celebration of his release that his socialist companions started to call him Il Duce, Romagna dialect for 'the leader'). Overnight he became a national figure, with a pressing invitation from the Italian Socialist Party leadership to rejoin the party from which he had resigned because, in his view, it was not revolutionary enough. Mussolini's stance brought him to notice in international socialist circles, particularly in France and Germany, and even Lenin expressed his approval by saying that with this action Italian socialism had taken 'the right road'. Mussolini assumed control of *Avanti!*, the prestigious Socialist Party newspaper, on 1 December 1912, fourteen months after entering prison as a relatively unknown provincial journalist and socialist agitator.

Almost at once the PSI (Italian Socialist Party) leadership realised that they had blundered. Mussolini used his probationary period to entrench himself in *Avanti!*, sacking all moderates and re-staffing with his followers. He then began to refuse to publish any article or letter with which he did not agree, or, if this was impolitic with a well-known contributor, he would skilfully savage it in his editorials, often by implying that it was not in tune with the party line. Having such a powerful platform at his disposal, within a few months he became a strong contender for the leadership of the party. Alarm bells really started ringing on 14 December 1913 when, during the election campaign, he wrote a highly inflammatory article entitled *Al marciapiede* (To the Streets), urging workers to abandon the democratic process in favour of revolutionary action. The majority of PSI activists were astonished at this, although many hoped or believed that having shot his bolt he would disappear from the political scene.

Eventually he went too far; he was sacked from *Avanti!* and expelled from the Socialist Party for opposing the party line of supporting Italian neutrality in 1914. In response, he founded his own newspaper, *Il Popolo d'Italia*, with

French secret service money. He then ran a strong campaign clamouring for Italian intervention in the war, culminating in Italy's declaration of war in May 1915. Increasingly, especially from 1917, the term 'fascist', which hitherto had meant nothing more than 'association member', became synonymous with 'patriot' and, in the eyes of the middle classes, 'socialist' with 'traitor', and progressively reference was made to 'internal enemies'. It is against this background that Mussolini founded his *Fasci di Combattimento* in 1919, a political movement which, despite its initial left-wing manifesto, soon became more and more right-wing. From the very outset the *Fasci di Combattimento* adopted violence instead of argument and Italy descended into almost outright civil war between the Socialists, and the offshoot Communist Party, and the Democratic Liberal parties, lay and Catholic, against the Fascists and their close allies, the Nationalists. In this bitter conflict, machine guns and even mortars were used and there were many deaths. It was during this period, and continuing up to 1925, that any anti-fascist, such as Amatore's father, was savagely beaten. Not that they needed much provocation; a beating could result from not doffing a cap quickly enough before the Italian flag. Arturo Toscanini, one of the great conductors of the twentieth century, was beaten up in public in 1931, prior to a concert he was about to conduct in Bologna, for refusing to play *Giovinezza*, the Fascist anthem.

The other notable event after my return to Musadino was the arrival of German troops in Porto Valtravaglia. The gradual infiltration of German troops into Italy began in November 1941, with the arrival and appointment of General Albert Kesselring as commander of joint Italian and German forces operating in mainland Italy and the islands, although German troops had been in southern Italy and Sicily since Rommel's intervention in North Africa. The Germans behaved like an unruly occupying force from the very start, but at this stage of the war they were generally well behaved in Porto Valtravaglia. Already, by January 1942, Mussolini was complaining about the behaviour of German troops in Italy, and Italian workers were being sent to Germany to the point of creating a labour shortage in Italy. As early as 12 January 1942, Ciano records in his diary:

> The Duce protests against the conduct of the German soldiers in Italy, especially the non-commissioned officers, who are presumptuous, quarrelsome, and drunken. Last night in Foggia two of them forced their way into a house where a man was about to go to bed, and said to him:

'We've occupied France, Belgium, Holland, and Poland, and tonight we are going to occupy your wife.' To which the man replied: 'You can occupy the whole world, but not my wife. I haven't got a wife, I'm a bachelor.' In their disappointment they smashed all his furniture before they withdrew.

And on 25 January 1942 he records:

Again Mussolini complains of the behaviour of the Germans in Italy. He has before him a transcript of a telephone call by one of Kesselring's aides, who, when speaking to Berlin, called us 'macaroni' and hoped that Italy, too, would soon become an occupied country. The Duce is keeping a dossier of all this, which 'is to be used when the moment comes'. In the meantime, he protests strongly against Clodius's[2] request to have still more Italian labourers sent to Germany. They would like to raise the number from two hundred thousand to three hundred and twenty-five thousand. It is too much …

I used to see German soldiers strolling along the water front, hiring boats and swimming at Porto's lido. We had a cinema in Porto; there was some resentment at having the back four rows reserved exclusively for Germans, but they behaved well. After their evening meal they used to wheel out two huge cauldrons with the dregs of leftover soup and hungry kids would gather waiting for it to be doled out. I went along a couple of times with a tin can but I stopped when I saw the Germans were laughing at us.

Food was indeed becoming a problem, particularly for us in the absence of my father. On 28 March 1942 Venice had the first demonstrations caused by bread shortages, and on 29 March there were bread riots at Matera, in the region of Basilicata in southern Italy, where groups of women broke into Fascist Party headquarters only to be dispersed by force with shots fired in the air. Commenting on the Matera riots on 29 March 1942, Ciano recorded: 'These are serious symptoms, especially as the harvest is far away and the available food supply scarcer and scarcer.' He took a short fishing break on 31 May 1942 and noted in his diary:

A day of rest and fishing. But this does not save me from complaints about food, which is very short. Wine is lacking, and so is everything else. Renato, my fisherman, has lost thirty pounds in a few months, and he tells me that the members of his family are losing weight at the same rate …

Earlier than this, during the school holidays in the summer of 1941, I attended the *colonia elioterapica* (Sun and Earth Camp) just outside Porto Valtravaglia, thanks to my teacher. These camps were a pre-war Fascist idea to promote healthy living, and as the name implies we spent a lot of time sunbathing at the lakeside. For lunch we were given a weak soup with over-cooked rice which many of the children disliked, but it all had to be eaten. So I would get the kids who couldn't eat it to quickly pass their bowls to me and I would polish the food off.

At the camp I grew very fond of a Jewish girl called Renata, known as *Mancina* (left-handed), because she had lost her right hand, and I used to try to lie near her in the sunbathing sessions. It may seem surprising that there was a Jewish girl in a Fascist holiday camp, but her family was probably in one of the many categories which were then exempt from the provisions of the various racial laws. But the fact that she was a Jew didn't arouse the least interest in the rest of us. One day, while we were all sunbathing, a boy of about my age appeared standing on the camp perimeter wall, taunting us all for being Fascists. It was Amatore, and that is how I first met him. He was still hanging around when we came out and I forget now how it came about, but I ended up walking home with him to his house in Prè. As we walked along he told me that the Fascists had killed his father whom he had never known and I told him about my life and how I had ended up in Musadino, although he had already heard about me.

One evening, a few weeks into our friendship, Amatore arrived at my house to bid me farewell forever. He announced that he was running away from home and had only stopped off to say goodbye. I told him to hang on a minute and I would join him. I found an appropriate red tea towel and a stick to tie it on, as I'd seen in cartoons of tramps. I put in a knife and fork and a few things, left a note for my mother telling her that I was off to make my fortune, and off we set. When we were out of the village and heading towards Domo I asked Amatore where we were going and he said he had no idea. I then suggested we first make for Milan and decide what to do when we got there. We passed through villages we didn't know and eventually got to the outskirts of Laveno as night was falling. There we met a man coming in the opposite direction with a horse and cart and we asked him what road we should take for Gallarate after Laveno. He stopped his cart and asked us where we were from and why we were going there so late. We told him that we were just passing through heading for Milan. He said something like: 'You lads had best save up and go by train. Come on, jump on the cart and I'll take you home.' I jumped on the cart straight away and we started off slowly, with Amatore trailing behind complaining, but eventually he jumped on too. As soon as he did so the carter whipped his horse into a brisk trot and I soon fell asleep on some sacks. When I woke up we were back in Musadino with a small crowd carrying lanterns gathered around the cart; my mother was in tears. I expected to be in hot water but all I got was a big hug from her. The carter said he couldn't go to Prè as it was out of his way, so someone took Amatore home. He got a similar reception to mine. We were banned from seeing each other for about a fortnight, each mother thinking that the other one was a bad influence on her son. Dino was furious with us for sneaking off without him.

10

WHILE MY FATHER WAS IN THE ARMY

My mother was a very gentle person. Moreover, she was a city person through and through and would have found village life strange even in England. Nothing had prepared her for life in Musadino; Italian village life was truly foreign to her in every way and even after months there she could barely comprehend the local dialect. Isolated as she must have felt, with two young children, she did her best to cope without my father. It would have been bad enough for a city woman had she spoken the language, but as it was, and with acute food shortages, it was a nightmare.

Cooking in particular was difficult for her. All cooking was done in the big fireplace over a wood-burning fire. Large pots were hung over the fire on a chain with a hook and you adjusted the heat by raising or lowering the chain. Smaller pans were placed close to the fire and required constant stirring to distribute the heat. With green wood there was lots of smoke and the fire was often on the point of going out, requiring constant blowing as we didn't have any bellows. We also lacked firewood and couldn't keep the fire lit all the time. Clothes were washed at the *lavatoio communale* (public wash house). In Musadino this was a fountain in the shape of a lion's head with incessant water running from its mouth (typical of fountains in nearly all the villages), and behind it stood two large stone troughs, one for scrubbing clothes and the other for rinsing. The same soap was utilised both for personal use and for washing clothes; it was bought in a long slab and you cut off a small block for use. There were always women at the fountain in summer and winter, washing clothes in the icy cold water. The *lavatoio* was only a couple of hundred metres from our house, but my mother hated going there and would do her best to wash our clothes at home. This meant bringing even more water in from the street tap outside our door.

My mother had also yet to learn how villagers washed their sheets, a process completely alien to her. The women would take the sheets to the public wash house like my mother did, but then they would return home with the wet rinsed sheets and place them in a wooden tub on a trestle; this would be lined with canvas and the sheets placed inside, with another piece of canvas covering the top. Then boiling water mixed with white firewood ash would be poured in, with the top canvas acting as a filter for the ash. After about an hour, a bung in the bottom of the tub was released and the water collected; the bung was then replaced and the liquid poured in and filtered once again. The sheets were left in the tub overnight then taken to the public fountain once more and rinsed in fresh water. This very old process removed all dirt and stains and whitened the bed linen, which was finally hung out to dry.

We had electric lighting but there were no power points and, consequently, neither we nor others had electric irons. The irons in use in those days were heated with charcoal; the entire upper half of the iron hinged open and inside it you would place hot embers from the fire and cover them with charcoal. Then, after closing the top, the iron was swung back and forth; the oxygen from the current of air thus created would liven up the embers and ignite the charcoal, raising it and the iron to a high temperature. At first, either the iron would go out and would rapidly get cold, or it got overheated and would scorch anything it touched. Ironing clothes, village style, was a bit of a nightmare for my mother until she got the hang of it.

As I previously mentioned, we wore *zoccoli*, crude footwear consisting of a hewn wooden sole and a leather strap in which to insert your foot. These took some getting used to and my mother and sister were constantly knocking their inner anklebones, causing them to ulcerate. My mother was completely unprepared for village ways and customs. We had only been there a few months when a middle-aged man caught a chill, which developed into pneumonia, and he died. On those sad occasions all the women would go to the deceased's house to say the Rosary. Virginia, our next-door neighbour, called on my mother to take her there. Not quite understanding what it was about, my mother took me and my sister Gloria along with her. When we got there we were ushered into an already crowded room with the women – some seated, others kneeling – reciting the Rosary in Latin. Chairs were brought in for us and we were placed near a double bed, our knees almost touching it. There, lying on the matrimonial bed, was the man's cadaver. My mother had never seen a dead body before and it came as quite a shock to her; Gloria probably thought he was sleeping and I, utterly fascinated, couldn't

take my eyes off him. The women must have been puzzled as to why my
mother had brought us along.

But some village ways and customs were pleasurable. Before the war, many
of the women in the village earned a supplementary income by raising silkworms. They had done this for many generations and were still doing so in
1940 and were very expert at it. The silkworms had to be fed daily with fresh
branches of mulberry, the only food they will eat. At that time there were
hundreds of mulberry trees around the Valtravaglia area grown solely to feed
silkworms. After about two months eating the leaves they stop feeding and
spend approximately five days spinning a cocoon, each one made of a single
thread of golden-yellow silk, tens of metres long. We used to help Virginia
and the other women pluck these lovely cocoons from the stripped mulberry
branches, which were then sold to a silk factory in Germignaga.

Early summer was haymaking time. The village men cut the long meadow
grass with scythes; this was heavy, back-breaking work and the men were
supplied constantly with wine mixed with water as they toiled without a
break under the hot sun, pausing only occasionally to hone their scythes
with their whetstones, which they carried on their belts in a cow's horn half
filled with water. We children and the women followed them, spreading the
newly mown hay with large wooden rakes, called *rastrelli*. In the evening the
men would spend an hour or so resetting their scythe blades by hammering
them to razor thinness with a special steel hammer, a *martello battifalce*, on
a distinctive chisel-shaped steel anvil, hammered into the ground or into a
piece of timber.

The other joy was chestnut time. The entire Valtravaglia was covered in sweet
chestnut trees, some very ancient. Chestnuts mature between September and
October and the longer they are left to mature the sweeter they are. The men
of the Valtravaglia used very long, slender and supple poles, almost as long as
the trees were high, to beat the laden branches, and the chestnuts would come
tumbling down to be collected by the women and children. The poles were
themselves made of chestnut and were specifically grown to a great height by
trimming all branches, keeping them very slender by blocking the light from
all except the tip. The men who used them to beat down the chestnuts wore
leather protective clothing and stout gloves to prevent injury from the falling
spiny chestnut casings. The chestnuts were known as the poor man's bread
and were eaten in a variety of ways: boiled in a pot or roasted in a special
padella per castagne – this was like a stout sieve with a longer handle than a
frying pan and a looped handle about a third of the way down. It was hooked

over hot embers and every so often the pan handle was flicked, causing the roasting chestnuts to bounce over so they were roasted evenly.

Two local dishes made with chestnuts were *mac* and *castagnaccia*; *mac* was made with chestnuts, rice and milk, and was absolutely delicious. *Castagnaccia* was a type of cake made from the ground flour of dried chestnuts. I recall wonderful evenings at Virginia's when she and her daughter Ilda would invite us to share a big *padella* of roasted chestnuts with them. Also, there were large expanses of the hillsides covered with blueberries and fragrant wild strawberries, and in summer Gloria and I would go with my mother to pick them.

Every house seemed to have their own wine; we were there when wine was still made in the traditional way, with men crushing the grapes in huge tubs with their bare feet. I recall watching the wine fermenting and bubbling, and savouring the fresh sweet smell before it was bottled. If you visited a neighbour you were always offered a bowl of wine to drink. Some of the wine was excellent, but a lot of it was rustic plonk of poor quality and quite acidic. My dad used to jokingly tell me to make sure to sit near the corner of a table so I could grab a table leg to face the 'ordeal' of the quick swig, before praising it and swiftly passing the bowl on.

My mother received a small allowance while my father was in the army, but since there was little food in the shops and the money was insufficient to buy it on the thriving black market, it was spent on other things such as going to the cinema in Porto about twice a month. We never went alone, but usually with a crowd of women from Musadino; it was very rare for the men to go. The seats were all at the same level, so the screen was rather high up. There was only one projector so a three-reel film show had to stop twice for the reel to be changed. The lights would go up, and if the projectionist wasn't quick enough in changing the reels the audience would get restive and there would be whistles and cat-calls for him to get a move on.

About once a month we would walk the 8km to Luino's outdoor market. The road was more or less at a level height from Muceno and on to Brezzo di Bedero. We would always stop for a rest at a point aptly called Belvedere, from where there was a magnificent view of the whole of Lake Maggiore, and from there we would make the long descent. The road, like all mountain roads, snaked back and forth to lessen the gradient for carts to Germignaga and nearby Luino. Occasionally, on our way to Luino we would call in to visit my father's paternal uncle in Germignaga. He was then in his mid-seventies, lived alone, and was in no position to help us financially or otherwise; in fact, more often than not we would take him some fruit. Then we would walk on to Luino where, on hot days, my mother would buy us big slices of iced watermelon or cool water from the street sellers.

On a darker note, the army started using the lower slopes of Pian Nave as a firing range, and all day during these exercises you would hear the rat-tat-tat of machine guns and rifle fire, and the explosion of mortars. Little care was taken over safety, and when the soldiers had finished and cleared off, boys from the surrounding villages went to look for spent bullets and discarded live ammunition. Inevitably there were accidents, and one afternoon a boy had his hands blown off when a small mortar bomb he was playing with exploded. But even after that, and with warnings from our parents, we still went up to look for rounds of ammunition.

One day I was coming back from Porto along the main road to Muceno. Just outside Porto this road passed Boltri, an engineering factory where I was to work on a lathe in 1944. On the other side of the road there was a quite a large field and I saw a crowd gathered there watching an army exercise. There were two tanks and the soldiers were lying on the ground letting the tanks run over them, after which they would jump up and attack the tanks from the rear. They were also doing this from one-man slit trenches, ducking as a tank approached, then, after it had passed harmlessly over their heads, springing out to attach explosives to it. It all seemed so neat and well choreographed, and appeared to make tanks completely vulnerable to infantry with small arms. Years later, when I was in the army myself, I realised how pointless and impracticable that training had been.

For the 1942/43 scholastic year I was moved up to the fourth elementary class; the fourth and fifth classes were held in Porto. I remember that it was a very wet autumn and I used a heavy hessian sack to protect me from the pouring rain walking to and from school. Although I didn't possess a coat, I did have a pair of swimming trunks, and during hot weather, either towards the end of the school term or during the long summer holidays, we all used to go to the lido (the same stretch of beach used by the *colonia elioterapica*) to swim and sunbathe. We all taught ourselves to swim here.

When it was too cold to swim, after school we would go to a newsagent's near the Albergo del Sole. The newsagent was a kind man who seemed very old to us boys; unfortunately I have forgotten his name. He owned several pleasure rowing boats, and before the war no doubt had a good income in the summer, hiring them out to tourists and city people on holiday. Now all the boats lay covered in Porto's harbour opposite his shop. We started out by hiring one for an hour, but eventually we were taking out three or four boats at a time for two or more hours. Of course we had no money to pay for all this, but he let us hire them on tick, and soon we owed him an astronomical sum. He would chuckle about this and although it was never said, we all knew it would be written off. I suppose letting us use the boats helped keep them watertight.

We also used to play at *lippa*. This was a very popular but simple game played outdoors. All you needed was a stout stick and a similar piece of wood about 20cm long with both ends tapered; you simply hit one of the tapered ends, sending it spinning vertically up, and you struck it as hard as you could in mid-air. In one dangerous version you aimed it at your opponent and he did the same in return. Small pieces of carbide were fairly easy to come by, at least in the earlier part of the war. A winter pastime on dark nights was causing explosions with a tin can and carbide. Carbide was used in lamps; it generates acetylene by reaction with water. You would get a tin can and punch a hole in the bottom with a nail; then you spat on your piece of carbide and covered it with the can, placing your thumb over the hole. When you felt the can lifting with the acetylene gas pressure, you removed your thumb and applied a lit match to the hole. There would be a flash and a loud bang and the can would go flying. The dare was to see who could keep his thumb over the hole the longest and produce the loudest explosion.

On 27 July 1942 Cardinal Schuster, the Archbishop of Milan, came on a pastoral visit. This was a very important event for Domo and Musadino. His last visit to the parish had been in 1930, one of about thirty pastoral visits to Domo from a Milanese archbishop since the eleventh century. I was one of a group of children he confirmed. This is a Catholic sacrament in which you are confirmed in the Catholic religion and given a new name in addition to your baptismal name. I was much looking forward to this and had chosen the name Julian. We were all lined up in a row outside the church. When he came to me, the cardinal confirmed me by making the Sign of the Cross with his thumb with consecrated oil on my forehead, and to my surprise and disappointment named me Peter; he then spoke a few words to me which I now can't remember. Whether our parish priest had made a mistake or whether the archbishop had rejected the name Julian because the Roman Emperor Julian, known as Julian the Apostate, had rejected Christianity, I shall never know. But Peter I was and Peter I remained. Nor did I ever imagine that Cardinal Schuster was destined to play an important role of mediation between Mussolini and the Partisan leadership, in trying to arrange for the surrender of all Fascist forces in April 1945.

It was at Porto on 28 October, the anniversary of the March on Rome when the Fascist year began, either in 1941 or 1942 (I now forget which) that I took part in a great Fascist rally in Porto Valtravaglia. The whole school had to attend in black shirts and were drawn up in ranks along the broad lake front, which was festooned with flags and banners, combined with a military parade of soldiers from the local barracks. The Balilla (us) were led by those teachers who were members of the MVSN (Voluntary Militia for National Security). In Porto the municipal doctor, Dr Ballerò, was a middle-aged man, small and with a paunch. I was astonished to see him and the local chemist as MVSN officers in full Fascist uniform, with their stomachs pulled in by blue cummerbunds, looking quite ridiculous. There was a lot of smirking and suppressed giggles among my school chums at the sight of them. At the end of the parade we were all, except for the soldiers, marched off to church for a solemn Mass and a blessing of the flags. All the flags and banners were held by MVSN or *carabinieri* bearers in full uniform, including their fascist 'fez' or matador-type headwear. At first it surprised me to see men wearing hats in church and the priests not objecting to this, but then I realised the whole thing was a farce.

II

MY FATHER'S RETURN HOME

My father was unexpectedly released from the army and arrived home on 8 December 1942. I can accurately pinpoint the date he came back because it was the feast of the Immaculate Conception, a public holiday and an important day in the Catholic calendar. Mussolini had already released 600,000 servicemen in November 1940 at the very time he was invading Greece; general mobilisation was never declared, with up to a million men exempted from call-up for various reasons, and various categories continued to be discharged.

My father told us that he should have been home a week or two earlier, but the first train he was on was ambushed by Tito's partisans, the line was blown up and the train machine-gunned. He also told us that since they were being discharged they had little or no ammunition with them, so they had jumped down from the carriage and lain down on the track behind a train wheel for cover. By this time my father's eyes had been opened; plain and simple, he had left as a Fascist and returned as a committed anti-fascist.

During my father's absence we had all slept in the main bedroom: me in a normal single bed and my mother and sister in a double bed. But when my father returned my sister Gloria got my single bed and I was moved upstairs to the top bedroom. Here my bed consisted of a pair of iron bars on legs, with three planks laid on them and a palliasse on top; it was a type of bed dating back centuries but actually very comfortable. The only trouble was I had to go outside on to the balcony to access the stairs to my room.

My mother explained to my father that she had been forced to get food on credit and had run up quite a hefty bill. Angry though he was, he immediately went to see Mino, the shop owner. Mino agreed that he could settle the bill by sawing and preparing firewood for him. My father also immediately got a job at Boltri's, the factory on the outskirts of Porto Valtravaglia, as a specialist grinder. Factories were then working a ten-hour day, except for Saturdays when they closed at one o'clock. This was officially called *il sabato fascista* (Fascist Saturday) and was introduced by Mussolini in June 1935. It was not meant to be an afternoon of leisure, but was designated for pre-military training and Fascist cultural and sporting activities. But factory workers simply ignored this and it became known as *il sabato inglese* (the English weekend). Gian Franco Venè, the Italian social historian, records that before the war in offices and factories there was an undeclared understanding that politics were not for the workplace, and there was a tacit truce between convinced Fascists, opportunistic Fascists and anti-fascists. However, in the early days of the *sabato fascista* Fascists took to coming to work on Saturday morning in full uniform so as to be ready for the one o'clock parades; this proved embarrassing both for Fascists and anti-fascists and created a rigid atmosphere on the shop floor which badly affected production. Over time the opportunistic Fascists came to work in their civilian clothes, which isolated and pinpointed who the true Fascists were.[1] By the time we worked there, no one ever turned up in Fascist uniform or, as far as I know, attended Fascist rallies.

My father would return from the factory, do a few hours' work for Mino, and on top of that do work for us, either digging our land or cutting firewood. He also bought a wood-burning iron stove with four cooking rings, each consisting of several cast-iron rings which you removed with a hook depending on the size of pan being used or the amount of heat required. Additionally, it had two small inefficient ovens and heated about 5 litres of water. The stove was placed on the wall opposite the fireplace and the smoke was carried through connected tin tubes across the room to the fireplace chimney. This was all very well with dry wood or a well-lit fire, but if we burnt green wood, as was sometimes necessary, the smoke tubes used to drip with a smelly brown liquid. But this was an improvement from having the house full of smoke from the fireplace. Another advantage of the stove was that every spring my father would carry it out on to the balcony and set it up there, so that cooking was more bearable in the hot weather.

Soon after my father's return I got a long lecture from him. He told me that my days of playing about were over and that from now on he expected me to do my share of the work. After school I was to bring home at least a bundle of wood per day. He was incensed to hear that for the past two winters we had sat in the house freezing and that I had done little to help. I was 12 years old then, and I should point out that all country boys in Italy from the age of 10 and even younger helped with work: tending to animals, picking fruit, collecting wood, hoeing and many other tasks. So there was nothing unusual in my father insisting I did some work at 11 or 12 years of age. It was probably my not working which had raised some eyebrows in the village.

Within a few days he had bought me a *falcetto*, a spade and a good penknife; and day after day we went up into the mountains cutting wood. He showed me how to tie a bundle of wood properly using a slender branch. We worked many weeks together until we had enough wood to see us through the winter. My dad also showed me how to saw logs and to use wedges to split them. He could bring down truly massive bundles of brushwood too heavy to lift. He would cut a long pole with a fork midway, thrust it in the bundle of wood and then shoulder it, holding the pole and dragging the heavy load along.

My father also taught me what was edible in the wild – how to recognise edible mushrooms and wild herbs and where they could be found, and also frogs and snails; in fact, every small or large wild mammal, bird, amphibian or fish. He showed me how to find birds' nests, usually blackbirds, and keep an eye on them until the fledglings were almost ready to leave the nest; then how to quickly dispatch them and clean them. Over the next three years, thanks to my father, we were never in any danger of starvation. He would cook up really tasty meals, using squirrel, hedgehog or the like. As for frogs, we ate the whole thing, not just the legs.

A few weeks after he returned, he and a village friend set some meat as bait for freshwater shrimps in a nearby stream. They took me along with them at nightfall, with lanterns, to find the bait surrounded with shrimps there for the taking; it was nearly dawn when we got back home. My father showed me how to pull the head off neatly and eat the shrimp raw, and also how to find them in daylight by feeling under stones in pools away from the main current. But best of all he showed me how to look for trout in larger pools and then watch where they went when they darted for cover, and how to tickle one and scoop it out. Every time it rained I would take a bucket and collect snails from the stone walls. My poor mother couldn't bring herself to eat small birds, frogs or snails, but at least it left the more conventional food for her.

Recounting these events in such a condensed fashion makes my father appear to have been an outdoor survival expert, but this wasn't the case. He had learnt his skills as a boy from his father, just as he had handed them on to me. Some he had forgotten and was himself shown by the other villagers. No one in Musadino, as far as I remember, ate frogs; this was something my father knew about from France. And we only ate a cat on one occasion, for strangely they all disappeared from the village, despite everyone vehemently denying that they would ever eat a cat.

Although you wouldn't starve to death on such fare, you couldn't rely on eating frogs and snails alone. You also needed carbohydrates such as potatoes, cereals and rice. Flour, pasta and rice were rationed from the autumn of 1940. Bread rationing was introduced in October 1941 when each person got 250g (about five thin slices of bread) per day, but even that was progressively reduced to 150g (three slices) during 1942.

After he had saved up the train fare, my father took two suitcases and went to the rice fields on the Po plains, around Novara and Vercelli, to see if he could buy rice or any other cereals there. Late that same night he returned with nothing more than a kilogram or two of rice which, taking into account the train fare, he could have got cheaper in Porto on the black market. This was the first and only time that I saw my father break down in tears. A few weeks after this he repeated the journey, only this time he took me with him plus two extra suitcases. On my last train journey I had travelled in a second-class passenger carriage, but now the wooden-seated third-class carriages were upgraded to second and first class. Freight wagons, fitted with improvised wooden benches and straw on the floor, were used for third-class passengers. We travelled third class.

When we finally got to the rice fields I thought the day would never end. The farmhouses lay at considerable distance from each other in the dead flat plain; the day was hot, and we tramped along dusty and seemingly interminable roads. When we asked to buy rice or maize we had many refusals; some polite, some not. Some offered to sell us any amount we wanted but at prices we could not afford. Finally, when I was beginning to think that we would return empty-handed, we found a farmer who sold us both rice and maize at a high but reasonable price, almost filling all four cases. We had three full cases, but my dad put half of one into the empty case so that we had two full ones and two half empty. I carried the two half-empty cases, but I had to stop frequently on the long slog back to the railway station.

The journey home with the four suitcases was no doubt a nightmare for my father, but after we got to the station it was very exciting for me. The worst bit was getting on the train to Novara from a small country station. There was a large crowd waiting and when the train finally arrived it was already crowded with passengers hanging on the sides. We managed to push through the throng and get on the train by climbing between two cattle wagons and standing over the buffers between them. I remember my father clutching me tightly, his arms around me, with the two half-empty suitcases he held banging on my knees. The two full ones he secured to the carriage with his belt. We stopped at one point and a long train passed by slowly, heading south: flatcar after flatcar loaded with tanks all covered with camouflage netting and tree branches, and on every flatcar, seated at the rear, there was a steel-helmeted German soldier with a rifle. Although I didn't know this at the time, the tanks were probably an advance consignment for the newly reformed and renamed Panzer-Division *Hermann Göring*, which had been quickly formed from the few survivors of the Division *Hermann Göring* destroyed in the final battles in Tunis, and from scattered elements from France, Holland and Germany. The division was worked up in France and then transferred by rail to the Naples area, where it gradually gathered in June 1943 before moving on to Sicily. Later it was to play a key role in disarming Italian troops. But whether it was that particular division or not, it was quite an impressive sight. Finally we got to Novara where things were less chaotic, and on the train journey from Novara to Porto Valtravaglia we actually found seats on the crowded benches.

We had been offered maize flour, but we had only bought a few kilograms. What my father had searched for, and found, was dried maize grain taken directly off the cob. My dad's plan was to grow our own maize by planting this seed. We had the use of three pieces of land which all had names: Mulin, Vignascia and Noèlla. The first two were owned by the Ghiringhelli family, but Noèlla belonged to my father's uncle, Peter, who was in Leeds. Noèlla had a big pear tree and an old fig tree. My father planted peach trees there and showed me how he grafted them. He dug up Noèlla, which had run wild, and we used it for growing vegetables. Mulin was a larger piece of land, a meadow with lots of mulberry trees for silkworms. My father felled all the mulberry trees and dug over the entire meadow by hand. Here he planted the precious maize which we had bought in the Po valley.

It seemed a long time getting the first crop, but once we got it we dried the cobs, strung them up in my bedroom at the top of the house, then stripped them and took the maize corn to the Musadino miller (he was the carpenter who had made my stilts), and there it was ground to flour. From then on we lived mainly on polenta. Polenta, now a dish served in top restaurants, is simply cornmeal (ground maize) cooked in boiling water. Traditionally it was cooked in a big cast-iron pot and constantly stirred with a big thick stick until all the water was either absorbed or boiled off, leaving a stiff porridge-like mixture; this was tipped out on a board and slices cut with string. We had polenta with every meal; or rather at every meal we had something to accompany our polenta. My sister Gloria, now in her seventies, still cannot stand the sight of polenta after eating it morning, noon and night for three years. It ensured that we didn't starve, but every year it meant that my father and I had to dig Mulin all over again, with me digging perhaps only a third or less.

On one memorable occasion I went high in the mountains to cut wood; normally we stayed in the foothills where the hazel bushes grew, and most of the firewood we cut was, in fact, hazel wood. But beyond a certain height hazel doesn't flourish because of the colder temperature, and on this particular day I pressed on above the hazel wood line. Just below the summit of Pian Nave in a sheltered area there were birch trees. These were grown for timber and harvested every ten to fifteen years. I was about to return to a lower level when I saw a young birch I thought I could carry and I started to fell it, cutting it with my *falcetto* on the side I wanted it to drop. This took me far longer than I expected, but eventually I got it down and lopped off all the branches, leaving the trunk stripped. I then discovered that I had miscalculated and it was far too heavy for me, and I lost more time cutting the trunk in two. Again I had misjudged and the lower thicker piece was still too heavy and I could only drag it.

As it seemed to be getting late, I decided to take the wood over to the Rià to see if I could perhaps float it down rather than retracing my steps. This was a big mistake. First, the torrent was far further over than I had judged and it took me the best part of an hour to get to it, carrying the lighter piece then going back to drag the heavier one. Eventually I got to the torrent only to find that the sides were far steeper than they seemed from a distance looking up. However, there did seem to be enough water to float the two pieces of wood, so I pressed on. I got one down then had quite a struggle getting back up the crumbling sides, and it took me some time to find where I had left the other. Finally I was back down with both pieces and off they floated, with me following along the side of the torrent. Suddenly, I heard the water getting louder and louder as I went through a gorge and the wood gathered speed. I ran after it only to see it disappear over a series of waterfalls.

I tried to climb down to where I judged the logs to be, but I had come too far down and had to follow the torrent upstream until I found both pieces. After this it was a slog back and forth, moving the two pieces along, and as the torrent bed got wider, the water – spreading out – got shallower. I would have been better off just going straight down the mountain as there was no way I could get the logs up out of the torrent bed. Occasionally I would get to a deep pool, and in one I saw trout. I was tired and hungry so I watched where the trout went when disturbed; I tickled one and scooped it out. I usually lit fires using a magnifying glass, so I left the logs and climbed up into the sunshine, lit a fire and cooked and ate my trout – I felt a lot better after that.

I went back to my wood and pressed on, reaching a point near Sarigo when it was beginning to get dark. To my surprise and great relief I saw my father coming up the riverbed, having spent a couple of hours searching for me. He asked me if I was alright, then shouldered the larger piece while I took the other, and we set off home. When we got back I was expecting great praise, but far from that I got a real ticking off for not sticking to the mountain paths and for chopping down the tree. He told me it was common knowledge that all the birches high on Pian Nave were private property. I spent the next two afternoons sawing the logs then splitting them up into firewood with an axe. I thought that was the end of the matter, but that tree was to come back and haunt me a couple of years later.

It wasn't hard work all the time. I still went to the beach and always kept my bathing trunks in my school *cartella*. None of us had a towel, and to dry off we would lie in the sun after patting ourselves down with hot flat stones, sending them skimming across the water afterwards to see who could get the most hops. However, I would sometimes cut my stay short, and after a quick dip, still half-wet, I would dash home and get my *falcetto* for wood or do some hoeing.

I was also reading a lot at this time. Amatore was my main source for books and we both used to devour the swashbuckling tales of Sandokan by Emilio Salgari, with the pirates of Malaysia battling the White Rajah, and the renowned hunter Tremal-Naik living in the Black Jungle, teeming with tigers and other dangerous beasts, where few other men but he could live. Dino, Amatore and I would build secret hideaways by bending over and interweaving branches; here we would act out episodes of the adventures of Sandokan and his trusty band. We swore that after the war we three would go to Malaya and China and follow in the steps of our hero.

Gloria and I had stopped getting birthday and Christmas gifts (more properly *Beffana* gifts on 6 January, when Italian children got their presents), but for my very last birthday gift in June 1942 my mother surprised me with a copy of Dante's *Divina Commedia*. Around this time I also first read Manzoni's *I promessi sposi*. Other books I subsequently had from Amatore were Victor Hugo's *Notre-Dame de Paris* (*The Hunchback of Notre Dame*), which I had seen as a film in Leeds with Charles Laughton, and *Les Misérables*. These books enthralled me and opened up a whole new world to me, and I have never quite recaptured the pleasure I had on first reading them, by candlelight in bed, in those troublesome days.

12

FALL AND RISE OF IL DUCE

At 2.40 a.m. on 25 July 1943, following a ten-hour meeting, the Fascist Grand Council passed a motion proposed by Dino Grandi of no confidence in Mussolini, with nineteen votes in favour and seven against. That the motion was put to the meeting and debated is truly astonishing, because the Grand Council was controlled by Mussolini and designed by him as an instrument of his personal power. Mussolini decided who the members were and, since there was no quorum, he could hold a valid meeting with just one person if he so wished. He called it into session when and with whom he liked. In fact, the last meeting before the fatal one was on 7 December 1939, when the Grand Council had declared Italy's non-belligerency. What brought about Mussolini's downfall was that he had overplayed his hand by vainly taking on too many ministerial posts and armed forces responsibilities. By 1943, as well as being head of the armed forces, he was Prime Minister, Foreign Minister (having sacked Ciano), Home Affairs Minister, Minister for War, Minister for Naval Affairs and Minister for Aeronautical Affairs. Furthermore, Mussolini's bizarre decision, on 17 January 1941, to send off all the regime's ruling members – the *gerarchi* (hierarchs), the key persons in the Fascist Party – to serve for three months at the front, caused bewilderment and resentment. As Ciano recorded:

> The topic of the day is the Duce's decision to mobilize by the first of February all the high Fascist officials – Government, Grand Council, Chamber, and Party. When Serena[1] made some objections about the practicality of the matter, he replied that it will be an interesting experiment in government with he, the Duce, working directly with the bureaucracy ...

It not only caused resentment, but more seriously it showed them at first hand how ill-prepared and under-equipped the armed forces were and how incompetent the Ministries, run directly by Mussolini, had been. This simmering bitterness came to a head with the Allied conquest of Sicily and the clearly imminent invasion of the mainland. Pressed by a delegation of *gerarchi*, led by Grandi and Bottai,[2] Mussolini agreed to call the Grand Council into session; Bastianini (who had taken such an interest in my broken arm) also attended and voted for the motion. No one at the meeting envisaged the fall of Fascism. What the *gerarchi* wanted was for Mussolini to relinquish control of the army and for command to be restored to the king. Three motions to this effect were put forward; the one by Dino Grandi won. Mussolini still believed he was in control and that he could disregard the Grand Council, his own creation, and he was fully confident when he went to Villa Savoia at 5 p.m. the same day for his usual meeting with the king. But in a pre-arranged coup, the king had him arrested and appointed Marshal Pietro Badoglio[3] in his place.

This extraordinary turn of events was completely unexpected and everyone was stunned at the news. As 25 July was a Sunday all factories were closed. The whole country erupted in jubilation with crowds in the streets. Newspapers, overnight, free from Fascist censure, had banner headlines covering most of their front pages. Sledgehammers came out and the *fascio littorale*, the Fascist emblem, was smashed and hacked off walls and monuments everywhere. The ubiquitous Fascist white-painted slogans, such as *Mussolini ha sempre ragione* (Mussolini is always right), which I had first seen in Rome, were obliterated. Caught up in the fervour, I painted *VV Badoglio!* (Long Live Badoglio!) on the outside wall of our living room. Everyone seemed to be convinced that the war was about to end, and Badoglio's broadcast saying that it would continue was taken with a pinch of salt.

A phrase from his speech was *La guerra continua* (The war continues), a phrase which stuck in my mind because just about every newspaper headlined it. Mussolini was said to be under arrest in a secret place and it was assumed by all that the Fascists were finished. The Fascists in the Valtravaglia vanished overnight; some, such as Ezio Galante, the *Podestà* (Fascist mayor) of Luino, fled to Switzerland, and many others were arrested. There was a blaze of red flags everywhere and the Musadino village band brought out their hidden instruments and played for the first time since 1922. The band was headed by Carlin, who lived next door to Amatore in Prè; a man full of fun who had always been very kind to me. He, like Amatore's father, had been severely beaten and made to drink castor oil by Fascists in the 1920s. A celebratory dance, with the band playing, was held in the village school which was festooned with bunting and flags. I remember walking home as dawn was breaking, tired but very happy – the first time I had ever been allowed to stay up all night.

However, under Badoglio between 25 July and 8 September 1943, inexplicably the *carabinieri* retained the Fascist authoritarian mindset and in many locations in cities and towns all over Italy they opened fire on workers' anti-war demonstrations, killing well over a hundred people, with many more wounded. In one incident, and not the worst by far, on 29 July in Milan, the army and the police opened fire, killing three demonstrators and wounding three others. A day later a general strike was held in protest, when again the army and police killed five strikers and wounded four. In view of the unrest, real or imagined, Badoglio imposed a general curfew, from 10 p.m. until 5 a.m. in all areas, and any gathering of more than three people was made unlawful. At Laveno, near us, a man was shot on the night of 5 August for breaking the curfew. It was never rescinded, but was simply continued by the Germans. Even the times remained the same in most places, although with local variations; in the Valtravaglia, possibly because of its proximity to the Swiss border, it started at 9 p.m. All public venues, such as cinemas, cafes and taverns, had to close, with all customers off the premises half an hour before curfew; exempted night workers required special permits with designated routes.

On 1 September news came through that the Allies had crossed unopposed from Sicily to the Italian mainland at Reggio Calabria (where we had arrived in June 1940), and on 8 September 1943 Badoglio announced what had been expected all August, that Italy was unable to continue the war and was seeking an armistice. We then learnt that Badoglio's government and the king had fled from Rome. In order to explain how this affected the Valtravaglia it is necessary to go back a few months.

In early 1943 a military garrison was set up in a requisitioned section of the *Vetreria Lucchini*, the glass factory in Porto Valtravaglia. It was manned by a staff of about thirty from the 7th Infantry Regiment to train air force ground personnel recruits to form a battalion for the defence of airfields against possible Anglo-American attacks. The garrison commander was a remarkable man, destined to receive Italy's highest award for valour: Lt-Col Carlo Croce, a reserve *Bersagliere* officer who had been recalled to service in 1940. On 8 September the armistice announcement was heard by chance on a civilian radio by a group of his officers in the Albergo del Sole hotel in Porto. This caused confusion in the garrison since they were unable to contact any higher command to find out precisely what was happening or what they should do.[4]

Lt-Col Croce realised that something had to be done and done quickly before the Germans occupied the zone. On his own initiative he decided at once to dissolve the garrison and form a voluntary clandestine military group (they were not yet called partisans). Those under his command who did not wish to take part he discharged with leave to make their own way home, and over the next two days the majority did so. Moreover, there were neither arms nor ammunition in Porto and Croce's first problem was to get some quickly. At a hastily arranged meeting in Varese, between officers from the garrisons at Luino and Laveno, nothing conclusive was agreed on what course of action to take, but Lt-Col Croce did manage to procure 10,000 rifle rounds and some arms. He also obtained nine Breda machine guns from a battalion of *Bersaglieri* which passed through Porto Valtravaglia on the night of 11 September, heading for the Swiss border; they also dumped their rifles and bicycles.

On the morning of 12 September a small group of four officers and seven other ranks, together with their commanding officer Lt-Col Croce, who had adopted the *nom de guerre Colonello Giustizia* (Colonel Justice), took all the weapons they could carry on two armoured cars, intending to make their way to the territory of Duncana, near the Swiss border. But at Brezzo di Bedero, on the back road to Luino, one of the armoured cars got wedged under an arch. They freed it with the help of the villagers and then moved back to the mountains behind Luino and Porto Valtravaglia, into the complex of First World War military fortifications near Cascina Fiorini. From there, in the following days, they were able to access the abandoned garrisons at Luino and Laveno from where they secured rations and further arms and ammunition. On 19 September, now well provisioned, they moved on to Vallata di San Martino.

This early Partisan band assumed the name 'Italian Army Formation' – *Cinque Giornate Vallalta di San Martino*[5] – with the motto *Non si è posto fango sul nostro volto* (No dirt has been flung on our face). Unlike the majority of later Partisan groups, *Cinque Giornate* was apolitical. Croce also showed that his allegiance to the king and the House of Savoy was at an end by cutting out the royal coat of arms from the Italian flag. In the following weeks and months, this small nucleus grew to over 150 men, including ten Italian army officers, as it was joined by other disbanded soldiers, civilian anti-fascists – such as the brothers Aldo and Giovanni Emilio Diligenti (Giovanni Emilio was later to become the president of the Italian Partisan Association at Monza) – and Allied and Greek prisoners of war, who had been released by the Italians and were trying to make their way to Switzerland. Croce set up his headquarters in the old Cadorna Barracks, a fortified two-storey building known as *il Forte* (the Fortress), at Vallata di San Martino; a building which, in the inter-war years, had been renamed Villa San Giuseppe and used by the Deaf-Mute Institute of Milan as a summer retreat.

Lt-Col Croce divided his group into three companies of fifty men: 1st Company, to operate mainly in the lower defensive galleries, under the command of Lt Giorgio Wabre; 2nd Company, under the command of Capt. Enrico Campodonico, in *il Forte* itself; and a headquarters company, under the command of Lt Carlo Hauss, to operate in the immediate vicinity of *il Forte*. A fourth officer, Lt Germano Bodo, became the group's adjutant. The formation's chaplain was Don Mario Limonta, a priest from Concorezzo, who also acted as medical officer for the group.

The Partisans now strengthened the old barracks further, with machine guns emplaced to the south, dominating the approach road. The road itself was made impassable to vehicles by a deep trench and a barrier across it, making *il Forte* inaccessible to an attacking force without bridging equipment. About 3km above this was the small church of San Martino; running underneath all were interconnecting galleries and tunnels. These fortifications, known as the Cadorna Line, had been built in the 1915–18 war as a precaution against a possible Austro-Hungarian attack through neutral Switzerland. I had seen the church and the impressive old fortifications when I had been to San Martino in happier days.

Mussolini, following his arrest and a series of moves, was under *carabiniere* guard in the ski resort hotel at the top of Gran Sasso, the highest Apennine peak. But from there on 12 September, in an audacious SS airborne raid led by Col. Otto Skorzeny, he was rescued. He was flown to the German air base at Pratica di Mare and from there, on direct orders from Hitler, he was immediately transferred to a Heinkel and flown to Vienna; he was taken the next day to Munich, where his family and Hitler awaited him.[6]

On 15 September the official Roman news agency, now under the complete control of the Germans, issued a short communiqué: *Benito Mussolini ha oggi ripreso la suprema direzione del fascismo in Italia* (Benito Mussolini has today reassumed the supreme direction of Fascism in Italy). There followed a list of ministerial appointments of some of the most feared names in what was now called *il Partito Fascista Republicano* (the Republican Fascist Party), and instructions that all institutions of the party and state were to support the German army. People were incredulous to learn that two frontier areas, Venezia Giulia and Alto Adige, the former Habsburg territories in South Tyrol and Carinthia, fought for in the First World War, had been incorporated into the Reich and placed under two *gauleiters*, directly responsible to Hitler. These were Friedrich Rainer at Trieste, and Franz Hofer, the *gauleiter* of Tyrol. At a stroke, Venezia Giulia became *Adriatisches Küstenland* and the South Tyrol *Alpenvorland*. But all disbelief vanished on 18 September when Mussolini himself broadcast from Munich. Almost in mockery, Mussolini's newspaper, *Il Popolo D'Italia*, repeated Badoglio's words with a banner headline *La guerra continua*, but sarcastically added: *L'Italia mantiene fede alla parola data* (Italy faithfully maintains her given word).

So we found ourselves living in the RSI (*Republica Sociale Italiana*, the Italian Social Republic), the puppet state officially set up on 27 September 1943. The RSI had no specific governmental centre; the various ministries were deliberately widely scattered by the Germans around Lake Garda and various northern towns, with the Germans controlling the telephone lines between them. The Ministry of 'Popular Culture' (a euphemism for propaganda) was located in the small town of Salò, near Brescia, and because this Ministry issued all RSI communiqués, journalists regularly used phrases such as 'Salò has announced' or 'Salò has reported', to such an extent that historians now refer to the RSI as the Republic of Salò. However, I do not recall anyone using that term at the time.

We also had a new flag based on the national *tricolore* of green, white and red. The royal Savoyard arms were removed and replaced by a Roman eagle with spread wings in grey, clutching the *fasces* in gold, the device being exactly like the metal *fez* badge of the Balilla and senior Fascist *gerarchi*. Staunch Fascists who flocked back to the party were clearly as surprised as anyone at its resurrection; this was evident from the shortage of black shirts and Fascist uniforms, as nearly all Fascists had destroyed them after July in an effort to melt into the background.

Mussolini proclaimed himself Head of State, Head of Government and *Duce* of the new Republican Party, but it was the Germans who were firmly in control. As General Albert Kesselring made clear, 'the territory of Italy is a war zone', and was under his military command. In a very revealing letter to Hitler regarding his new status, Mussolini complained:

It is my duty, Führer, to indicate to you the reasons which obstruct the reorganization of Italian life, and they are the following. The German military commands issue a continuous stream of orders on matters which concern civilian life. These orders are often contradictory from province to province. The civilian authorities are ignored and the population has the impression that the Republican Fascist government has absolutely no authority even in matters totally extraneous to the military sphere ... In the three [sic] provinces of Emilia, Piacenza, Parma and Reggio, the German military authorities have taken over the civil administration, and issued instructions that every request made by an Italian citizen must be accompanied by a German translation. In peasant provinces such as these, this is impossible to put into practice ...[7]

But neither Mussolini nor Kesselring wielded real political or policing powers. Those powers lay with the Gestapo and the SS in a complex but deadly grip, with a chain of command headed by Reichsführer-SS Heinrich Himmler. Directly under Himmler was his liaison officer, the German military governor for north Italy and plenipotentiary to Mussolini, SS-Oberstgruppenführer Karl Wolff. Under him was SS-Gruppenführer und Generallieutnant der Polizei Dr Wilhelm Harster, head of the police and Gestapo in Italy. Harster was sent to Italy by Himmler on 29 August 1943 and, with his headquarters in Verona, he remained in Italy until the end of the war. Prior to that he was in Holland where he was implicated in the death of 104,000 Dutch Jews. Harster's tentacles reached out from Verona through a network of *Kommandure Sipo-SD* (KdS – Regional Commands) and, finally, *Aussenkommandos* (SS Commissariats), followed by SS-*Aussenposten* (Forward Commands), the last link in the SS command chain. The *Aussenkommandos* in Milan was headed by the sadistic SS-Hauptsturmführer Theodor Saevecke,[8] Chief of the Gestapo in Milan. He controlled the whole of Lombardy with *Aussenposten* at Bergamo, Novara and Pavia.

13

GERMAN OCCUPATION AND THE BATTLE OF SAN MARTINO

On 25 July 1943 there were six German divisions in Italy. By 8 September eighteen had poured over the undefended Alpine passes, with four more on their way. On 10 September they began shelling Rome, occupying the city in the evening. From then on they began stripping Italy of anything they could lay their hands on.

The province of Varese, in which we lived, was occupied by the Germans on 12 September, and martial law was imposed on the 14th. It was to be the start of persistent and ferocious repression, with Republican Fascists working hand in glove with the Germans. The head of the party, Pavolini,[1] in a speech at Verona on 14 November, made this abundantly clear. He exhorted all Republican Fascists to obey the Germans and to show no mercy to the Partisans. The *Guardia di Finanza* (Italian Customs Officers) were removed from the Swiss border and replaced by the *Zollgrenzschutzes* (German Frontier Guards), later joined by Italian *Guardia di Finanza* of proven Republican Fascist credentials, but under German control. In November 1943 180,000 young men were called up, but only 87,000 presented themselves for service; the rest deserted, the bulk of which took to the mountains to swell the growing ranks of the Partisans. Droves, amounting to many hundreds of soldiers, *carabinieri* and customs officers, obtained political asylum in Switzerland.

It is against this background that the Partisan *Cinque Giornate* group began to operate in the Valtravaglia. Initially, Lt-Col Croce tried to avoid direct contact with German and Fascist forces as he tried to build up his group and get arms and supplies for them. In the week before they arrived at San Martino, and before the Germans were established in Porto Valtravaglia, the Partisans returned to the garrison to remove as much material as possible and take it to San Martino before the Germans could get it. Angelo Lazzarini (who I always knew as 'Angiolin'), from Musadino, helped them in transporting it, and in particular a load of bayonets. Some other lads and I went to the garrison and we got in easily. The Partisans told us to help ourselves to any clothing they were not taking. There were heaps of shirts, breeches, caps, mess tins and army webbing. I tried to find something to put them in, but seeing only a small army pack and having stuffed it full, I then put on several shirts and a couple of caps. I took everything home and ran back to Porto for more, but by the time I returned, barely an hour later, I couldn't get in. From then on I dressed in an assortment of army clothing.

On Saturday 30 October several Partisans arrived in Musadino and cut off our village for a few hours. By now we were already getting German patrols at irregular intervals, so the Partisans must have watched them and slipped in to Musadino shortly after a patrol had passed through. They arrived quietly, reportedly in mid-morning, and went directly to Mino, our grocer and baker, handing him a formal requisition note which was headed with the group's motto and designation:

Non si è posto fango sul nostro volto – Esercito Italiano – Comando Gruppo Cinque Giornate-Zona d'Onore, 29 ottobre 1943.

The text continued:

To the baker at Musadino.
You will deliver to the bearer of this note, commissioned by us, 6 quintals [600kg] of foodstuff (rice) currently located in your premises and which is the property of the Italian Army. On completion of the handover you will endorse this note in ink with the amount delivered and which will serve as a normal requisition voucher. You will verbally inform him of your total stock in hand.
The Commandant: Lt-Col Giustizia.
Long live free Italy in a free world![2]

They then went to Enrico Vaiani, who ran Musadino's co-operative store, and there requisitioned 600kg of pasta. It was agreed that Enrico and Mino could report the 'theft' after allowing sufficient time for the carter and Partisans to clear the area; which is what they did. The matter was reported to the *carabinieri* at Luino, and their commandant, Lt Federico de Feo, in turn telegraphed details to the Germans:

> At 11 o'clock yesterday 29 inst in Muceno [sic], in the municipality of Porto Valtravaglia, six civilians, armed with pistols and hand grenades penetrated the grocer's shop owned by Giacomo Isabella [Mino] and the workers' co-operative managed by Enrico Vaiani ... It would seem that the Partisans are part of an armed gang hiding in the mountains at the back of the town of Luino, as the attached note given to Isabella would indicate.

At the time I knew nothing of this, and neither did any of my friends. Indeed, my close friend René, who worked for Mino and always baked the morning bread, starting at around 4 a.m., and who I helped on several occasions, never mentioned it, and I suspect that the reported time of 11 a.m. by Mino and Enrico was deliberately misleading. In all probability, the Partisans came in the small hours before 4 a.m.

At this stage neither the Germans nor the Fascists knew who 'Giustizia' was or where he and his group were located, other than 'in the mountains'. The first clash came by chance on 2 November, when a few members of the group ambushed a German patrol they had almost bumped into. A hunt for them was organised by the Varese *carabinieri* under the command of the Republican Fascist Salvatore Sinisi, but they were unable to locate them. There was a second attack on 9 November when the Partisans ambushed a small car, a Fiat 500, used by the SS. Of the three German occupants, one was killed and another wounded.

As Partisan activity increased, so the repression tightened. For the Germans, the Partisan action of 2 November was the final straw. What follows regarding the action they took to eliminate the Partisans at San Martino is my own personal recollection, combined with details established after the war. By early November the group had been infiltrated by informers, Fascists posing as refugees seeking help to get to Switzerland, allowing the Germans to build up a picture of the number of Partisans and their defences. The diary of the German Frontier Guards records: 'On 1 November Commissioner Knop gave the commander of the company of mountain police highly detailed documents regarding the location of partisan gangs.' And on 5 November:

> The presence of a large gang of partisans armed with heavy weaponry in the military fortifications in the vicinity of San Martino has been sufficiently

1 My Grand Tour: 1940–46. *Based on a map courtesy of the University of Texas Libraries, Austin, USA*

2 Lake Maggiore and some locations mentioned in the book.

Left 3 My mother's first birthday, February 1906. *Author's collection*

Right 4 My grandfather returned to Italy for military service in the *Alpini, c.* 1899. *Author's collection*

5 Italian immigrants from Manchester and Leeds, 1910. My grandfather is seated second from the left, holding a walking stick. His brother, Chiarino, seated first on the right, same row, was killed in 1915 in the First World War. *Author's collection*

Left 6 My dad at the wheel of his Uncle Peter's Austin 7 in George Street, Leeds, 1923. *Author's collection*

Right 7 My father's motorised grinding machine. *Author's collection*

Left 8 My father returned to Italy for his military service in 1925. *Author's collection*

Right 9 My parents and I, June 1930. *Author's collection*

Left 10 Typical Valtravaglia village public laundry fountain. *Courtesy of Pancrazio De Micheli, Porto Valtravaglia, Co-ordinator for Calendario Artistico della Valtravaglia e dintorni*

Right 11 A girl from the Valtravaglia, 1925. *Courtesy of Pancrazio De Micheli, Porto Valtravaglia*

12 Taken in 1914, not a great deal changed in thirty years. The women have *sciuere* on their backs, and one is holding a *falcetto*. *Courtesy of Pancrazio De Micheli, Porto Valtravaglia*

13 The *colonia elioterapica* at Porto Valtravaglia. *Courtesy of Pancrazio De Micheli, Porto Valtravaglia*

14 'Imbarcadero' cafe-bar, Porto Valtravaglia in 1945. Notice the short-wave radio mast and the German *Splugen Bräu* beer sign. *Courtesy of Pancrazio De Micheli, Porto Valtravaglia*

15 It was about here on the Laveno–Luino coast road that the ILH-KR hand grenades were disposed of. *Courtesy of Pancrazio De Micheli, Porto Valtravaglia*

16 The shrine of the Pietà in Musadino, just outside where we lived. Taken in 2009 much has changed: the road used to be cobbled and the house to the right is new. *Courtesy of Clara Fortunelli, Vicenza, Italy*

17 Our house in Musadino in 2009, renovated almost beyond recognition. *Author's collection*

18 This is the small chapel of San Pietro, Musadino. Taken in 2009, it has been extensively restored. The road leads to Muceno. *Courtesy of Clara Fortunelli, Vicenza, Italy*

19 A pair of young oxen.
*Courtesy of Pancrazio De
Micheli, Porto Valtravaglia*

20 Taken in 1925, this
photo shows Musadino as
it was in the 1940s. The
first large door is that of
the *Dopolavoro*. Next is the
Co-operative, with typical
brooms and a *sciuera* outside.
The down pipes for the rain
simply run into the road.
The building behind the
woman is the school, and
the bell tower is that of the
church at Domo. *Courtesy
of Pancrazio De Micheli, Porto
Valtravaglia*

21 The electric
train-cum-tram, which ran
between Luino and Varese.
*Courtesy of Pancrazio De
Micheli, Porto Valtravaglia*

22 Taken in Luino in the 1940s before the occupation. A little banter with the greengrocer. Three women are wearing *zoccoli*, but one has bare feet. *Courtesy of Pancrazio De Micheli, Porto Valtravaglia*

23 Women doing laundry. Taken in Germignaga in 1940. *Courtesy of Pancrazio De Micheli, Porto Valtravaglia*

Top, left 24 A rare photograph showing *Bersaglieri* uniforms in the 1920s, including the light uniform of the cycle section, with folding bicycle. *Courtesy of Clara Fortunelli, Vicenza, Italy*

Top, right 25 The ideal – recruitment poster for the *Alpini* 'Intra' Battalion. *Courtesy of Museo e Biblioteca, Associazione Nazionale Alpini, Sezione di Domodossola, Italy*

Bottom, left 26 And the reality – soldiers of the *Alpini* 'Intra' Battalion bound for Albania in 1941. Many were destined to become Partisans and not return until 1945. Notice the battalion's motto '*O u rump o u muer!*' and the *Alpini* hat chalked on the crowded freight wagon. *Courtesy of Pancrazio De Micheli, Porto Valtravaglia*

Bottom, right 27 My ID card photo taken in 1944. *Author's collection*

28 Silk sash from the ill-fated *Conte Rosso*, given to my mother as a souvenir of our journey. *Author's collection*

29 The Prince of Piedmont's visit to Vicenza in June 1938. He is the tall figure in the foreground carrying a dress sword. To his right is a *gerarca*, a high-ranking Fascist Party official wearing the full dress black Saharan uniform with fez headdress; to his left is an officer of the Fascist MVSN. *Courtesy of Clara Fortunelli, Vicenza, Italy*

30 The ten Partisans standing at the undamaged entrance to Caserma Cadorna moments before they were executed. They are, from left to right: Giuseppe Pellegatta (defiantly with hands on hips), Mario Padovan, Franco Ghezzi, Angelo Ventura, Osvaldo Brioschi, Bruno Nassivera, Sergio Caminata, Idalio Spotti, Giovanni Battista Padovani and Lt Alfio Manciagli (Folco). *Courtesy of Signora Francesca Boldrini*

31 Forty-three Partisans on their way to execution. Intra, 20 June 1944. The placard reads 'Are these Italy's liberators or are they bandits?' The woman is Cleonice Tomassetti. *Courtesy of Pancrazio De Micheli, Porto Valtravaglia*

ILH·KR

ITALY.

XMAS. 1944.

32 ILH-KR 1944 Christmas card, used again in 1945. *Author's collection*

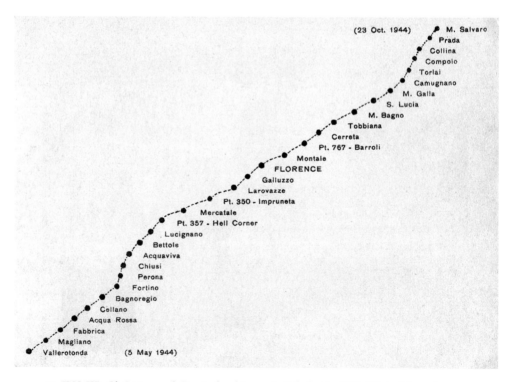

(23 Oct. 1944)   M. Salvaro
Prada
Collina
Compolo
Torlai
Camugnano
M. Galla
S. Lucia
M. Bagno
Tobbiana
Cerreta
Pt. 767 - Barroli
Montale
FLORENCE
Galluzzo
Larovazze
Pt. 350 - Impruneta
Mercatale
Pt. 357 - Hell Corner
Lucignano
Bettole
Acquaviva
Chiusi
Perona
Fortino
Bagnoregio
Cellano
Acqua Rossa
Fabbrica
Magliano
Vallerotonda   (5 May 1944)

33 ILH-KR Christmas card. Route fought over in Italy by the ILH-KR to November 1944. *Author's collection*

34 Classes 1, 2 and 3 of *scuola elementare*, Musadino, 1948. *Courtesy of Pancrazio De Micheli, Porto Valtravaglia*

35 *Scuola media* (middle school), Class of 1946. Anita Isabella, who died a few weeks later, is seated second on the left. *Courtesy of Pancrazio De Micheli, Porto Valtravaglia*

36 Dedication of the memorial stone to Benedetto Isabella at San Michele on 9 September 1945. The man facing the camera on the far left is my father. *Courtesy of Pancrazio De Micheli, Porto Valtravaglia*

37 Enlargement, showing my father. The officer at his side, wearing glasses, may be Major Theunissen, G2 (Military Intelligence) officer of the 6th SA Armoured Division. *Courtesy of Pancrazio De Micheli, Porto Valtravaglia*

Left 38 Monument in honour of Rudolf Jacobs at Sarzana. *Public domain*

Right 39 Lance-Bombardier Peter Ghiringhelli in Stanley Fort, Hong Kong, 1952. *Author's collection*

40 Memorial and ossuary of the fallen at the battle of San Martino. The rebuilt church is to the right. *Courtesy of Dott. Cesare Bottelli*

Above 41 My friend Roberto
Rivolta. He gave me his photograph
as a souvenir when I left Musadino
in 1946. *Author's collection*

Right 42 Anita Isabella, Amatore's
sister. *Author's collection*

43 My maternal uncle,
John Granelli, in July
1944. *Author's collection*

demonstrated … trusted Italian informers have delivered incontrovertible documents to Commissioner Knop regarding the gang's precise deployment … The available material was sufficient to give the go ahead to military intervention.

The Partisans were well aware that the Germans had discovered their location, and they were also warned well in advance of an impending attack. But Lt-Col Croce emphatically decided to stay put and fight it out. His concept of warfare was that of a regular soldier, defence of territory – a concept totally unsuited to guerrilla fighting – and although the military fortifications appeared impregnable, San Martino itself could be surrounded on all sides. The Committee for National Liberation (CLN) for the district of Varese held a meeting at Morazzone, a municipality like Porto about 40km north-west of Milan, and came to the conclusion that an attack on San Martino was imminent. In view of this, they sent Colonel Girolamo Laneve Albrizio, a regular officer in the *Alpini* regiment, who was the CLN's local officer in charge of military affairs, to forewarn Croce and try to dissuade him from remaining static at San Martino.

Croce steadfastly maintained that his group would stay firm where they were. At this, Laneve Albrizio made a proposal to lead a diversionary attack on the Germans from the adjacent mountainside above Cavorna, about a kilometre distant as the crow flies, if Croce would let him have two heavy machine guns. Again Croce refused, angrily saying that he would give up command before giving up his heavy weaponry. Finally, Major-General Bartolo Zambon, the CLN's senior military officer, personally went up to see him. Croce told Gen. Zambon that he was well aware he stood little chance of defeating a concerted German attack, but he also told the general that someone had to make a stand, and he and his men were determined to fight it out; all those who did not wish to stay were free to leave with honour.

In his report to the CLN, Gen. Zambon recorded: 'Nothing can be done with Croce. Irremovable. A hero. And heroes too all his men who are all irrevocably determined to stay with their colonel: determined to die on the spot.' Zambon said that at one stage he had spoken of giving him a direct order to move and that he was there at the order of the CLN, but Croce had replied: 'Revolutions are made with blood, freedom is won with blood and not with "orders" and talk.' It was a decision which affected all of us.

The CLN, I should explain, was formed in Rome on 9 September 1943 and was the political arm of the Resistance movement. In essence it was an informal alliance of all anti-fascist political parties. Committees were quickly established in all provinces occupied by the Germans. The committees comprised the representatives of the four major parties: Actionists, Christian Democrats, Communists and Socialists. By 1944 three major autonomous CLN groups had emerged. The largest of these was the CLNAI (*Comitato di Liberazione Nazionale per l'Alta Italia*, Committee for National Liberation of Northern Italy) which had its headquarters in Milan, right under the noses of the Germans, and extended its authority over all Italy north of Tuscany.

On 13 November the Germans declared a state of siege for the whole of Lombardy: all public places were to be closed until 21 November and the publication of all newspapers was suspended. On Sunday 14 November I awoke to a loud drone of engines; at that stage I was no longer used to traffic noise and at first I couldn't make out what it was. I opened my window and saw a stream of vehicles heading up the old military road. I could only see the south-west side of San Michele from Musadino, but about 2,000 German troops were involved from the 15th German Police Regiment and German Frontier Guards, with Fascist *carabinieri* and GNR (*Guardia Nazionale Republicana*) members. An advance German force had already set out from Arcumeggia, to the south of Monte Nudo, out of my sight and hearing. The German troops on our side of the mountain were to complete the encirclement. However, the convoy to the south of Monte Nudo was in for a nasty shock. About 2km north of Arcumeggia the Partisans had laid a trap for them on the outskirts of Duno, a tiny hamlet on the road to San Martino, where they had set up the two heavy machine guns behind large piles of logs, waiting to be carted out. It was here at Duno that the Germans suffered their most heavy losses. Taken by complete surprise, and expecting their drive to San Martino to be unopposed, they were mown down in droves.

This was the first gunfire I heard, as the noise echoed back and forth in the mountains. No one knows exactly what happened to the ambush Partisans, but it is thought they got away via the nearby San Gottardo torrent. Witnesses remember the Germans being thrown into turmoil, the road strewn with smashed vehicles and ambulances coming and going. They also recalled that some men suddenly drove up and started to spread out white sheets, which they believed were a signal to the approaching attack planes not to bomb Duno, where they were temporarily stranded. Meanwhile, probably unaware of what had happened, the Germans on our side of the mountain pressed on.

As the gunfire died down, three Junkers JU87s, the dreaded crank-winged dive-bombers known as Stukas, appeared in formation. I should have realised that men were dying, but I must admit I was quite fascinated watching the planes circle round, then come screeching down in a steep dive to release their bombs, followed by machine-gunning. Stukas carried two heavy machine guns but only one bomb, so there was a lull every so often as they went off to some nearby airfield to reload and return to repeat their air strikes. But despite the pounding, very little damage was done to the fortified barracks; the church, their main target, was surrounded by craters but had been missed completely, possibly due to the difficulty and danger of dive-bombing in a mountainous area. The Germans also must have got careless and overconfident because, although I didn't see it, one of the Stukas was shot down.

The battle lasted two days, but eventually the Partisans ran out of small-arms ammunition and had to surrender. Before they did so they blew up their armoury and explosives dump in the main tunnel to stop any equipment falling into German hands; Lt-Col Croce, the last man to leave, lit the fuse. Casualties are difficult to establish, but the Germans and Fascists paid the heaviest price; sources give various numbers, the maximum being 200. Incredibly, the fort was so well built and the defences so strong that the Partisans lost only two men during the battle, some sources say one, giving his name as Italo Corazza. Ten Partisans surrendered at the fort. They were Lt Alfio Manciagli (Falco), Osvaldo Brioschi, Sergio Caminata, Franco Ghezzi, Bruno Nassivera, Mario Padovan, Gian Battista Padovani, Giuseppe Pellegatta, Idalio Spotti and Angelo Ventura. These ten were shot in front of Cadorna Barracks and their bodies left there. They appear in a souvenir photo taken by a German soldier, showing them dazed and tired standing before the barracks' main entrance just before their execution. A further twenty-six Partisans were taken prisoner during the battle, mainly in the lower defensive tunnels. They were taken to Luino where, after barbaric torture, they were shot in Luino's cemetery. The Germans encouraged people to view the bodies but forbade anyone to go near them. They were publicly exposed for two days before burial was permitted. As for the ten Partisans executed at San Martino, initially the Germans ordered their bodies to be left where they had been shot. But following an outcry they relented with ill grace, and late on 17 November their bodies were brought down on a donkey drawn cart and buried in unmarked graves. However, the ring the Germans had hoped to snap around San Michele failed to close, possibly because of the Duno ambush. This allowed Lt-Col Croce and about a hundred Partisans to melt away.

While the battle was taking place the Germans combed the mountains, treating anyone they came across as either a Partisan or a Partisan sympathiser.

Benedetto Isabella from Musadino, the brother of our baker Mino, was found in San Michele on 14 November and shot. Benedetto was in his forties and had absolutely no connection with the Partisans. It was a Sunday morning and he had gone up at first light, just before the battle started, with a pot of varnish to do some maintenance work and to collect some potatoes which he had hidden there to avoid them being confiscated. He had intended it to be a short call; later he was to become the godfather of his niece Francesca, who was being baptised after High Mass a little before midday, as was the custom then.

His body was brought down the next morning after the firing at San Martino had mainly subsided. Led by our parish priest, Don Carlo Agazzi Rota, Benedetto's brothers, my father, Valdo, Mario Cip and other men, accompanied by some women who were telling their Rosary beads, went up to San Michele. Benedetto was found in his house with a single bullet hole in the middle of his forehead, his potatoes looted and the house ransacked, as was the rest of San Michele. As they arrived there a German armoured car appeared from the Brissago section of the military road and, advancing slowly, drove the men off without firing, ignoring the praying women. It then reversed at the start of the Muceno road and drove back down on the Brissago road. The women feared a trap if the men returned, so without waiting, they themselves took the body to a spot known as *scupèl biòt*, where they correctly surmised the men would have taken refuge. From there Benedetto's body was brought down to Musadino, by the men, strapped to a ladder. Don Carlo contacted the Germans and they gave permission for Benedetto to be buried, but without a funeral. However, this was ignored; as his coffin passed through Musadino, from his house to the cemetery in Domo, led by Don Carlo, more and more people spontaneously followed until at the cemetery there was a great throng of mourners from villages all around Musadino. I remember the cemetery being packed and there was a great silence as I watched his coffin being put in a wall niche, as is the Italian custom.

Unbeknown to us, four other civilians from Musadino had been caught at San Michele: Angelo (Angiolin) Lazzarini, his wife Anna, and his two cousins Augusta and Redegonda. He had a small *osteria*, a tavern-cum-restaurant, at San Michele, and it was here that the Germans found them. Angiolin was badly beaten up and his *osteria* completely and methodically trashed. Every bottle, glass, plate and ornament was smashed before his eyes, and his pig stolen. The four of them were taken to the German headquarters at Rancio for interrogation. Angiolin was savagely whipped. When I went to work for him in 1944, as I shall recount later, he told me that the German sergeant who had flogged him with a bullwhip had to stop to rest and strip to the waist before resuming. The three women were made to clean up the blood on the interrogation room walls and floors where some of the Partisans were tortured before being taken to Luino to be shot.

Torture was used extensively by the Germans and Republican Fascists to get information, but more importantly to spread terror, and at that stage of the war they openly boasted of it. Some of the torture methods used by the Republican Fascists were extremely sadistic. Torture and summary execution of Partisans stopped to a certain extent later in the war when the Partisans began to take German prisoners, who were kept alive and used in exchange for captured comrades.

Two days after the battle of San Martino the Germans returned there, and for no reason whatsoever they blew up the church dedicated to St Martin. It had stood there for over 1,000 years, and when I saw it many months later it was just a pile of rubble; Caserma Cadorna, which appears remarkably undamaged in the photograph of the ten Partisans about to be executed, was razed to the ground. As for Lt-Col Croce and his surviving men, they made their escape at nightfall through the labyrinth of communicating tunnels and walkways to Ponte Tresa, and from there they crossed the Swiss border to safety. In the following months most of these men, including Croce, returned to Italy to join other Partisan bands. In 1944 Croce was wounded in his arm in another action and was captured by the Germans in the Valtellina mountains above Sondrio. His arm was amputated but he died on 24 July 1944, following torture by the SS at his interrogation. In April 1945 he was posthumously awarded the Gold Medal, Italy's highest award for valour.

As to the fate of other Royal Italian Army troops from the Valtravaglia area, *Alpini* (known as *le penne nere* – the Black Quills – from the eagle quills in their Alpine hats), recruited locally, served in the *Intra* Battalion of the 4th Alpini Regiment. The battalion's motto was, in Piemontese dialect: *O u rump o u moeur!* (*O rompo o muoio!* – 'Either I break through or die!') In 1941 they were sent to Albania to take part in Italy's disastrous attack on Greece, and in 1942 they were moved to Yugoslavia and there, when the armistice was declared on 8 September 1943, the 4th *Alpini* Regiment disintegrated. However, the *Intra* Battalion, under the command of Capt. Piero Zavattero Ardizzi, joined Tito's partisans and fought the Germans in Serbia-Montenegro and then north-east Italy for fifteen months, ending up, in April 1945, in Bolzano as part of a Garibaldi Partisan division.

The Republican Fascists set up a rival *Alpini* '*Intra*' Battalion, but the only connection this Fascist battalion had with Lake Maggiore and the Valtravaglia was its name. It was formed on 15 February 1944 and was made up of Fascist volunteers recruited from Italian soldiers held in prisoner-of-war camps in Germany, and after training at Münsingen in Baden-Württemberg, the battalion was incorporated into the Fascist *Monte Rosa* division. At the end of July 1944, the division was moved to Liguria, and that August took part in the fourth anti-Partisan raid on Santa Maria del Taro, as I shall recount in Chapter 17. The Republican '*Intra*' Battalion surrendered to the Americans on 29 April 1945 at Fornovo Taro.

The battle of San Martino, and in particular the shooting of Benedetto at San Michele, was the very first incident of its kind, and so made a great impact on all of us. None of us dreamt that these events were just the curtain-raiser, a mere taste of far worse slaughter and suffering to come in the terrible year of 1944. The Germans themselves made this abundantly clear; in the days following the battle a notice in German and Italian was pasted up on our courtyard door. I cannot now remember the exact wording, only that it made very grim reading. It had about twenty or more paragraphs, each one starting with 'Anyone that …' and ending with '… will be shot'. The last paragraph I do remember; it read: 'Anyone found defacing this notice will be shot.' It was signed by General Kesselring. Here is another example, an extract from 'Order by German 5 Corps, 1S. No. 391, 9 August 1944':

> The public must be made to realise that any sign of partisan activities in their midst will have the most unpleasant consequences for them as well.
> 111. In areas where partisans are found in large numbers, or where acts of sabotage are of frequent occurrence and the criminals cannot be found, the following steps are to be taken:
> (a) *Arrest of hostages* …
> (b) If there is a recurrence of acts of violence, an appropriate number of the hostages will be shot. I reserve the right to order the shooting. This is to be brought to the notice of the population in advance, so that their responsibility in this matter is established and brought home to them.
> (c) If crimes of outstanding violence are committed, especially against German soldiers, an appropriate number of the hostages will be hanged. In such cases the whole population of the place will be assembled to witness the execution. After the bodies have been left hanging for

12 hours, the public will be ordered to bury them without the assistance of any priest.[3]

But this sort of order was often completely disobeyed and hostages were frequently bayoneted to death or burnt alive in crowded barns with flamethrowers turned on them.

Massacres became endemic; here is an extract from the Report of British War Crimes Section of Allied Force Headquarters on German Reprisals for Partisan Activities in Italy:

The British War Crimes Section of the Allied Force Headquarters has investigated fully a number of cases of German reprisals for partisan activity in Italy, committed between April and November, 1944. In addition it has been established that information received from many sources on a further large number of atrocities committed between March 1944 and April 1946, is substantially correct.

A study of all these cases reveals that there is a striking similarity in the facts. The incident invariably opens the killing [sic, opens with the killing] or wounding of a German soldier or soldiers by partisans; reprisal activity is then initiated either by the troops immediately on the spot or, in more serious cases, by the arrival of definite units and formations specially detailed for the purpose. There is no taking of hostages in the normal sense of the word, but a number of people are selected haphazardly from the local population and are killed by shooting or hanging, whilst whole villages or certain farms or houses are destroyed by fire. In a number of cases an announcement is then made to the population that the action taken was a reprisal for the death of a German soldier and will be repeated should further attacks on Germans take place.

A typical example is the Civitella atrocity, one of those cases which has been completely investigated. Partisan Bands had been operating in the area, attacking lone German lorries and motorcycles. On June 18th, 1944, two German soldiers were killed and a third wounded in a fight with partisans in the village of Civitella. Fearing reprisals, the inhabitants evacuated the village, but when the Germans discovered this, punitive action was postponed. On June 29th, 1944, when the local inhabitants were returning and were feeling secure once more, the Germans carried out a well organised reprisal, combing the neighbourhood. Innocent inhabitants were often shot

on sight. During that day 212 men, women and children in the immediate district were killed. Some of the dead women were found completely
naked. In the course of investigation, a nominal roll of the dead has been
compiled, and is complete with the exception of a few names where bodies
could not be identified. Ages of the dead ranged from 1 year to 84 years.
Approximately 100 houses were destroyed by fire; some of the victims were
burned alive in their homes.[4]

14

RACE LAWS AND
PERSECUTION OF THE JEWS

lthough I did not know it at the time, Italian officers of the calibre of
Croce were few and far between. Matters might have been different had
Marshal Badoglio acted swiftly and given decisive orders to the army to
resist the Germans. The result of his indecision and flight to Brindisi with
the king on 9 September, left the armed forces in chaos and many units just
remained in their barracks waiting for orders that never came. The result was
that around 800,000 were quickly disarmed by the Germans and taken away
in long cattle wagon trains to detention camps in Germany and Poland, their
status much lower than that of regular prisoners of war. The same inertia
affected many Allied POWs detained in Italian camps; the many who decided
to sit tight, expecting a rapid, unopposed advance of Allied forces, were simply
rounded up and taken off to Germany. General Montgomery, as he then
was, issued an order to the head of MI9, the military intelligence service for
escaped prisoners of war in occupied Europe, which was secretly communi-
cated to the Italian POW camps: they should 'Keep fit and stay put' and await
the arrival of Allied troops – aptly described by one historian as 'rather stupid
advice',[1] it proved to be very helpful to the Germans.

As soon as the puppet government of Salò was set up, everyone from
the age of 12 had to have new identity cards, and those issued before
25 July 1943 were declared invalid. These new Republican Fascist cards
were in Italian and German. They also stated which race you belonged to
– *Razza: Ariana* – which seemed a bit superfluous since no ID cards were
issued to Jews. My father obtained ID cards for my mother and me, which
gave my mother's birthplace as Pianlavagnolo and mine as Musadino
instead of Leeds. These were probably issued by Callogero Marrone; a very

minor detail compared with the hundreds of Jewish lives that this brave man saved.

A life-long anti-fascist, Marrone was the head of the Varese Register Office, and from there he issued a large number of false identity cards to Jews and anti-fascists. He was betrayed (it is believed by a Fascist employed in his office) and arrested by the SS on 4 January 1944. He was held for nine months in a succession of prisons, first in Varese, where he was badly tortured in an effort to get him to reveal the National Liberation Committee network, but he refused to say a word. Then he was taken to a prison in Como for daily inter-rogation; and on to the notorious San Vittore prison in Milan after a failed attempt by Partisans to free him. After this the SS seem to have given up interrogating him and he was sent to the Bolsano–Gries transit-concentration camp, run by the Butcher of Trieste, Odilo Globocnik.[2] There he managed to get a letter smuggled out on a scrap of paper, writing in tiny letters to his 17-year-old son Domenico, who had joined the 'Poldo Gasparotto' Partisan brigade led by Luciano Comolli:

> Here I am in my new residence, still as always in the best of health and high morale. I'm in a concentration camp for political prisoners where there is no lack of cool fresh mountain air to fill my lungs. There is a problem with not having woollen clothes, but you can't have everything, and I'll get used to it. Don't worry about me, I can truthfully say that the past nine months have strengthened my character. Suffice it to say I can now adapt myself to any kind of labour. I shall return with calluses that would honour any man. I've a ravenous appetite and the tar-black bread they give us seems like cake to me … If you could see how I'm now dressed you would burst out laugh-ing: sheared like a sheep, a self-made paper hat on my head against the cold and the sun, a sort of overall with a large cross on the back and a red triangle on the front, the sign of a political prisoner, and underneath the number 4317, dirty shoes, and so on. But what is important is this: excellent health and morale as high as ever. I'm called 'the Philosopher'. Have courage and be constant … On Monday or Tuesday we shall be taken further north. Do not worry about me for wherever I go I shall know how to survive this foul bestial existence.[3]

For safety reasons, he signed smuggled notes with the pseudonym Peppo Coppula. 'Taken further north' for him meant the extermination camp at Dachau, where he died of typhus on 10 February 1945. There is a marble plaque on the Varese Register Office in his memory and honour, put up jointly by the Jewish community, the National Association of Partisans and the Varese municipality. It reads:

> At this site Callogero Marrone, Head of the Register Office of Varese, operated clandestinely to save our Jewish brothers from the Nazi-Fascist ferocity. Betrayed and arrested on 4 January 1944 he was deported to Germany to the extermination camp of Dachau where he died just as the dawn of liberty was breaking. May the name of this righteous man be blessed for all Eternity.
> Favara, Agrigento, 8 May 1889
> Dachau, February 1945

Anti-Semitism had become official Fascist policy shortly after the publication of the *Manifesto of Fascist Racism* in July 1938, when all Jews were expelled from the party. Mussolini had introduced anti-Jewish laws in 1938, aping the infamous Nazi Nuremberg Laws. Under the Italian racial laws all foreign Jews were to be expelled from Italy; additionally, all Jews who were Italian citizens were expelled from the Fascist Party, the civil service, the armed forces and the teaching professions. Also, no Jew was allowed to own a business with more than 100 employees or own land above 50 hectares, and all Jewish children were excluded from Italian schools. But it was also decreed by law that all Jews dismissed from public service were entitled to full pensions and that Jewish children should attend Jewish schools. Eight categories of Italian Jews and their families were fully exempt from the 1938 racial laws, ranging from early Fascist membership to families of soldiers who lost their lives or were wounded in the Great War and colonial wars; and probably my friend Renata, the girl who was with me in the *colonia elioterapica* of Porto Valtravaglia, fell into one of these categories.

Up to 1938 there was little or no anti-Semitism in the Italian Fascist Party, and certainly not outside it. However, there had long been an underlying streak of anti-Semitism within Fascism, and foremost of a minority was Giovanni Preziosi,[4] whose rabid anti-Semitism dated back to 1919. But he found scant support in the party and, prior to the alliance with Hitler, was marginalised by Mussolini, who ridiculed his views. Indeed, it may come as a surprise to many that the 1938 Fascist census of Italian and foreign Jews in Italy recorded that there were 22,756 Fascist Jews of which 10,370 were full party members. Of these, five had been *San Sepulcristi* (i.e. founder members of the Fascist movement) and 210 Jews held the coveted certificate awarded to Fascists who had participated in the March on Rome.[5] Against this, the majority of Italian Jews were anti-fascists but purely for political reasons, not for religious or other reasons. In general, upper- and middle-class Jews tended to favour Fascism, whilst proletarian Jews tended to be anti-fascist – the same pattern as for non-Jewish Italians.

Mussolini had famously said that 'the question of race does not exist in Italy', and had gone on record over the years denouncing racism as 'unscientific', 'ridiculous' and 'absurd'. But this in no way excuses Mussolini; he implemented a policy he did not believe in purely, it seems, to ingratiate himself with his new friend Hitler and, as De Felice says, 'to remove any glaring source of discord with his ally'[6] – in 1938 he made Preziosi a Minister of State. Thus his complete volte-face in 1938 came as quite a shock and took everyone by surprise. The racial laws were particularly punitive for foreign Jews who had sought refuge from persecution abroad and had settled in Italy; all those who had immigrated since 1919 were ordered to leave the country, but after 1931 most of the other western countries had closed their doors to Jews and they were unable to leave.[7]

But repressive and unjust as these measures were, that was as far as it went; no Jews were arrested, Jewish children could attend Jewish schools and all Jews were free to attend their synagogues. Many Fascists were opposed to these measures; Italo Balbo,[8] for example, refused to sign the Racial Manifesto. How seriously Italian Fascists took anti-Semitism can be judged from an entry in Ciano's diary for 4 June 1938: 'The Duce was very annoyed with Farinacci,[9] the head of current anti-Semitism, who has a Jewish secretary: Jole Foà.' Farinacci pleaded that he couldn't sack her as she had been his secretary for many years and at her age would be unable to find another job. That may have been the case in 1938, but already Italian Fascism was on the slippery road to Auschwitz, and in the Republic of Salò Farinacci, like all Republican Fascists, fully embraced Nazi racism.

When the regime fell in 1943 Preziosi fled to Germany where, together with Farinacci and Pavolini, much to the annoyance of Mussolini, he made a series of vitriolic broadcasts inveighing against Jewish and Freemason 'traitors' within Fascism and calling for the severest measures against them. Preziosi did not return to Italy until December 1943, and at first, although a minister in the Salò Republic, he had little effective power. This was until 15 March 1944 when, under pressure from Berlin, he was made head of a new racial office and named Chief Inspector of Race. However, in a futile effort to control him he had to report to the presidency of the Council of Ministers; a move deemed by the historian De Felice as 'a last desperate attempt by Mussolini to avoid losing complete control of anti-Semitic policy'.[10] But lose it he did, and from March 1944 the Germans took over full control of Republican Fascist racial policy through their agent Giovanni Preziosi.

When Fascism fell, thousands of Jews came to our province because it was the main route to the Swiss border. In the forty-five days' window of opportunity between the first fall of Mussolini and the German occupation, 6,000 Jews crossed safely into Switzerland from Italy, and of these 5,000 crossed from the province of Varese. Those first emigrations were organised by Delasem, an organisation founded in 1939 and which had been supported by the Fascist government; its function was to assist foreign Jews to leave Italy. It was a legal organisation until 8 September 1943, after which it fragmented and operated clandestinely, principally in Genoa, with the help of Cardinal Pietro Boetto and a number of Catholic priests, until Delasem's Jewish operatives themselves were forced to flee to Switzerland. After that the two main organisations in the Luinese territory for assisting Jews were OSCAR,[11] originally set up by four priests – Don Natale Motta, Don Franco Rimoldi, Don Aurelio Giussani and Don Andrea Ghetti – and a lay organisation set up under the auspices of the CLN, by Giuseppe Bacciagaluppi, who worked in Milan but had a villa on Lake Maggiore at Caldé, where his clandestine operation was based. Bacciagaluppi was a powerful figure in the Resistance but a very unassuming man. Operating under the code names *Joe*, *Anfossi* and *Ingeniere Rossi*, he was the military delegate of the CLNAI in Lugano, and representative of the north Italian Partisans to the Allies in neutral Berne. After the war he was the first appointed manager of the Monza race track.

But there were other more simple networks, many run by parish priests in the mountain areas, such as one run by Don Piero Folli at Voldomino di Luino in conjunction with Cardinal Boetta of Genoa. All these groups offered their services free of charge.

Guiding Jews to safety could be lucrative work, and this attracted professional smugglers, petty criminals and worse. The price for getting a Jew across the Swiss border ranged from 5,000 to 10,000 lire if the road was relatively easy, but it could be as high as 40,000 lire for a difficult and arduous mountain route. Avaricious guides would often threaten to abandon people in the mountains unless they paid more, and a few unscrupulous villains would be paid by the Jews then betray them at the border and claim the reward for capturing them. The CLN, which had to employ local guides, devised a system to counter this. A note would be torn in half and one half given to the person being assisted; once across the border he or she would write an agreed phrase not known to the guide and sign it. No money was paid until the guide produced the signed torn note to the CLN and it was matched up with the other half. But determined criminals still betrayed many. Agata Herskovitz, a 20-year-old woman of Czech origin who survived the death camps, gave a vivid account of such a betrayal. On 1 May 1944, along with her father and brother, she had almost reached the border at Cremenaga, on the road from Luino to Ponte Tresa. The guides accompanying them kept urging them on across the difficult terrain:

> Come on, just a little effort, they gave us their hand or their arm heartening us: in a few hours you will be safe, all your problems solved. And in fact, at a certain point, before we got to the border, they showed us: Look, all you have to do is lift this wire netting and you are home and dry. We cannot go through it, give us your torn note and the best of luck. They turned and whistled. At that instant floodlights came on and customs' guards rushed out of a small barracks shouting Halt! You are all under arrest! We were dumb-founded, incredulous.[12]

All Jews had their possessions forfeited; the expropriations were unbelievably draconian and carried out with extreme rigour. At first, to pretend this theft was legal, all possessions seized were listed in detail in the *Gazzetta ufficiale d'Italia*. Here's an example dated 8 April 1944:

> Considering the legislative decree of the Duce n. 2, dated 1-4-1944-XXII:
> Considering the declaration of the property possessed by the Jew Somner, Antonio of Montecchio Maggiore;
> Decree:
> The property belonging to the Jew Somner Antonio is confiscated:

10 ladies hats	2 pillow cases
5 used pairs of ladies' shoes	4 small cotton towels of which one towelling
1 used pair of men's house slippers	1 ladies' cotton night dress
1 single cotton sheet	1 apron
1 girdle	2 feather cushions
2 bathrobes	5 coat hangers
1 dressing gown	1 rubber shopping bag

1 men's shirt	3 small aluminium pots
2 used pairs of men's socks	1 bowl
1 ladies' slip	3 shoe brushes
4 ties	1 packet of medicinal cotton
3 used ladies' silk dresses	1 bedside mat
3 silk shirts	4 suitcases
1 used ladies' suit	

The said property passes into the trusteeship of Ente Gestione and Liquidazione immobiliari.

But in May 1944 there were complaints about these lists from the Ministry of Education, describing them as 'negative propaganda', and following that, the lists were provided as special supplements of the *Gazzetta ufficiale* not available to the public.[13]

The terror against Jews started as soon as the Germans occupied Italy, well before March 1944. On 15 September 1943, only two days after they had occupied our area, soldiers of the 3rd Company, 1st Battalion, 2nd Regiment of the SS Panzer Division *Liebstandarte 'Adolf Hitler'* massacred fifty-four Jews at Meina, on the Piemontese side of Lake Maggiore. The majority of these were evacuees from surrounding cities, with a group staying at the Meina Hotel owned by Mr Behar, a Jewish citizen of neutral Turkey and therefore exempt from Germany's racial laws according to an agreement between the Reich and the Turkish government.

The Jewish guests at the hotel were the Fernandez Diaz family (Pietro Fernandez Diaz, his wife Liliana, and children Gianni 15, Roberto 12 and Bianca 12, and their grandfather Dino Moise, aged 76); the Masseri family (Marco and Ester, their son Renato, aged 22, and his wife Odette, aged 19); and a married couple, Mario and Lotte (*née* Frölich), who were simply there from Milan as the dinner guests of the hotel owner. Two other Jewish guests staying there were Daniele Mediano, aged 52, and Vittorio Pombas, aged 35. In addition, the hotel barman, Vitale Cari, aged 26, was a Jew. According to witnesses, at dusk on 22 September, SS-Hauptsturmführer Krüger ordered that the Jewish hotel guests be served their evening meal in their rooms. He then went from room to room telling the Jews that he would have to take them to Borgomanero (a distance of about 14km) for interrogation. At about 9.30 p.m. the Jews were made to leave their rooms and were lined up in the corridor. They were taken away for execution in small groups of three or four, because the SS only had a small van to transport them in. The final group was driven away at about 3 a.m. Their bodies were bound with wire and weighed down with heavy stones; they were taken out to the middle of the lake in a boat requisitioned from Ernesto Giuliani and thrown overboard. The next morning some of the cadavers had floated to the surface, so the SS went out in boats and sank them again using boathooks. They then returned to the hotel and took the slaughtered Jews' possessions. At this point they discovered that the three Fernandez Diaz children, Gianni, Roberto and Bianca, and their grandfather Dino Moise, had been overlooked and left locked in their room. All the 'Aryan' hotel guests were subsequently ordered to their rooms and told to remain there all night. The children and the old man were shot in their room. Witnesses reported that the children were heard screaming and the man shouting; then there was silence.

I have given details of this early massacre because it happened on Lake Maggiore. But it is typical of many hundreds of massacres of Jews and non-Jews, both civilians and Partisans, in Italy at that time.

15

THE REPUBLIC OF SALÒ SLIDES
INTO CIVIL WAR

s well as the Partisan band led by Lt-Col Croce, other Partisan bands, all officially designated *Gruppi di azione patriotica* (GAP, Patriotic Action Groups), were active in the province of Varese. In the zone of Gallarate, Saronno, Busto and Varese there were small Partisan groups hiding in the surrounding countryside, dispersed among peasant families and re-entering the towns to sabotage and attack barracks. In fact, it was the group from Gallarate which had provided Croce with his three heavy machine guns, two of which had been used in the ambush at Duno with such devastating effect. The heavy machine guns were taken in a raid in early November from fighter aircraft parked at the military airfield at Lonate Pozzolo. These groups were part of the 121st GAP Garibaldi Brigade '*Gastone Sazzi*' (all Communist Partisan formations were designated 'Garibaldi Brigades'). This group was later renamed '*Walter Marcobi*', in honour of Walter Marcobi, *nom de guerre* Remo, the Communist leader of the formation who was betrayed and killed near Varese in October 1944.

Another early Partisan band was formed and led by 'Captain' Giacinto Domenico Lazzarini of Mesenzana (a village almost opposite Musadino, but on the other side of the Valtravaglia mountain chain), who lived and worked in Milan. Initially his group was based in Milan and was dependent on the Milanese branch of the CLN, and it was only in the late summer of 1944 that it became active and was transferred to the CLN of Varese. The Lazzarini band of Partisans had about thirty members: soldiers from the disbanded army, RSI army draft dodgers and local anti-fascists, including a 20-year-old kinsman of mine, Luigi Ghiringhelli from Luino. The band had been in contact with Croce's group but, after the debacle of San Martino, had been ordered to lie low.

From mid-1944, the Lazzarini band took part in several actions in the province. But, during the early hours of 8 October 1944, following information given by an informer, the main section were taken by surprise in their sleep and captured by a 100-strong company from the GNR officer training school at Varese. Four of the Partisans – Giacomo Albertoli, a 19-year-old student from Castelveccana; Alfredo Carigniani, a 24-year-old railway clerk from Lucca; Pietro Staliviero, a 26-year-old worker from Montegrino Valtravaglia; and Carlo Tapella, a 29-year-old haulage carter from Samirate – were all severely beaten and then executed on the spot. Five others, covered in blood from their beating, were taken to Brissago and shot in the cemetery. These were Gianpiero Albertoli (Giacomo Albertoli's cousin), aged 24 of Castelveccana; Flavio Fornara, aged 23, a factory worker from Omegna but resident in Luino; Dante Girani, aged 20, from Montegrino Valtravaglia; Sergio Lozzio, aged 18, and Luigi Perazzoli, aged 23, both from Milan. Three others were shot at Bettole di Varese; these were Elvio Copelli, aged 20 from Voldomino; Evaristo Trentini, aged 23 from Clivio; and my father's young cousin Luigi Ghiringhelli. Their bodies were left lying for hours in the rain before the Republican Fascists allowed them to be taken away for burial.

This parading round of captured Partisans at different locations and executing them in public was deliberately done to give repression maximum publicity, and, more importantly, to strike terror in the population. Captain Lazzarini himself, and some of his followers, managed to avoid arrest and were able to make their way to Switzerland.

As for the Republican Fascists, their numbers were swelling too in our area. On the one hand, as the Allies advanced up through Italy and the territory of the RSI shrank, more Fascists from central Italy were compressed into northern Italy. On the other hand, many Partisans remained in their local home areas as the front line swept over them.

Mussolini tried to reconstruct the Italian army, under General Graziani,[1] as soon as he returned to Italy. Initially, it was intended that it should be built around the core of the surviving MVSN, the Fascist militia, and mainly from the thousands of ex-soldiers languishing in German internment camps. Graziani had no objection to incorporating the militia into the new army provided that the army be non-political and not subject to Fascist party control. Mussolini himself did not object to this, but the party, and in particular Ricci[2] and Pavolini, did, insisting that disbanding the MVSN would destroy Fascism and place the RSI at the mercy of Graziani. The matter was settled by forming the *Guardia Nazionale Republicana* (the GNR previously mentioned), a political police force formed from the fascist remnants of the *carabinieri* and the MVSN. The GNR was answerable to the Ministry of the Interior and not to Graziani.

The new army under Graziani, the *Esercito nazionale repubblicano* (ENR), was trained in Germany and ultimately consisted of four divisions: the 1st *Alpini* Division '*Monterosa*'; the 2nd Infantry Division '*Littorio*'; the 3rd Marine Division '*San Marco*'; and the 4th *Bersaglieri* Division '*Italia*'. All four ENR divisions were used almost exclusively against Partisans and not on the front line against the Allies, since the Germans never quite trusted them and had initially opposed raising them.

In November 1943 Himmler set up an Italian SS Legion of ultra-Fascists, the *Italianische Freiwilligen Verband/Legione SS Italiana*, under the direct control of Germany with an oath to Hitler. These Italian SS, more Nazi than fascist, were formed around the *XIX Battaglione Camicie Nere*, of the Fascist militia, who were in Greece at the time of the armistice and immediately placed themselves under the orders of Major-General von Stetner, the commanding officer of the 1st Division *Alpenjager*. The brigade consisted of two battalions: *Debica*, named after the Polish town where they were trained, and *Vendetta*. These initially were under the command of Waffen-Brigadeführer Pietro Manelli, and first saw action against Partisans in February 1944, after their training in Germany and Poland.

In March that year they were sent to fight at Anzio where, in recognition of their performance, Himmler fully integrated them into the Waffen-SS. In the second half of 1944 they returned to our area in northern Italy and spread out to fight the Partisans. Later, in March 1945, they became the *29. Waffen Grenadier Division Der SS (Italianische Nr. 1)*, having absorbed other RSI units.

In July 1944, to counter the growing number of Partisans, Mussolini decreed that all Republican Fascist male party members between the ages of 18 and 60 should bear arms. These new forces were called *le Brigate Nere* (the Black Brigades). The Black Brigades should have numbered a few hundred thousand, but only about 30,000 were recruited, probably with less than half of these actually bearing arms. However, what they lacked in numbers they more than made up for in fanatical zeal, and they were very much feared. They gloried in death as a cult, symbolised by their black flag emblazoned with a skull and crossbones. They were organised into fifty brigades, named after Fascist 'heroes' and the Italian provinces, but these 'brigades' were never more than companies in strength. The three Black Brigades that were active in our area were the *VIII 'Aldo Resega' – Milano*, the *XI 'Cesare Rondini' –*

Como, and the *XVI 'Dante Gervasini' – Varese*. Aldo Resega had been the head of the Republican Fascists of Milan and was assassinated by Partisans on 18 December 1943.

In addition, there were a number of private Fascist militias more or less controlled by different Fascist leaders. The two that operated in our province were *La Decima Mas* (*X-Mas*) and the dreaded *La Muti*. The *Decima Mas* was formed from the pre-July 1943 *Decima Flottiglia Motoscafi Antisommergibili* (Tenth Anti-Submarine Torpedo Boats Squadron), commanded by the flamboyant figure of Junio Valerio Borghese. Borghese himself didn't join the Republican Fascist Party, but he devoted himself to savage reprisals against the Partisans. Bad as these groups were, the worst by far was *La Muti*, named after Ettore Muti, the Fascist Party secretary 1939–40, dismissed by Mussolini as 'inept and corrupt', who had died escaping arrest in 1943 and was regarded as a Fascist martyr. *La Muti* was the largest and most criminal of many freebooting groups and had about 2,000 gang members operating mainly in Milan and our province.

Most British and American books on the war in Italy mention the Ardeatine Caves massacre of 335 Roman civilians, ordered by Kesselring in retaliation for the killing of thirty-three German SS soldiers in Via Rasella in Rome on 24 March 1944. But this appalling atrocity was only one of many hundreds of massacres in Italy, and was certainly not the first, as recently stated by military historian J. Holland.[3] On 21 November 1943, at Limmari di Pietransieri in the province of Chieti, 109 civilians, including women and children, were shot and their houses torched for protesting and refusing to give up their homes and belongings, purely as an example and demonstration of German superiority. And at Francavilla al Mare in the same province, in December 1943, twenty-three civilians were executed in reprisal for the death of a German soldier.[4]

The worst atrocity occurred between 29 September and 1 October 1944. After an orgy of killing and burning, which had started on 12 August, *16. SS-Panzergrenadier Division 'Reichsführer-SS'*, led by SS-Sturmbannführer Walter Reder, together with elements of the *Brigate Nere*, moved on to Marzabotto, a small town near Bologna, where:

Two regiments of the Adolf Hitler SS [sic] surrounded the part of the town beyond the River Reno. In the suburb of Casaglia a crowd took refuge in a church to pray for safety. The Germans burst in and killed the officiating priest and three old people who could not obey the orders to get out quickly enough. The remainder, 147 in number, were then killed with machine-guns in the cemetery. Twenty-eight families were completely wiped out. A hundred and seven were killed in the Caprata suburb.

At Casolari 282 were killed, including thirty-eight children and two nuns. At Carpiano nearby, forty-nine, including twenty-four women and nineteen children, were assassinated, and the Nazis killed a further 103 in the neighbourhood, scouring one house after another. The final total killed at Marzabotto was 1,830, including five priests.[5]

There were also frequent searches and round-ups. The Italian term is *rastrellamento*, for which there is no exact English equivalent; it was the word used to describe all anti-partisan operations carried out by Republican Fascist and German forces, as well as extensive area searches. These combined searches and round-ups were similar to those of the eighteenth-century navy press-gangs, but on a much larger scale. They served several purposes: to strike terror into the population; to round up draft-dodgers; to draft males between 14 and 60 for work in Germany or for digging defences such as anti-tank ditches for the Germans in Italy; and to get a reserve of hostages to shoot if any German was harmed or German equipment damaged.

I was in the courtyard of our house when one of these searches took place in Musadino. I was unaware that the Fascists had arrived until a young member of the newly formed *Brigate Nere* came into the courtyard holding a sub-machine gun at the ready. I must have looked very nervous because I remember him telling me not to be afraid in a very patronising manner. He asked me how many people lived in the courtyard and who they were, and I told him. As I pointed out where I lived on the first floor I suddenly remembered that when Mussolini had fallen from power the year before, I had daubed *VV Badoglio!* (Long Live Badoglio!) on the whitewashed wall to the left side of our door; it was covered by bundles of firewood, but they could easily be cast aside in a search. I knew that people had been imprisoned for writing anti-fascist slogans on walls, even before July 1943, and that in the RSI you could be shot for it. It would have been particularly ironic getting shot for a slogan praising such a pathetic figure as Badoglio.

We also had an old muzzle-loading shotgun, with the ram-rod slung under the barrel, which was still hanging on the wall in the living room where we had found it when we moved in. From time to time there had been notices posted up in the village demanding that all firearms be handed in, but we had ignored them. I now dreaded him going up to the first floor and searching through the bundles of wood or, worse still, going into the house and finding the shotgun, so I started playing for time. He had a dagger on his belt and I asked him if it was a real weapon or just for ceremonial use, and he unsheathed the dagger to show me. I then asked him how long he had been in the GNR. This seemed to please him and he began chatting away. He took great pride in telling me he was only 16 and a volunteer. But I was only half-listening as the shotgun, the slogan and my mother's foreign accent spun through my mind. He had just started to show me his sub-machine gun when someone from his group called out his name and he shouted back something like 'All clear here' and abruptly left. I was shaking with fear, but as soon as I heard the group leave I dashed upstairs and quickly obliterated the slogan as best I could; it had been covered with firewood for months and my father hadn't realised it was there. That evening the gun was taken down and its outline on the wall and the slogan outside whitewashed over. The shotgun was packed with cart grease and firmly wrapped up; the next day it was taken to Noèlla and buried near a cherry tree, and for all I know it's still there.

One day I was searching for mushrooms fairly high up Pian Nave, when suddenly I came across an empty packet of Player's cigarettes. I recognised it immediately from the familiar figure of a bearded sailor framed in a lifebelt. I was completely flabbergasted and was unsure of what I should do. I didn't understand how anyone could have been so careless to have dropped it, and then it flashed through my mind that it might have been deliberately left there as some sort of signal. I went several yards away to the cover of a tree, from where I could still see it. After about fifteen minutes, when nothing had happened, I realised I had to do something; if it wasn't a signal then I had to remove it. I whistled; no reply. Then I called out; again no reply. I went back to the packet, picked it up and carefully examined it. It was damp but not wet, so I assumed it must have been dropped within the past twenty-four hours. I put it in the lining of the army cap I now wore, in case I was stopped, and returned home with the few mushrooms I had found. I didn't tell my parents about this – the less said the better I thought. Then at the first opportunity I steamed the packet open. Under the glued part were some letters and num-bers. Now I thought I had really messed things up and I had half a mind to take it back to where I had found it; in the end, however, I destroyed it.

In 1946, when I got back to England, one of the first things I did was to steam open a packet of Player's, and much to my relief I found that it had a similar set of letters and numbers; it was simply either a printer's number or a batch code. More than likely it had been dropped by an Allied POW making for the Swiss border who had been rather careless.

Another incident which stays in my mind happened when I was sent on an errand by my father to collect a bottle of medicine from a friend of his who had served in the army with him in Yugoslavia and lived on the other side of our mountains. My father had written to him so he was expecting me. I had never crossed directly to the other side of the mountain chain before. To do so by level road you had to circumvent it either from Luino or south from Laveno, so I was quite keen to go. By now I knew the path to San Michele, but after that, down the other side, I stuck mainly to the old military road to Brissago. I finally located the house and my father's friend. He asked me how my father was and I told him he was still suffering from severe stomach cramps almost daily; he then gave me the bottle of medicine for him. He wanted me to stay overnight, but I said I would set off back immediately to get home before curfew. All in all, I couldn't have been more than fifteen minutes with him before I set off on the return journey.

It was a long haul back to the San Michele pass, along an unfamiliar route, but I made it and at the top I paused for a rest. I could see most of Lake Maggiore spread before me. I was admiring the view when I heard the sound of an aeroplane, and I saw it as a distant dot in the sky near Intra, a town on the western shore opposite Laveno. In what seemed like a matter of seconds, the noise of its engine grew louder and louder, rising to a screech. I now saw that it was a fighter and that it was heading straight towards me. I didn't question why a fighter plane should single me out; I instinctively threw myself down at the side of the road. I lay with my head buried in my arms, expecting the pilot to open fire, but the fighter carried on with its engine screaming. It seemed to pass only inches above me, but was probably about 50ft up. It flew straight on and within a split second crashed into the mountainside. There was a massive explosion, which shook the ground beneath me. It had all taken place so fast that for a minute or two I didn't quite realise what had happened. Though very shaken, I was alright, and I got up and dusted myself down. I was so inured to war by then that I didn't even bother to go and look at the crashed plane; I just carried on home. When I got back I was told that an airman had bailed out further down the lake, but I didn't see him. There was a brief report, a mere paragraph, in the paper.

After my father's discharge from the army, and for the remainder of the war, most days we bought a daily paper, the Milanese *Corriere della sera*. This was not an extravagance as the price remained low throughout the war, although it gradually shrank in size from a full-size newspaper to two sheets, and eventually to a small single sheet. Old newspapers were used for many things, such as lighting the fire, wrapping for drying fruit and toilet paper.

It was around this time that I witnessed a rather bizarre event. The men of the village used to gather in the evening at the village *osteria* to drink wine and play cards; not in the public area at the front but in the innkeeper's living room at the back. I was there one evening with my father, about an hour before the curfew, watching him play scopa, a popular card game like whist which the village men played very noisily, slapping their cards down on the table. The *osteria*, as well as being a tavern, also served as a shop for the sale of salt and tobacco, which in Italy were state monopolies and could only be sold in premises licensed to do so. We heard the main entrance door-bell go and the *osteria* owner's wife went out to see who was shopping so late. She returned to the back room with a couple of German soldiers who were on patrol. Everything went quiet as the two Germans entered with rifles and wearing steel helmets. I cannot now remember what unit they were in, but I do remember that they looked middle-aged. They were probably *Zollgrenzschutzes* frontier guards, as the unit's personnel were all in their mid-thirties and forties.

The Germans seemed to quickly accept that we were all quite harmless and they warmed themselves before the fire where the landlady was roasting some chestnuts. The card game started again, but in silence, as the Germans continued to stand by the fire. They had a couple of chestnuts and one of them asked for a glass of water to wash them down. At this, the *osteria* owner offered them a glass of wine instead of water. After an initial show of reluctance, and indicating that they were on duty, both accepted the offered glass of hospitality. One of the Germans sat down near me and the other opposite, with me at the outer end. Speaking a few words in broken Italian, they began showing us photos of their wives and children, and revealing that they too lived in mountain villages. They had taken their helmets off and placed them on the ground, with their rifles propped up at the end of the table.

Seeing me looking at the steel helmets, one of them picked up his helmet and handed it to me, showing me the leather webbing inside. While I was looking at it, and the two were showing their photos to my dad and the other card players, I became aware of an almost whispered argument going on in dialect. One young man was urging that we should kill them and dump their bodies in the countryside; others were saying that by doing so we would only bring disaster on the village. While this muffled argument continued I felt my hands, still holding the helmet, begin to shake. As it happened, nothing came of the incident; the soldiers drank up and left, smiling, to continue their patrol. Someone must have tipped off the Fascists about this, however, because one night shortly afterwards the house of the young man who had urged the killing of the Germans was raided. Fortunately, as they came up the steps he managed to get out of a bedroom window and hung by his hands from the house rafters. After they had left he got away, but I don't recall seeing him again.

16

FOOD SHORTAGES AND
A BRUSH WITH THE SS

In Mussolini's Italian Social Republic there was a new twist. Ration cards were only issued to Fascist Party members. I remember one day we were all called out of school to see a company of *Decima Mas* lined up, with a band playing for us in the school playground. The company commander gave a short speech and then handed out pamphlets to give to our parents. In brief, it promised food to all who joined the Republican Fascist Party and, as far as I am aware, no one took up the offer. Not having a ration card didn't really make much difference since there was nothing in the shops anyway. Our grocer, Mino, now mainly sold matches and candles, and bread made with a little flour and all sorts of additives and flour substitutes. In mid-1944 my father had bought a pair of guinea pigs from a man in Muceno. We kept them in a recess under the stone stairs from the courtyard, where they bred very rapidly. They provided lots of fresh meat, and along with polenta we had little need of ration books. Sometimes Virginia, our next-door neighbour who kept hens, would give me a newly laid egg to suck. The trick was to make a small hole in the top of the egg without breaking the shell, then suck out and swallow the contents in one gulp.

The main reason the shops were bare was because the Germans were now raiding everything. All factories were now producing for the Reich, but they even disrupted this by pillaging machinery. As the front advanced, all salt-producing areas were cut off. What salt there may have been in northern Italy was not distributed, as this was very low on the German priority list. In our province salt became like gold as a means of exchange. Nowadays there is more than enough salt already in the foods we buy, but total salt deficiency is an entirely different matter. After a few weeks it leads to severe headaches, dizziness and back cramps. At first all the ground salt went, then the rock salt vanished, and finally the low-grade rock salt given to animals went too. Parts of barrels which had held salted fish were sold at a premium; the wood was boiled and the salty fishy water used as a condiment, or even boiled away to leave a salt residue. One of my father's friends seriously proposed cycling all the way to the Ligurian coast to boil seawater until he had a bag of sea salt to bring back.

At tremendous risk, my father managed to smuggle a length of narrow copper tubing out of Boltri, the factory where he worked. He did this by carefully coiling it around his body. With the copper tubing, and after much trial and error, he built and perfected an illicit still, which he set up in the basement of our house. For the distillation flask he stripped the straw from a 2-litre wine container, the Chianti flask so loved by British wine drinkers, and about a litre of wine lees was boiled in it at a time, with the steam from the boiling wine going from the flask through the coiled tubing into a small barrel of cold water. The steam from the boiling wine would condense as it passed through the cold water and drip into a bottle placed under the coil end. The result was the spirit grappa. My father was nothing if not enterprising and he used this to barter for salt.

In the spring of 1944 I tried my hand at being a porter. I had heard there was money to be earned at the station at Porto by carrying the bags of wealthy Milanese coming to visit their evacuated families. For my first venture I took the wheelbarrow my father had made. A train of the usual cattle and freight wagons came in and there was a surge forward of lads as the passengers struggled off, but only one or two got bags to carry; I got nothing. As I waited for the next train, I suddenly thought of the lad who had carried our bags when we arrived in Italy. I remembered his ragged clothes and bare feet. Now, four years on, here was I barefooted, my clothes much more ragged than he had worn, and I was far less successful as a porter than he had been. I went a couple more times but found that pickings were very few and far between, as were the trains, with many cancelled or subject to long delays. One afternoon, after I had stopped going, a young man arrived from Milan and at the station checkpoint he was shot through the head and killed instantly. Apparently he had been ordered to raise his hands, but with one hand in the air he had put his other hand into his inside pocket to get his wallet out to show his ID card; at which point a German soldier, thinking he was going for a gun, shot him.

In June 1944, having reached the age of 14, I started work full time. My first job was as a builder's labourer in Caldé, south of Musadino on the coast of

Lake Maggiore. I had to leave the house early to get there for eight as it was a walk of about 6km. My first task was to move a large pile of rounded stones in a wheelbarrow from a demolished wall to a small building site. The stones were very heavy to lift into the wheelbarrow and it would sometimes tip as I was loading it. I had to then wheel it along a series of planks, but the wheel often slipped off into sand, tipping the load out. It was very hard work and afterwards I had the long walk home. I also had to keep the builders supplied with mortar; I had to mix the cement, sand and lime with a shovel as there was no fuel to run a cement mixer. I think I was only at this job for about three or four weeks when my father found me a less heavy job at the factory where he worked. Here I was put to work on a lathe making threaded bolts and screws. There were three lathes in a row operated by me and two other lads. The bolts were cut from long rods of metal which made a deafening noise as they spun and rattled in supporting stands. Initially, the lathe settings for the required screws were set up by our foreman, but I was quickly able to do this myself from a blueprint like the other two experienced boys could. We also made and sharpened our own cutting tools, and my father showed me how to temper them by heating them red hot and then quenching them in oil.

The lathes we worked on had their own electric motors, which was unusual in those days. Most of the machinery in the factory was driven by long leather belts from overhead pulleys from a central engine. The work was interesting enough but the noise was deafening on our three lathes, and when we switched off at break time the sound would still be ringing in our ears. If we could find a piece of stainless steel rod we would filch it, and between finishing one type of bolt and setting it up for another, we would quickly make stainless steel signet rings. The eldest of the three of us, nicknamed *Re Barbuto* (the Bearded King – after the kings on playing cards), smuggled them out of the factory by simply slipping a ring on his finger.

One morning we got tipped off that the factory was going to be raided by the Germans, rounding up workers for Germany. We were actually warned of this by the management who were desperate to keep their workers to meet production targets set by the Germans themselves. A whistle went and we all streamed out quickly and made for a hillock facing the factory from where we could see what was going on. On that day I was on the same shift as my dad and we had our lunch together at the top of the hill. In due course, a couple of German trucks rolled up, but soon left empty-handed; there was little they could do with the management playing innocent. All they had succeeded in doing was stopping the factory's production for about three hours.

We worked five and a half days a week, ten hours a day, Monday to Friday; on Saturday work finished at midday. The factory was just outside Porto, and to get there we would cut down past Noèlla, through a small wood, down to Prè, where my friend Amatore lived, then through a denser wood and on to the main Porto–Muceno road. I used to hate the walk when I was on an early shift on my own, and my father on a later shift. Work started at seven and it would still be dark when I left the house. I particularly hated going through the two woods in pitch-black darkness and I would whistle to keep my spirits up. I would get to Prè just as dawn was breaking and Amatore's mother would often bring out a bowl of fresh goat's milk for me to drink. Amatore, lucky lad, would still be asleep tucked away in a warm bed.

Work was frequently interrupted at the factory either due to small-scale sabotage or to major power cuts. We could easily bring our lathes to a halt either by shorting out the electric motor or by not reversing the lathe fast enough as a screw thread was being cut, making the threaded section of the screw shank break off inside the thread cutter. This was liable to happen genuinely with smaller screws, so a deliberate action was difficult to detect, providing it wasn't done too often. I think our foreman was well aware of this but turned a blind eye to it. I must admit I often did it just to get a break from the deafening noise of the rattling steel rods, rather than to bring down the Third Reich.

On one occasion, during a short break in the factory, I was fooling around with my two workmates. We were kicking a ball of paper around between our lathes when I aimed a kick at it but missed; my wooden sandal flew off and, with the full force of the kick, my bare foot landed on the narrow edge of the lathe stand, deeply splitting the gap between my little toe and the next toe. I was in excruciating pain and the men realised I was badly hurt. I was hurriedly carried to the first-aid room and my dad informed. After the dirt and grease was cleared out, my father held my foot while iodine was poured in the injury to cauterise it. I cannot remember now how I got home; it might have been by horse and cart. Later that afternoon Amleto, my Milanese evacuee friend, came to the house. When he saw what had happened he offered to take me on his bicycle to Doctor Ballerò in Porto to see if it needed stitching. My mother was anxious about the injury and agreed I should go, and we set off with me sitting on the crossbar of Amleto's bike.

Instead of going direct to Porto, which would have meant a steep descent from a point above Porto called the *Altipiano*, Amleto thought it best to make a detour via Muceno and cycle past Prè and the factory, the gradient being less steep. We were on the long straight stretch from Prè, gathering speed on what appeared to be a clear road, when a group of German soldiers stepped out and formed a roadblock less than 50m before us. This time there were no smiling middle-aged soldiers – it was an SS group, with a Republican Fascist GNR member acting as interpreter. We heard a German shout 'Halt!', but as we were going too fast we carried on a good few metres towards them before stopping and falling off. We were told brusquely to put our hands up and walk towards them. Amleto got up off the ground immediately, but I couldn't. He went to give me a hand up but was ordered to keep his hands raised, so I ended up sitting on the ground with my hands up with Amleto standing by my side.

Amleto was shouted at to move away from his bike, and the SS came over to us. We were asked for our identity cards and also where we were going. I told them what had happened and I was ordered to take the bandage off my foot so that they could look at it. I remember the Italian fascist saying to Amleto, 'Your story doesn't make sense. He would have been taken from the factory to the doctor if he needed one, not from Muceno', or words to that effect. I said the wound had got worse since I had arrived home in Musadino, but he asked me how was it possible for a cut to get worse and why had we gone to Muceno. By this point I had stopped listening and I felt certain that we would both be carted off to work in Germany. I wondered if my mother would ever find out how I had vanished. Even my foot had stopped hurting, it just felt numb. The SS were immaculately dressed, particularly the haughty NCO in charge; he was either an SS-Rottenführer or an SS-Scharführer, and other than occasionally talking in German to the GNR man, he looked down on me as if I were a piece of dirt.

At this point, seeing things were not going well for us, to my complete surprise Amleto pulled out a Republican Fascist Party membership card and gave the Fascist raised arm salute. The GNR man was taken aback and, after checking that the party card was genuine, he started chatting amicably with Amleto for a few minutes and finally we were let through.

I was stunned and bewildered by this turn of events and could hardly speak to him. Throughout the years of our friendship I had confided in Amleto, and now I feared I might have put my father and others in danger. Amleto, seeing my worried face, said to me, 'Don't worry, things are not what they seem', and I didn't see him again until May 1945. As for the doctor, he said that foot injuries such as mine were best left unstitched and that it would heal if I rested it and kept it clean. He cleaned it up further with methylated spirits and re-bandaged it for me, and I hobbled back home by the short route, which was far too steep to cycle.

17

DEATH AND DESTRUCTION FROM LAKE MAGGIORE TO SANTA MARIA DEL TARO

Lake Maggiore was targeted yet again in 1944. A *rastrellamento*, carried out by the SS and Republican Fascist forces between 12 and 20 June, was typically brutal. A force of around 17,000 advanced, burning and pillaging and leaving destruction in their wake. Four hundred Partisans were in the mountains of the Verbano and the Cannóbina, above Cannóbio (where our parish priest had taken us for a day's outing in 1941). The majority of the Partisans fought their way out but forty-one were captured. First they were taken to the *asilo* (kindergarten) of Malesco, where they were tortured; then early in the morning of 20 June they were loaded on a truck and taken to SS Headquarters in Villa Caramora at Intra. Here a witness already imprisoned there described how they were sadistically kicked, punched and hit with rifle butts as they were shoved into the room, their faces swollen from the beatings they had already endured. Two others were put in with them: Cleonice Tomassetti, a Milanese schoolteacher and Partisan courier, arrested in Intra as she got off the ferry from our side of the lake; and Marino Rosa, an Intra workman arrested two days earlier.

At 3 p.m. on the same day the forty-three prisoners were taken outside and made to form a column. At the head of the column was Cleonice Tomassetti, flanked by two Partisans who were made to carry a placard which read SONO QUESTI I LIBERATORI D'ITALIA O SONO I BANDITI? (Are these Italy's liberators or are they bandits?) The witness[1] who was imprisoned with them recalls that their escort had smartened themselves up, laughing and joking, combing and brushing their hair, to give maximum contrast between their smart appearance and the sorry state of the Partisans they were about to execute. They were then made to parade along the road from Intra to Fondotoce, passing through Pallanza and Suna, with the entire population turned out to watch at each location. Along the canal, which joins Lake Magazzo to Lake Maggiore, the place of execution, they were made to lie down in rows of three, then shot three at a time with a sub-machine gun. They started shooting them at six o'clock, finishing about an hour later.

One of them, Carlo Suzzi, aged 18, was shot but not mortally wounded. Surviving by a miracle under the bodies of the executed until nightfall, he escaped with the aid of local people and, on recovery, rejoined the Resistance, adopting the name *Quarantatré* (Forty-three) as his *nom de guerre*.

A German soldier took photographs of this macabre march as a souvenir and took the film to a chemist in Intra to be developed; the chemist kept copies of three photographs, one of which appears in this book. This callous behaviour and execution shocked everyone on our side of the lake; the Germans themselves making sure that everyone knew. The executed Partisans who have been identified are Giovanni Alberti aged 20, Giovanni Barelli aged 24, Giglio Battelli aged 31, Carlo Antonio Beretta aged 31, Angelo Bizzozzero aged 21, Emilio Bonalumi aged 21, Luigi Brioschi aged 22, Luigi Brown aged 24, Dante Capuzzo aged 30, Sergio Ciribì aged 18, Giuseppe Cocco aged 18, Adriano Marco Corna aged 21, Achille Fabbro aged 20, Olivo Favaron aged 18, Angelo Freguglia aged 20, Franco Ghiringhelli (no relation) aged 21, Cosimo Guarneri aged 21, Giovanni La Ciacera aged 26, Franco Marchetti aged 20, Arturo Mezzagora aged 20, Rodolfo Pellicella aged 30, Giuseppe Perraro aged 18, Ezio Rizzato aged 35, Marino Rosa aged 26, Aldo Cesare Rossi aged 22, Carlo Sacchi aged 35, Cleonice Tomassetti aged 32, Renzo Villa aged 19, and Giovanni Volpati aged 41. Sadly, the names of the remaining fourteen are not known.

In Milan, on the morning of 10 August 1944, fifteen men were shot by a platoon of Republican Fascists of the *Legione 'Ettore Muti'* in Piazzale Loreto (Loreto Square). Their bodies were piled up on display in a heap, but relatives were forbidden to pay any last respects to them. The Fascists who guarded the bodies, preventing access to the relatives, are on record as spending the day laughing and joking at the 'pile of rubbish'. These fifteen are now known as the martyrs of Piazzale Loreto. They are: Andrea Esposito, Domenico Fiorani, Gian Antonio Bravin, Giulio Casiraghi, Renzo del Riccio, Umberto Fogagnolo, Tullio Galimberti, Vittorio Gasparini, Emidio Mastrodomenico, Salvatore Principato, Angelo Poletti, Andrea Ragni, Eraldo Soncini, Libero Temolo and Vitale Vertemati. The youngest was 21, the oldest 46.

Some were badly tortured, and the Partisans vowed then that Piazzale Loreto would be where Mussolini and fourteen senior Fascists would one day be taken to atone for their desecration. When Mussolini was informed of the massacre by the Germans, he is reputed to have said: 'We shall pay dearly for this blood.' The man who ordered the massacre was Theodor Saevecke, the chief of the SS security police in Milan, and *SD Aussenkommando* in Lombardy. It was Saevecke who had also ordered the murder of the fifty-four Jews at Meina on Lake Maggiore. He was renowned for his sadistic torturing and was responsible for sending at least 750 Jews to extermination camps.

Over in Santa Maria del Taro and the surrounding area, where my mother's sister Rosa lived, and with whom we had stayed on our arrival in Italy in 1940 in what now seemed blissful days, there were four *rastrellamenti*. The first was from 22 to 28 May 1944. At about 2 a.m. on 22 May, Santa Maria's inhabitants were woken up to the sound of German troops pouring in on half-tracks. There were about 8,000 Germans supported by Fascist militias. Having established themselves in requisitioned houses they proceeded to sweep Monte Penna, which they believed was a Partisan stronghold. All men, young and old, found away from their homes were arrested and taken to Santa Maria's saw mill, which the Germans had occupied and set up as a temporary prison for SS interrogations. Those found to be of military age were deported, the rest released. This first operation was, however, relatively mild; a Fascist was wounded and in retaliation a house was burnt down and three captured Partisans put against a wall of the same house and shot. On 14 June the Partisans returned to the area and demolished all road bridges leading to Santa Maria, isolating it completely, and the town could only be supplied or accessed by pack-mules or on foot.

The second *rastrellamento* started on 7 July 1944, and this one was the most terrible. Arriving from Chiavari, this time the Nazi and Fascist troops met with armed resistance and had to fight their way to Santa Maria, where they arrived in the afternoon of 10 July. On the previous day, Sunday 9 July, the parish priest of Santa Maria had interrupted Mass and advised all young men of military age to leave at once and take refuge on Monte Penna. He himself remained behind with Dr Cesare Pighini, hoping to calm the Germans, believing that no harm would come to the remaining old men, women and children. The Germans, however, had other ideas. They ordered everyone to assemble in the church square with no exceptions; they then searched and ransacked every house. The old men were ordered to assemble at six the next morning, to be used as forced labour in rebuilding all the demolished bridges. Both the parish priest and the doctor were arrested, and the priest was told that should any harm come to a single German soldier he would be held personally responsible. The Germans then advanced out of Santa Maria on the road to Bedonia, but they were ambushed by Partisans, and in a three-hour battle their losses amounted to thirty-four killed, with more wounded and fifteen taken prisoner. The Partisans' losses were three killed and one wounded.

The following day more troops poured into Santa Maria. Enraged at their losses, the Germans now had everyone assemble again and, severely beating many of the old men, continually threatened all of them with death. All were crowded into a large hall and locked up. On 12 July the Germans brought their thirty-four dead comrades and laid them out on the road outside the cemetery. They then made the entire population, old men, women and children, file past them in a column two abreast. The women and children were then released, but their joy was short lived, for when they returned to their houses they found that in their absence their furniture had been smashed and anything useful removed. The priest and the doctor were carted off to a concentration camp at Bibbiano in Reggio Emilia.

Starting on 16 July, the Germans and Fascists fanned out to the surrounding villages in an orgy of murder and destruction. In total, 61 civilians, including some priests, were shot; 20 young men were deported to Germany; 196 houses were completely destroyed (the villages of Menta and Bruschi were burnt down); 76 houses were partially destroyed; 200 farmhouses were razed to the ground; 500 head of cattle were stolen; and many houses were ransacked and the contents stolen, to an estimated value of tens of millions of lire. Fields were left desolate; a scorched earth policy because the local population was accused of aiding Partisans. On 20 July the Fascists and Germans moved on to other areas, leaving a trail of desolation.[2]

There were two further *rastrellamenti* in Santa Maria; the third, on 24 August 1944, was carried out by the SS and a contingent of Fascist *Alpini* of the 'Monte Rosa' division, which included the Fascist 'Intra' battalion, but there wasn't much left to destroy. Meanwhile, my Uncle Luigi had dug out and constructed a concealed recessed room by tunnelling from inside his stable; although cramped, it provided the men of Pianlavagnolo with a safe hiding place. Once they were inside, my Aunt Rosa covered up the camouflaged entrance with cow dung and cattle bedding. The Germans never discovered this and the men were spared having to flee up into the mountains during the searches for slave labour.

A company of *Alpini* arrived with their baggage and set up a garrison at Passo del Bocco above Santa Maria, where they remained until 10 April 1945, despite several Partisan attempts to dislodge them. On 17 December 1944, the Fascist *Alpini* raided the *Trattoria Nando* in Santa Maria del Taro and detained six young men, who were playing cards there, as hostages and imprisoned them at Borgonovo. On Christmas Eve two of them, Berto Lusardi aged 21 and Luigi Squeri aged 27, were bound and dragged to the entrance of Borgonovo cemetery, with the inhabitants of the town in tears and loudly begging for mercy on their behalf. But the two men were shot in reprisal for a minor Partisan action. Their families only learnt of their execution on Boxing Day, when their sisters returned distraught to Santa Maria from Borgonovo, where they had gone to visit their brothers on Christmas Day evening. As had happened at San Michele in 1943, courageous volunteers immediately set out for Borgonovo to recover their bodies, returning with them on the evening of 27 December. The remaining four hostages were released at the end of January 1945 and promptly joined the Partisans.

The fourth and final *rastrellamento* started on 30 December 1944, when the church at Valetti was ransacked and the parish priest, Don Bobbio, was accused of collaborating with Partisans and arrested. He was taken to Chiavari where, after a summary trial, he was shot on 3 January 1945. In this last anti-Partisan action the Germans brought in the Cossacks, known to the local population as *mongoli russi*. My Aunt Rosa and her family had their fields ruined and food and livestock stolen, but they did survive the war, unlike many of the villagers we had met in July 1940.

Of course, not all Germans were ardent Nazis; a small number were clearly shocked by Nazi bestial behaviour, and there were desertions well before it became evident that Germany had lost the war. Few, however, were as determined and resolute as Kapitänleutnant Rudolf Heinrich Otto Max Jacobs, a German naval officer who commanded the *Ingenieurskorps* of the *Kriegsmarine* in La Spezia, and Stabsunteroffizier Johann Fritz, a Wehrmacht NCO on his staff. In late 1943 Jacobs, who had done the best he could to supply food to the local population, having been wrongly informed that his wife and two children had died in an air raid, loaded up an armoured car with jerry cans of petrol and as much ammunition as it would carry and, together with Fritz, drove it over to the Partisans and joined them. Rising quickly through Partisan ranks after he had established their trust, he became a Partisan leader in the *Brigata Garibaldi 'Ugo Muccini'*, fighting for nearly a year under the assumed name 'Primo'. Finally, in a daring action on 3 October 1944, posing as German army officers, he and Fritz led a group of three Russians and five Italians, in German uniforms, into a hotel in Sarzana used by the Republican Fascists as a barracks. But the surprise attack failed and Jacobs lost his life in a fire-fight, his gun having jammed. He was posthumously awarded the *Medaglia d'Oro*, Italy's highest award for bravery. His family only learnt of this in February 1957, when they were traced by the former commander of the Partisan '*Muccini*' Brigade, Paolo Ranieri. A plaque was unveiled in Rudolf Jacobs' honour at Sarzana on 29 November 1953.

18

A New Job

On his day off, on Sundays, my father had got himself a job clearing several large tree stumps from a piece of land between Porto and Luino, adjacent to the railway track and only a few metres from the lake. As I had nearly recovered from the injury to my foot, I went a couple of Sundays to help him as it was very hard work removing the deep roots with axe, pick and shovel, in the days before chainsaws were invented. At this time in 1944, northern Italy was within Allied fighter plane range, and anything that moved was being strafed and machine-gunned. The steamship *Milano*, launched in 1930, was sunk by a fighter in the waters off Intra. These boats used to run up and down Lake Maggiore, criss-crossing alternately from the ports on either side of the lake, but by now the few left were barely running. Trains were a particular target, and to protect themselves engine drivers attached the engines to the front of the trains as usual, but with the engines reversed, so that the driving cab was leading, as invariably they were machine-gunned from the rear to compensate for the speed of the train. I was quite fascinated watching the trains pass slowly by in this fashion as we worked on the tree stumps.

Very early one morning, while we were working at the site, I saw a fishing boat heading back to Porto. As soon as I told my father he stopped work and called out to the fishermen who rowed inshore, within speaking distance. My father offered them firewood in exchange for fish, to which they readily agreed; I waded into the lake to get the fish as they loaded the wood. We already had a good fire burning as the weather was bitterly cold, so we gutted a couple of fish there and then and ate them by the fire, before taking the rest home for my mother and sister to share. There was no way of preserving them, so we had fish and fish soup at every meal for a couple of days.

When my foot had healed I didn't return to work in the factory. Angiolin, who had been badly beaten up by the Germans in 1943, agreed to give me a job. I was to work for him without pay, but I would be housed and fed. I also got a pair of his boots thrown in! Angiolin was one of the wealthier men of the village; he had a pair of fine oxen, a horse, mule, cattle and goats. He was very hard working, and I always remember him from when I first arrived in Musadino, driving his ox team pulling huge loads of wood, and his timeless cries of 'Heu! Heu! Vallah!' to spur them on (Italian carters' cries which dated back to Roman times). And so, at the age of 14, I left home. I didn't realise it at the time but, apart from visits and an occasional night's stay, I had left home for good.

The work took some getting used to. I had to get up very early to clean out the cowshed, put in new bedding of dried chestnut leaves, then feed the cows, which meant going up to the hayloft, opening trap doors and dropping hay down into the feeding trough; then back and forth with buckets of water for them, each cow drinking a bucketful. After that I milked them. The cows were not let out of their stalls until the spring, when they were herded high up to San Michele for the summer's rich pasture. Angiolin also taught me how to harness and drive the horse, mule and oxen.

The oxen were used for really heavy loads, mainly logs. The wood was sent down the mountain by a system of cableways: long stretches of steel cable on which the load would be hung by a wheeled pulley or a hooked piece of wood. If a wooden hook was used it had to be greased, otherwise it would simply burn through from the friction; wooden hooks were mainly used for hay loads. You couldn't see the distant loading point up the mountain so signals were passed by tapping the cable. As soon as the load was on its way and gathering speed, the cable would ring out. For safety you had to stand well back because if the cable broke it would whiplash, and would more than likely cut you in half. One day we were working away; the wood was whizzing down and I was unhooking it and carrying it to the ox cart. I was impressed at the speed of the wood coming down and I recalled how much I had struggled to bring down the large birch tree high in the mountains soon after my father had returned home. I said something like 'This is a lot faster than dragging a log down', to which Angiolin said: 'So it was you who chopped down one of my birches, was it?'

'No, no,' I said. 'Not me.'

'Well, that's very funny,' he said. 'Your dad told me it was you', and he started chuckling while I felt my face go crimson.

Angiolin was already trying to restock his *osteria* at San Michele and I took a few things up by mule and cart, including a large demijohn of *marsala*, the dark sweet dessert wine made in Sicily. To get to San Michele you had to go up by the military road which started beyond Muceno. Then it was a tedious journey as the road snaked back and forth up the steep face and you seemed to be forever turning corners and seeing the winding road ahead of you. About halfway up I stopped for a rest and became intrigued by the *marsala*. Curiosity played its part, and I managed to get the large cork stopper off the demijohn. I twisted the bark off a sapling of wood so that I had a hollow tube, and with it I sucked up a good swig of wine. I intended to leave it at that, but as the morning wore on I took more and more swigs, until the level of *marsala* was visibly low. Just before I pulled into San Michele, I topped it up with fresh mountain water and hammered the bung back in tight.

At San Michele I took my meals with Angiolin and his wife Anna. However, the *osteria* was small with a lack of sleeping accommodation, so I slept in an attached empty stable. There was a draught from the door, but I was comfortable and warm once I was in bed. The only part of my job I disliked was bringing the goats in at sunset. They would be stalled overnight, then milked and let out to roam freely during the day. There was a dominant goat in the herd, and once you had got it and set off home, the rest of the goats followed. The bells they wore could be heard over long distances so it wasn't too difficult to find them.

About the third time I was out I quickly located them and felt a great sense of achievement – it looked as if I would be heading home in ten minutes. The herd was strewn just below the military road on a steep section. As I called they started coming towards me, but as they got near the leader turned and headed off down a narrow path, and the rest followed him. After that it was stop and start all along the path, as it got narrower and narrower, until I found myself staring down a sheer drop of a couple of hundred metres. To make things worse I now found that there were a couple of goats behind me blocking the path back and the thought flashed through my mind that I had survived so far in the war and now I was in danger of falling to my death because of a silly goat. I edged my way back along the crumbling track and returned dejected along the road to San Michele, only to meet Angiolin coming to look for me. At a distance behind me, the goats were now out on the road, and literally within a minute Angiolin had them all following him. Fortunately the season was closing in and San Michele was abandoned for the winter, with all the animals driven down to Musadino, ending my brief career as a goat herder.

On 9 September 1944 the Partisans on the west side of Lake Maggiore set up the Republic of Ossola, having cleared the entire area of Germans and Fascists following a battle at Domodossola. Its territory included thirty-five municipalities, including the towns of Domodossola, Bognanco, Crodo, Pieve Vegante and Villadossola. The tiny republic lasted until 22 October, when it was invaded and inevitably defeated by superior German forces. For about three days during its existence, the area around Oggebbio was shelled by an 88mm gun set up between Porto and Luino. I could see the flash as the shells exploded in apparent silence, and then the sound followed seconds later. There was a Milanese evacuee about a year or two older than me who, just outside my house, told me that he had been to watch the gun firing. I said that it was typical of the Fascists to shell a defenceless village, at which he grabbed me by the front of my coat and, cursing me, he tapped my chest hard with his fist and said he could smash in my rib cage with one blow. I remember his exact words: '*ti spacco la cassa toracica.*'

I went into the house badly shaken and my father asked me what the matter was; after some hesitation I told him. Usually he was quite cautious in his dealings with Fascists, but on this occasion he rushed out of the house and asked me which one it was who had threatened me. He then yanked him out of the group and, with his face only an inch away, told him in no uncertain terms that if he ever threatened me again he would knock his head off. I was afraid that something unpleasant might come of this, and I regretted telling my father, but to my surprise the lad and his group completely avoided me after that.

A small incident shows just how suspicious the Republican Fascists could be. One Sunday in October 1944, Pancrazio, a 9-year-old boy from Domo, a schoolmate of my sister Gloria, accompanied his grandmother to graze some sheep in the foothill woods above her village of Torre. As was usual with all boys then, he began looking for discarded rounds of ammunition, just as I used to as a schoolboy (this being an area which the army had used for live exercises before the armistice of September 1943). Under a bush in some soft muddy ground, he saw a red object protruding and carefully dug it out. It was a hand grenade. He saw that the safety pin had been removed and, realising that it was dangerous, threw it as far as he could, which unfortunately wasn't far enough. It exploded on impact, injuring him with splinters of grenade casing, earth and fragments of rock. The deafening explosion brought his grandmother and some men working nearby running, and he was carried down to Torre. Fortunately for Pancrazio, who was bleeding profusely, one of the Milanese evacuees who had a small van was with his family in Torre for the weekend and had a can of petrol, a scarce commodity in 1944, and he was rushed in the van to hospital in Luino for an emergency operation.[1] A day or so later, when he was able to speak, two Fascist militiamen, accompanied by two men in plainclothes, came to interrogate him. They went over his story again and again, telling him that they did not believe him as the area had been cleared years ago; they said he must have met Partisans or acted as a courier for them. They told him that if he didn't tell the truth, as soon as he was better he would be taken away and shot. Needless to say, the men who had saved him, and his grandmother, were also questioned repeatedly before the Fascists were satisfied. Fanaticism certainly deprives all of reason.

Meanwhile, the Allies were only very slowly advancing up the leg of Italy, and after the capture of Rome in June 1944 it became clear that the Italian campaign was secondary to the invasion of France. The Allied commanders, General Eisenhower and General Montgomery, had already left Italy at the end of December 1943 – Eisenhower to be Allied Supreme Commander of 'Overlord' and Montgomery to take command of 21st Army Group, which was then preparing in England for the invasion of Western Europe. Seven Allied divisions were taken away from Italy to take part in Operation Anvil, the landings on the French Mediterranean Sea coast. Also, the Allies failed to appreciate how much the Partisans were doing and only a small proportion received drops of arms, and from late 1944 that assistance was curtailed as the Resistance in France, Holland, Yugoslavia and Greece was believed to be more militarily important.

This was bad enough for Italian Partisans, but worse was to come. On 14 November 1944 Field Marshal Alexander, now Allied Supreme Commander, personally broadcast on radio *Italia Combatte* that the Partisans should lay down their arms and go home for the winter and await the Allied spring offensive. There is no doubt that Alexander believed this would save Partisan lives, but it was unbelievably foolish. The radio broadcast drove the Partisans to the brink of despair. Partisan bands could not pack up for the winter and go home, to do so would mean immediate arrest and they would be picked off one by one. As the *Action Party* newspaper in the south pointed out, the battle against the Germans and Fascists 'was not a summer sport that could be called off at a moment's notice'.[2]

Once the Germans realised the broadcast was genuine it assured them that there would not be an Allied major offensive in Italy in the immediate future, and they were able to temporarily withdraw troops from the front line to concentrate them on fighting the Partisans. In addition, they now brought in two Cossack cavalry divisions from Russia, from the Don and Kuban country. These arrived with a huge baggage train of camels, as well as an estimated 6,000 horses and all the Cossacks' families, numbering about 50,000 in all. Hitler promised them permanent settlement in north-east Italy in return for wiping out the Partisans, and they were particularly brutal and ferocious in all their actions. The majority were Orthodox Christians but there was a strong contingent of Cossack Muslims. Inevitably, given this explosive mixture of cultures, Catholic churches were desecrated and torched in the many villages they settled in, and each village had a Cossack Ataman who ruled like a king. Many British historians seem to have no idea of the terror that the Cossacks spread through northern Italy in their ruthless fight against the Partisans. Indeed, one recent historian regards them almost as wronged civilian refugees and says:

> The Germans had tried to settle them in Byelo-Russia but, after the defeats of summer 1944, the Cossacks were forced back on the road again, ending up in northern Italy. There they had successfully defended themselves against Italian communist partisans. They were armed, but only as a militia, not as an army.[3]

Some militia!

He goes on to say that the majority of the Cossacks were women, children and old men. But even a cursory glance at the many photos of them on the internet shows young uniformed men in their twenties and their officers, men in full vigour, in their thirties and forties.

Another unfortunate consequence of Alexander's announcement was that it allowed the Germans to strengthen their defensive line using Italian slave labour. As Philip Morgan puts it: 'the whole disastrous episode showed how little the Allies thought of the Italian resistance at this point, and how little they thought of the Italian campaign.'[4]

A mistaken perception of Italian Partisans, and what they were contributing in 1944, lingered on long after the war, and is only now becoming clearer as Wehrmacht documentation is released. As late as 1986 two British military historians, who had both served as officers in Italy, described the Italian Partisans as being 'lavishly armed by the Allies, and capable of little more than murder and noisy fire-fights with fellow Italians of a different political hue'.[5]

However, an official report from Alexander's 15 Army Group headquarters in May 1944 tells a quite different and more balanced story. It is headed 'Partisan Movement in Italy':

There are three Allied armies in Italy. The Fifth and Eighth in front of the enemy need no introduction but the partisans fighting in the enemy rear have been the subject of so much tainted enemy propaganda and much extravagant and ill-informed scribbling from this side of the line that it is not surprising to discover how little the truth is known about them by most people ...

The winter of 1943/44 was hard for the partisans, and the numbers dwindled for a while. But then when the warmer weather coincided with the large-scale call-up of Italians for military service or labour in Germany, masses of evaders sought out the nearest partisan band and joined up. Since then the movement has grown steadily ...

The Communists are at present without doubt the strongest political influence in the movement, followed by the Action Party, the Socialists and the Christian Democrats, and the Liberals ... The only thing which all parties have in common is the desire to see the Allies beat the Germans in Italy. They are an astonishing mixture; Italians who may be elderly lawyers, ex-army men, youths in search of adventure; Russians, Poles, Slavs, Alsatians who have deserted from the Germans; American airmen, British, Indian, Canadian, New Zealand and French officers and men who have escaped from Italian prison camps, and in the north-east, tough Slovenes ... Other bands are good militarily but also obsessed with political aims – Moscatelli, a strong Communist Division SW of Lake Maggiore, is an example ... Bands exist of every degree, down to gangs of thugs who don a partisan cloak of respectability to conceal the nakedness of their brigandage, and bands who bury their arms in their back gardens and only dig them up and festoon themselves in comic opera uniforms when the first Allied troops arrive ...

Assistance to the Italian partisans has paid a good dividend. The toll of bridges blown up, locomotives derailed, odd Germans eliminated, small groups of transport destroyed or captured, small garrisons liquidated, factories demolished, mounts week by week, and the Germans' nerves are so strained, their unenviable administrative situation taxed so much further, that large bodies of German and Italian Republican troops are constantly tied down in an effort to curtail Partisan activity. Occasionally pitched battles have been fought, with losses to the enemy comparable with those they might suffer in a full-scale Allied attack.

The CLN

A word on the Comitato Liberazione Nazionale. The one at Milan, called the CLNAI, is the 'GHQ' of the partisan army. Under it Regional CLNs hold sway over various zone commands. Bands operate under the Zone Command. Owing to a lack of rapid communications this hierarchy has little military control, but has to be content with broad policy directives. But – it should be noted that not every band acknowledges the supremacy of the CLN; a few remain sturdily independent.

What have the Allies done?

When the partisan movement emerged as a fighting force, the Allies began to supply them with arms and equipment, principally by air. Begun at the end of 1943, this supply was stepped up throughout the spring and summer of '44, during which time many hundreds of tons of stores reached the bands.

In addition to the stores, the Allies have sent considerable numbers of Italian and American and British officers and men, all with wireless sets, to the leading partisan bands. These men organize and train, act as military advisers, pass intelligence and assess requirements. Often, indeed, they become leaders in all but name.

All the mountains in the quadrilateral Genoa to the Po to Bologna and down to the front, and the mountains SE of Turin to the sea and SW, west and NW to the French frontier, are firmly in partisan hands, the Germans only controlling the main roads and railways – and even these are subject to constant sabotage. In all, 100,000 armed partisans is a conservative estimate, and if arms could be delivered in unlimited quantities that number could be trebled.

If anyone is heard saying 'Those partisans are just an infernal nuisance' or 'What do partisans do, anyway, beneath all this swagger?' he might be asked 'Have you thought what it might be like if we had them to cope with instead of the enemy?' Large areas over which we could never motor except in protected convoy; in which no small body of men would dare to camp alone; a constant trickle of men who just disappear from the unit; all roads liable to be mined; bridges blown; supply and troop trains derailed from coast to coast; the necessity of strong guards on every installation; the exhausting business of combing hills far in the rear for an enemy whose earth is never stopped and whom nothing may be seen or heard but a sniper's bullet now and then.[6]

Partisans were also very much appreciated by the Allies in the Apennines and gave strong support to the attack on the Gothic Line in September 1944. The official British history of the Second World War illustrates this succinctly:

> 2nd US and 13th Corps were not the only enemies with whom the German troops had to contend. The Italian partisan bands in the Apennines had grown in strength, activity and effectiveness during the summer. Their operations had become such a menace to AOK [army headquarters] 14 that [General] Lemelsen [the commander of 14th Army] argued his case for the retention of 16th SS Panzer Grenadier Division less on the weakening of 14th Panzer Corps than on the need to deal with the partisan threat to his communications through the Apennines – a threat which was dramatised when the commander of 20th Luftwaffe Field Division was ambushed and killed by partisans on 12th September.[7]

But despite the Allies breaching the Gothic Line the war in Italy dragged on; the front line was close but never seemed to get any closer.

I was at home in Musadino for Christmas 1944. There was a surprise on Christmas Eve when news got round that the butcher at Porto had the carcasses of three donkeys. My dad grabbed a couple of bottles of his illicit grappa and we dashed down and managed to get a good portion of fresh meat. So that Christmas was a special treat, we had roast donkey and, as a change from polenta, roast potatoes and cabbage. My mother had peeled the potatoes, but we retrieved the skins and roasted them too.

19

THE WAR ENDS IN ITALY

The winter of 1944–45 was one of the coldest in living memory in northern Italy; the temperature plummeted to −16°C in the Po valley and far lower in the mountains. Consequently, the return to San Michele, in preparation for taking the animals up to the summer pastures, was later than usual and there was still snow on the ground as we went higher up. Several villagers came with us to help Angiolin after the long winter. In the evening they all went back to Musadino, set to return early the next morning. On a whim, I opted to stay behind. I watched them go off and then took a turn around the empty village. It was an odd feeling, completely alone with not another human being for miles, but it felt exhilarating. When night fell, however, my old idiotic fear of the dark came rushing back, my imagination running riot – thoughts of *The Face at the Window*, the horror film I had seen in Leeds all those years ago. The wind got up and the inn sign hanging outside the *osteria* started creaking. I even imagined that poor Benedetto, the man who had been shot in 1943, was walking about the village. Just after eight the next morning I could hear singing in the distance, and shortly afterwards Angiolin and the rest came into sight. They asked me how it had been all alone at night. 'Great,' I said. 'I wouldn't have missed it for the world!'

In early April 1945 the Allied offensive was finally in full swing again. The Allies had broken through the Gothic Line in September 1944, but had then remained entrenched following Field Marshal Alexander's injudicious broadcast. On 5 April the American 9th Army shattered German defences on the west of the line and advanced on Liguria. And on 9 April, the British 8th Army on the eastern side of Italy advanced east of Bologna towards the

Argenta Gap, the key to breaking out of the Apennine mountains and on to the Po plain. But the Germans fought tenaciously and showed no signs of capitulating. I heard all of this on the radio in the *Dopolavoro*, the working men's club, now strangely deserted and with only a caretaker. I became apprehensive as the front line grew closer; it seemed inevitable that unless the Germans gave in the battlefield would come to us. Being so close to the Swiss border we would have nowhere to go to avoid the fighting.

Then on 23 April there was a general Partisan uprising. Indeed, in Turin it had started on 18 April with a series of general strikes, during which Partisans from the hills entered the city and lay low; zero hour was set for 1 p.m. on 27 April for the insurrection and the two armoured divisions, commanded by General Hans Schlemmer, harassed by the Partisans, moved out of Turin.

Mussolini had transferred his puppet government to Milan on 16 April. On 24 April Cardinal Schuster arranged a three-way meeting between Mussolini, the Germans and the CLNAI to discuss the surrender of Milan, but the Germans didn't show up. The terms the CLNAI put to Mussolini were unconditional surrender within two hours. Mussolini refused and left Milan the next day for the last time. In the week that followed the Partisans continued with the uprising all across northern Italy, with Milan and Genoa quickly falling.

On 24 April I was walking up to Musadino from Porto Valtravaglia. I was on the steep section below the Hotel Altipiano when a group of Partisans came whizzing by on bicycles, their guns slung across their shoulders. I shouted to them that Porto was full of Germans and one at the back of the group shouted back 'We know'. Later I went back up to San Michele. From the valley bellow I could hear sporadic firing from time to time, but not from Porto Valtravaglia or Luino, which by then had been cleared of Germans.

The following morning I was standing just beyond San Michele, at a spot overlooking the valley, when I heard a great pealing of bells, with church after church joining in, and I knew at once that the war was over. I ran down the mountain and at the first village, Sarigo, people were outside cheering and shouting *La Guerra è finita! La Guerra è finita!* (The war is over!)

I dashed home and hugged my mother who was crying with joy. She told me to go down to Porto; British troops had arrived and my father was with them and wanted me to join him. I ran all the way to Porto, and when I got there I saw at the waterfront dozens of troops in khaki tropical kit. I strolled up and down for a bit not knowing where my father was, and, hardly being able to take in this astonishing sight, I sat down on the harbour wall beside two soldiers who were admiring the lake. To the day I die I shall always remember my exact words to them; I said in English: 'Do you know a man called Peter?'

They looked at me in surprise, and then one said: 'There's a Peter at every station, son.'

He asked me where I had learnt to speak English and I said, 'I'm from Leeds'. He then asked, in what sounded to me like a German accent, 'Leeds? Vere's that?'

At that I became rather alarmed, thinking that they might all in fact be Germans posing as Allied soldiers. Fortunately, a few minutes later my father spotted me and explained that they were South Africans and that their accent was South African, not German. He took me into the Albergo del Sole, Porto's main hotel, where he said he was now based and where he wanted me to join him. This had been the hotel where German officers had stayed, but now it was the officers' mess of the Imperial Light Horse and Kimberley Regiment (ILH-KR), and my father was already engaged as their interpreter.

It was still mid-morning and he asked me if I had eaten; I said no. He said, 'Just wait 'til you see this', and he took me to the hotel kitchen and sat me down at a table.

Lunch wasn't ready yet but there was some still-warm porridge left over from breakfast, and I remember eating several bowls of it. As I took the first bowl I sprinkled rather a lot of salt on it and, before I started eating, thinking I had made a mistake, one of the cooks said, 'That's salt', and pointed out where the sugar was. I thought he meant that I had taken too much precious salt. It took some getting used to being able to have as much salt as I wanted. That night, for the first time in many years, I slept in a real bed with sheets. When I awoke everything seemed so unreal. I didn't have any real work to do, just help a little in the kitchen. But it was only an excuse for me being there, and sometimes it was just twenty minutes a day, perhaps helping to clear tables or go on errands.

Contrary to what I remember regarding the date, *Victory in Italy* by Neil Orpen states that on 1 May 1945, the 6th South African Armoured Division was ordered to cross over from Mestre, near Venice, to the Milan area, to help the America IV Corps, where Lt-Gen Hans Schlemmer's LXXV Mountain Corps was still holding out north-west of Milan. Orpen says, 'It was a very long drive, mainly at night, of 320 kilometres across the widest part of Italy', which implies that the South Africans could not have been in Porto Valtravaglia before 2 May. Nevertheless, I am pretty sure that at least an advance party of the ILH-KR battalion was there a couple of days before that date.

Either on the evening of their arrival or a day later, I was sitting near the waterfront with them when there was a buzz of excitement as some large photographs were passed around. My dad came up to where I was sitting and showed me two A4-size photographs of the bodies of Mussolini, Claretta Petacci and the leading Fascist *gerarchi*; one showed them all lying in a group, and the other showed them strung up by their feet from a girder of the garage in Piazzale Loreto. I asked my dad about Hitler and he told me that he was still alive – no one contradicted this.

Mussolini had been shot on 28 April 1945, and his body taken to Milan the next day. He was first laid on the ground and only much later strung up (for about three hours). The report of Mussolini's execution and the subsequent desecration of his body flashed around the world and the photographs were in Porto that evening or at the latest on 30 April. Hitler shot himself on 30 April, but the news wasn't made public until Doenitz broadcast it on 1 May. Within minutes of the German announcement, the news of Hitler's death went around the world like wildfire, with all broadcasts interrupted and newspaper 'extra' editions published within hours. It is from all this that I am reasonably certain the ILH-KR, or at least an advance contingent, was in Porto Valtravaglia before 1 May, i.e. before the news of Hitler's death was released.

It was only when I saw the two photos that it finally sank in that the war was really over. Of course the war was still continuing in Germany, which did not surrender until 8 May, but for me it was over that evening. Most people regard with repugnance and horror what was done in Piazzale Loreto, without knowing why the bodies of fourteen executed Fascists were taken to that fateful square. But for the Partisans it was a symbolic gesture of deep significance. It was the exact location where, eight months earlier, fifteen Partisans and civilians had been executed and their bodies piled up and mocked, with a placard proclaiming them to be a heap of rubbish with the Milanese forced to watch. At first the fourteen Fascist bodies were placed on the ground, as those of the Partisans had been (the fifteenth, Achille Starace, was still alive at that point). But as the crowds increased and pressed forward the Partisans decided to hang them up for all to see and to stop the surge. The bodies hung up initially, from left to right, were those of Nicola Bombacci,[1] Mussolini, Claretta Petacci, Alessandro Pavolini and Francesco Barracu.[2] But while the body of Barracu was being appended, the cord broke and he came crashing to the ground, just as Achille Starace[3] was being executed, and Starace was strung up in his place.

There were many Fascists who survived that day who were far worse than Starace. Following his dismissal as Party Secretary in 1939, he was marginalised and ignored by the party. In July 1943 he followed Mussolini north and lived, overlooked, in poverty. He was also in and out of concentration camps for having written letters to Badoglio. Unfortunately for Starace, as the bodies of the Republican Fascists were being strung up, he went out jogging. He stopped at a cafe just as some Partisans were passing and is reputed to have called out 'Good morning boys!' Arrested on the spot, he was taken to Piazzale Loreto, still wearing his tracksuit, and saw Mussolini swinging overhead minutes before his own execution.

The decision to hang the bodies has been much criticised as verging on barbaric, but a British historian is of the opinion that it was done to stop attacks on the bodies, of which there had been a number as they lay on the ground and the crowd surged forward. In his view it was intended 'to spare them further humiliation, not to prolong it'.[4]

The news spread rapidly through Milan and more and more people came to the square. As soon as Cardinal Schuster heard about it, he put through a phone call to Riccardo Lombardi, the new city prefect, and shouted down the phone: 'Either you cut down those cadavers, or I will go myself.'[5] After the cardinal's intervention the bodies were removed to the Milanese morgue; they had hung in Piazzale Loreto for just over three hours.

Before the Allies took control there was an orgy of killing; the suffering had been too great, the massacres too many, and now retribution was swift. The Fascists and Nazis themselves had inured the population to public executions. In Luino some Fascists were being taken by car to the cemetery to be executed, but a crowd stopped the vehicle and wrenched a door off in their eagerness to drag them out to be beaten before they were shot. The Fascists executed at Luino were: Vittorio (or Virgilio) Cattani, a 40-year-old driver; Sergio Napoletano, aged 33; Adamo Rolandi, a butcher from Brissago; and 46-year-old Angelo Vanetti. Other Republican Fascists from Luino who were executed were: Giovanni Bazzi, aged 60, shot at Varese on 28 April; Guglielmo Venturini, aged 37; Federico Zosi, also aged 37; and Gelindo Zuretti, aged 29, all members of the GNR and executed at Mulino d'Anna on 30 April. A 22-year-old woman, Tullia Sperani, was executed at Seveso on 10 May. Another two Fascists from Luino, Remo Camerini aged 22 and Angelo Corti aged 40, were taken by Piemontese Partisans across Lake Maggiore and shot at Verbania on 21 May 1945. In all, probably some 9,000 Republican Fascists were shot or otherwise killed in northern Italy between April and May 1945,[6] with about 40,000 across the country in prison awaiting trial in 1946.

Giovanni Preziosi, the rabid anti-Semite, escaped being executed by the Partisans. At the height of the uprising in Milan he took refuge in a fourth-floor apartment, from where, on the morning of 26 April, he and his wife threw themselves to their deaths.

General Graziani, the Chief of Staff of the Republican Fascist army, was lucky. He had the presence of mind to telephone General Raffaele Cadorna, an officer in the free Italian forces who was liaison officer for the Allies with the CLNAI. Cadorna arranged for Graziani to surrender to the Americans and was immediately placed under their protection.

Officially the war continued in Italy, although apart from a few sporadic outbursts all resistance came to an end on 25 April, a date which in Italy is now celebrated as National Liberation Day. However, on that date the Allied armies were still at the River Po, having started to cross on the 23rd. The contribution of the Partisans was unexpected in its intensity and most welcome. Britain's official history of the Second World War records:

> A notable contribution to the fragmentation of both German Armies was made by Italian Partisans. After the Allied breakthrough came with the crossing of the Po a general insurrection had been ordered by the C.L.N.I.A. [sic] in Milan on 25th April. Most of the big cities of northern Italy thereafter fell into Partisan hands before Allied troops could reach them and important public facilities, such as hydro-electric works, were thus saved from German demolition. In the field Partisan forces obstructed the Germans' withdrawal routes and waylaid the dispatch riders who often represented the sole means of communication between headquarters. 26th Panzer and 29th Panzer Grenadier Divisions had both to fight off attacks from strong bands as they tried to move across the country into the Venetian Line. Their dispersed and exhausted units were continuously beset during the subsequent withdrawal to and across the Brenta.[7]

The majority of the German forces in Italy had ceased fighting by 29 April 1945, although the official surrender wasn't signed at Caserta until 2 May. The war ended in Europe on 8 May, now celebrated as VE Day. But in our province that date was hardly noticed.

Within a week of the war ending, we got news via the Red Cross that my grandfather, my mother's father, had died of a heart attack in Leeds on 23 February 1945 at the age of 65. This was sad news for all of us, but it hit my mother particularly badly.

Although all armed resistance of German forces came to an end on 25 April, and they had ceased fighting the Allies by 29 April, incredibly that did not stop the massacres of Italian civilians. On 24 April 1945, at Villadose in the province of Rovigo, detachments of fleeing Germans, out of pure ferocity and rage at their defeat, rounded up twenty elderly people and children at dawn and shot them at the cemetery. In the end they also shot the Republican Fascist militia man who had evidently assisted them.

From 24 to 27 April, retreating Germans slaughtered twenty-seven civilians at Cortile di San Martino, Perugia.

On 26 April at Narzole, in the province of Cuneo in Piedmont, again out of pure vindictiveness, houses were torched and sixty-six civilians, including women and children, shot. The next day, possibly by the same German unit, thirteen civilians were slaughtered at Bivio di Moriglione in the same province.

Also that day, 27 April, at Saonara, Padova, fifty civilians were executed by retreating Germans for no reason; and nine were shot at Rodengo Saiano, in the province of Brescia.

At Lonigo, in the province of Vicenza, on 26 April, a column of retreating Germans of the 1st *Fallschirmjäger* (Airborne) Division (identified in the Italian sources as 3rd Btg. *Fallschirmjäger* Rgt. 10) captured five armed young men aged between 16 and 25. They did not belong to any official Partisan group but, in a wave of enthusiasm on the eve of liberation, had acquired antiquated weapons and were seeking to join the Partisans. News of their arrest spread quickly and the parish priest, Monsignor Caldana, and a Partisan leader, Luciano Bettini, went to see the German commander, a Major Alfred Grundmann, to request their release. Major Grundmann gave ample assurances that the five would be released in due course, but insisted they would be held temporarily as hostages to ensure the safe passage of his troops to the Italian border. Major Grundmann gave his word as a German officer to Monsignor Caldana that no harm would come to them.

The next day, after the Germans had been given a clear, unmolested passage, the five were found shot in a ditch in Via Marona in Lonigo. An Austrian woman, Ildegarte Polster, who had acted as interpreter for the priest and the Partisan, had a narrow escape. By chance from an open window, on the morning the Germans were leaving, she overheard an officer, in the presence of Grundmann, say to the two soldiers who were escorting the five young men: 'It might be best to shoot the Austrian woman as well.' She immediately fled and hid in a nearby house. The five shot were Pietro Burattini, Dino Fasolin, Alberto Zigiotto, Angelo Zigiotto and a Sicilian known as Mussopappa.[8]

On 29 April retreating SS troops, after they had been given permission to leave in good order to avoid further bloodshed and had been allowed to pass safely through by the Partisans, wiped out the tiny village of Castello di Godego in the province of Treviso. In total seventy-five villagers were shot in the main square in batches of fifteen by volleys of machine-gun fire. It has proved impossible to discover any reason or motive for this massacre. These same troops had already shot thirty-six at Sant'Anna Morosina, and, proceeding in their flight along the road from the abbey of Pisani to San Marino di Lupari, a further sixty people were shot. On that same terrible day there were other massacres: at Cervignano del Fruili, Udine, twenty-two were shot; and at the Villa del Conte, again in the province of Padova, fourteen civilians were killed.

At Grugliasco, in the province of Turin, during the night of 29 April, the population was celebrating the end of the war. Windows were festooned with flags and the streets were crowded with happy people. Then the vanguard of the German LXXV Corps arrived. The commander of this formidable German corps, General Hans Schlemmer, had gained immunity from Partisan attack by promising not to destroy Turin and other Italian towns. This was the German division, mentioned previously, which had triggered the move of the 6th South African Division from the Mestre area to Lake Maggiore.

The German corps retreated slowly, slowed down by their draught horses, and they could not shake off rings of Partisans who shepherded them on their way, as they were pursued by American forces. On reaching Grugliasco, however, the first German troops, apparently incensed by the joyous festive atmosphere, stopped and began destroying and burning houses. Sixty-six people were killed. Many of them, wounded and unable to move, were crushed to death under the tracks of tanks and half-tracks.

That same night, while negotiations were taking place for the surrender of the LXXV Armoured Corps, a detachment of SS broke off and, out of pure revenge, slaughtered fifty-two peasants who were peacefully resting in their own homes at Santhià in the province of Vercelli.

On 2 May, after the agreed surrender of all German forces in Italy, remnants of the *Brigate Nere* and German troops destroyed the village of Pedescala Valdastico near Vicenza, killing eighty-three villagers, among them the parish priest and nine women. On the same day, as a last parting gesture, a group of about 800 SS, en route to Austria, pillaged and burnt down the village of Maggio-Avisnis, Udine, and shot fifty-one inhabitants.

The final outrage perpetrated in the closing hours of the war was at Ovaro in the province of Udine. Strangely, it is the only one among the massacres I have listed which appears in non-Italian books, and is the only recorded case where the United Nations War Crimes Commission considered prosecuting a white Russian, a Cossack, of a war crime. It is also an incident that might well have been avoided had more sensible counsels prevailed. Here is the report from the British Archives:

TRANSLATION NO. 747
WAR CRIMES COMMISSION   Ovaro, 3 May 1945

On 2 May the *voluntari della liberta* [sic] fighting against a contingent of Cossacks grouped in Ovaro, were compelled after several hours to retire due to the arrival of a great number of Russian reinforcements. During the battle four *Voluntari della Liberta* were killed, while others were more or less seriously wounded.

After the retreat and firing was stopped, Major Vausico [? Nauziko in Italian accounts], commander of the Cossack unit, headed Russian reinforcements and ordered them to take reprisals against the civil population.

Following the order, the troops scattered savagely in all the homes of the Ovaro, killing barbarically all of the men they found in the houses. The greater part of the victims show horrible wounds in the head and is composed mostly of middle-aged and old men, among whom are two priests and an old woman.

The following are the names of those killed: Priests – Don Pietro Cortula and Don Virgilio Pavoni, engineer Rinaldo Cioni and his father-in-law Attilio Rossi, the father of the chorister Lavoni Tullio Silvio, the carpenter Fedele Elio, aged 70, Mrs Mirai Giuditta, widow Marcuzzi, the labourers Gressani Vittorio, Celman Matteo, Agrinis Antonio, Gettardis Matteo, Agarnis Dante, Gonano Antonio, Collinassi Gino, Pietra Giovanni, Pavoni Giacomo, Rupil Rinaldo and Truscoli Antonio, Traveschi Gio Batta, both aged over 70.

The persons listed above represent the great part of the men who remained in town, as the others had succeeded in fleeing.

Besides these barbaric massacres, they threatened women, robbing them and after burning all the broken articles, including the Communal Ambulance. The citizens were forbidden to make any attempt to extinguish the fire.

It is to be added that the prisoners (1 Patriot and 3 or 4 Georgiani [sic, Georgians]) were killed and the corpses of the georgiani, who were fighting with the Italian volunteers, were found barefoot and arranged in the shape of a star.

THE MEDICAL OFFICER

Covassi Luigi[9]

But there was much more to this and it would seem that the Cossacks were needlessly and ineffectively attacked, setting in motion their shocking reprisals. On 29 April there was a meeting of the CLN in Ovaro regarding what action should be taken against the Cossacks. In later years the communist Partisan Garibaldi Brigades claimed they had strongly advised against any action being taken against them. They pointed out that they had very few men, having been reduced to twenty or thirty over the winter, and that it was folly to oppose an estimated 30,000 heavily armed Cossacks who were desperate to reach the Monte Carnico Pass some 30km away – the still snow-bound route into Austria. Contrary to this, the anti-communist Partisans of the Osoppo Brigades argued that the Cossacks should surrender unconditionally to them and the entire lot should be prevented from reaching Austria until the Allies arrived. The Osoppo faction won the day, greatly augmented by a last-minute intake of young partisans, scornfully dubbed 'partisans of the last hour', who were eager to see action and who shouted down the Garibaldi Brigade representative. When he said '*al nemico che fugge ponti d'oro*' (to a fleeing enemy, golden bridges), he was booed. It would appear that industrialists of the area also backed the Osoppo Partisans.

There were Cossacks in Ovaro, and in the nearby *carabinieri* police station in Chialina they all gathered and moved their wives and children in with them for protection pending the arrival of the main body of Cossacks and Germans. Under a flag of truce, a Cossack officer, Major Nauziko, arrived and talks began, but it seems that both sides were playing for time, with Nauziko aware that within twenty-four hours the mass of Cossacks would be there. Nothing was concluded except agreeing to meet again on the following day. However, during the night a large amount of explosives was placed close to the police station and it was blown up, resulting in twenty-eight Cossack deaths, including two women. After this a full battle developed; the Partisans were defeated and retreated, leaving Ovaro to the vengeance of the enraged Cossacks.

20

MY TIME WITH THE ILH-KR

There were two distinct types of South African soldiers: those of British descent and the Afrikaners. Some of the latter spoke mainly in Afrikaans and their English had a heavy Afrikaner accent. But they mixed well and both were friendly, and I would ride around with them in jeeps; the drive up to San Michele, which had taken me hours with a mule, now seemed to take about ten minutes. These were wild days, and while driving along the military road, which snaked back and forth, we would suddenly cut across the scrub to rejoin the road lower down. Many of the soldiers were just three or four years older than me and I quickly formed some good friendships; I was then coming up for 15 and I had started drinking fairly heavily. In the evenings we would go to cafes in Luino and drink bottles of vermouth. I didn't have any money, but I was never expected to pay for anything by my new friends.

Nearly all the young South Africans seemed to get drunk very quickly, mainly, I think, because they tended to drink fortified wines, such as vermouth, as if they were beer. One evening's spree turned out to be a bit of a nightmare. I had been drinking with a soldier (who I shall call Garry) and we decided to row across the lake to Cannóbio, which I had told him I had once visited and liked. In the dark we took one of the rowing boats moored in the harbour at Porto and quietly set off, taking turns at rowing while the other steered. Cannóbio is near the Swiss border and would have meant rowing about 13km, so after crossing the lake we pulled in at Cannero Riviera instead, about 6km diagonally across from Porto.

By now it was well after midnight and we couldn't find any cafes still open, which was just as well for Garry was far more drunk than I had realised. We were staggering around almost lost when we heard an accordion being played and, following the sound, we gatecrashed a wedding reception which was in full swing. At first we were made welcome, and the Piedmontese dialect wasn't too difficult to understand, but Garry, in trying to dance, fell onto a long trestle table laden with wine and food and he and it crashed to the ground in a shower of broken glass. The mood changed, and we were told in no uncertain terms that we were no longer welcome. With Garry's arm around my neck, I managed to get him back to the lakeside but I had to leave him as I frantically began searching for the rowing boat. I finally located it and rowed it back to where I had left him, only now he had wandered off. Eventually I found him but I was feeling very drunk. I ducked my face in the cool water and persuaded him to get into the boat. He kept saying that he didn't want to go rowing but wanted to go to bed, and it took me a good five minutes to get him to half-understand that we were on the wrong side of the lake and that his bed was on the other side.

I had only rowed about a kilometre, and was about to wake him to steer, when I discovered that he had passed out completely; I shouted his name, shook him, flicked water on him, but there was absolutely no response. By now I had sobered up completely as I realised the mess we were in. It was pitch black, we were in the middle of the lake, and I feared that he might wake up and fall in the water and drown. I spent some time dragging him under a seat so that he couldn't suddenly jump up. I had to steer with my oars, but had my back to the direction we were going. I gave up trying to work out where Porto was and decided the best thing to do was to get to the other side and sort it out from there. I reached the Lombardy shore somewhere between Luino and Porto, although it took me some time to figure that out in the dark, but finally in the middle of the night I reached Porto and tied up. I left Garry in the boat and dashed to his dormitory; I shook awake a couple of his friends, managing to convince them to get dressed and sneak out with me. Still unconscious, they carried him to bed. When I next saw Garry he thanked me profusely and said: 'I don't know how I ended up in a rowing boat, but it's a good job you found me before I tried to row it.'

Pleasant as those days and nights were, very quickly I was made aware of a darker side of South Africa. On the top floor of the Albergo del Sole, where I slept, there were three young soldiers who were officers' batmen. I became friendly with one of them and would laugh and joke with him. One day one of the Afrikaners took me aside and asked me if I knew that the three batmen were coloured. I didn't understand what he meant by coloured since they looked whiter than some southern Italians to me. He said they may look white, but if you look at their fingernails you will see that they are pink, and he told me that it was bad for white people like 'us' to let them get over-friendly. He explained that coloured people had a black mother and a white father, and when I asked if they could have a white mother and a black father he told me that was impossible and the very idea was crazy.

A few days after this I moved out of the Albergo del Sole to the main body of troops in Caldé, and there I slept in requisitioned premises in a large room with about a dozen soldiers. I became quite friendly with a young soldier I knew as Shap. Another Afrikaner asked me if I was aware that Shap was a Jew. He told me that you could tell from his name, Shapiro, that he was Jewish. I told Shap about this and he told me just to ignore them.

Early on 14 May the ILH-KR were taking a trip and I went along for the ride. I thought we were going to Milan but instead we went to the auto-racetrack at Monza, where today's Formula 1 races are held. As soon as we got inside the racetrack I was dropped off and joined a crowd at the side. This was the South African army's Victory Parade, and the whole 6th South African Armoured Division was there with all its tanks, artillery and vehicles. There were a number of high-ranking officers on the saluting podium, who I learnt much later included General Mark Clark and General Lucian Truscott, who had taken over command of the 5th US Army from Clark in December 1944, together with other senior Allied officers, including Italians. Major-General Poole, the division's commander, led the parade, standing in his command jeep saluting as he passed the podium; then his jeep was parked and Maj-Gen Poole joined the group on the podium as his three brigades drove by. I now wish I had paid more attention, but at the time the names of Gen. Clark and Gen. Truscott meant nothing to me; neither, for that matter, did the name of Maj-Gen Poole. I must admit I was then as much interested in seeing the famous stadium as I was in seeing the parade.

A couple of weeks after this there was a big flap on, with helmeted soldiers forming up with rifles and half packs. I asked Shap whether they were having another big parade, and he said that this time it wasn't a parade – they were going to disarm the Partisans. He told me they were all Communists and there was a danger they would refuse to lay down their arms and there might be trouble. He seemed to know hardly anything about Partisans and I don't think he believed me, a young boy, when I told him they were not all Communists. I asked Shap if I could go with them again and he told me to go and ask the sergeant-major, who I knew well. I eventually found him and asked him, but he said no. I ran back to Shap who, by luck, was at the back of a half-track near the rear door. He asked me what the sergeant-major had said and I said it was okay, I could go. I'm not sure Shap entirely believed me, but he opened the door anyway and I jumped in. Then I saw the sergeant-major walking around as the engines were revving up, so I ducked down. Shap and the other soldiers in the half-track laughed and Shap said: 'You're going to get me shot, Peter, you know that?'

We set off in convoy and drove towards Monza. I can't remember now if we went to the auto-racetrack again or to a large field, but when we got there I saw many hundreds of Partisans, bearing arms, lined up in ranks with pennants flying. We were at a commanding spot on the periphery, with other units of 13th Brigade, but kept well back. Major-General Poole made a speech, thanking the Partisans for their service, and there on the podium, to my surprise, was my father interpreting the speech into Italian; at that moment I was extremely proud of my father.

I could hear the speeches from the general and from the leadership of the CLNAI clearly over tannoy loudspeakers. It was very emotional with a band playing. There was a minute of silence as they presented arms, after which, instead of shouldering their arms, they lay them at their feet, then marched away in squads, pennants flying. It all went very smoothly. My father never knew I was there, and I didn't tell him at the time because the sergeant-major was a great friend of his and I was afraid my father might mention it and get Shap into trouble; in the years afterwards we simply never spoke about the war.

Both my father and I were also very friendly with one of the dispatch riders. He used to ride his motorbike flat out between Porto and Luino, but late one evening he had a terrible accident and was rushed to hospital in Luino. My father had to go along to arrange an emergency electricity supply for an immediate operation. I went to see him as soon as visitors were allowed, and it seemed that he would recover, but sadly he died within the week. I felt very sad about this as he had come through the entire Italian campaign unscathed. I feel sad too because, although I can still see his face, I can no longer remember his name.

One night the South Africans arranged a dance at the officers' mess in the Albergo del Sole to which the mayor and the Italians he had recommended were invited. I was near the bar watching the couples dancing when I felt a tap on my shoulder. I turned round and there to my complete surprise was Amleto in full Partisan uniform, with the red scarf of the Communist

'Garibaldi' units around his neck. I hadn't seen him since we had been held up at the SS roadblock and he had produced a Republican Fascist Party card. Amleto smiled at me and said, 'I told you things are not what they seem.' This was very true. In the house at the side of ours, in the floor above René, there was a family of evacuees from Milan, a woman with her children. Her husband worked in Milan and would come to Musadino every weekend to visit his family. He had a goatee beard in the style of Italo Balbo, and from that we all called him Barbuto. He was very friendly with everyone, and would always greet me cheerfully and take an interest in what I was doing. Then in April he appeared in Musadino with his beard shaved off. A few days later he was arrested and taken back to Milan. It turned out that he was a Republican Fascist and had been instrumental in the arrest of many people in Milan. I was completely stunned to hear that after a short trial he had been sentenced to eighteen years in prison; later he was set free under the 1946 general amnesty. He was very lucky; had he been caught a few days earlier he would undoubtedly have been shot.

After a couple of weeks I got a more permanent job as batman to an officer of the ILH-KR in Luino. My duties were extremely light, and other than making up his bed in the morning and cleaning his Sam Browne belt and boots I had nothing to do; it was less than an hour's work a day and I was free afterwards to do whatever I wanted. By now I was practically dressed in full uniform, and I even wore an army-issue black beret. I also had a regimental cap badge of the ILH-KR; this was two flags on crossed lances, the royal standard and the Union Jack, with the regimental motto *Imperium et libertas* (Empire and Liberty) underneath. One afternoon I put the badge in my beret and set off to walk to Musadino to visit my mother. I had covered a few kilometres and had just got up the steep bit to Belvedere, the local beauty spot, when I saw a jeep coming towards me; in it was the battalion commanding officer who knew me well. As he passed I stood to attention and saluted. There was a screech of brakes as the jeep came to a halt; it was put in reverse and came back at high speed towards me. I thought for a moment I was going to be offered a lift, but instead the commanding officer bellowed out: 'Peter! Come here!'

I ran over and he ordered me to take the beret and badge off immediately. He proceeded to give me a dressing down, the gist of which was that under no circumstances could I wear the regimental badge or any other regimental insignia, and I was never to salute an officer again. He said, 'You are not in the army, do you understand Peter?'

When I replied 'Yes, sir' he blew up again, saying: 'Don't "yes, sir" me, you are a civilian!'

He impounded both the beret and badge and the jeep sped off in a cloud of dust, leaving me utterly crestfallen. Next minute the jeep came whizzing back again. 'What's that around your waist?'

'It's a belt,' I replied.

'I can see it's a belt! It's an army issue web belt, take it off!'

At this point his driver got the giggles and he got a telling off as well. After that I continued to wear army clothing, but it was the end of badges and webbing.

I had worn the Imperial Light Horse and Kimberley Regiment's cap badge with pride, however briefly, and I should like to give a brief account of what they, and the rest of 6th South African Armoured Division had contributed to the German defeat in Italy.

The division was formed on 1 February 1943 in South Africa from the depleted 1st South African Infantry Division, which had fought at El Alamein, and the remnant units of the ill-fated 2nd South African Infantry Division following its capture at the fall of Tobruk, with 10,722 South Africans taken prisoner. Thus, the main reason for converting these infantry divisions to armour was manpower shortage; an infantry division necessitated 24,108 officers and men, whereas an armoured division only required 14,195. The division, which trained for a year in Egypt to peak efficiency, was commanded by Major-General W.H. Evered Poole, a remarkable officer who inspired many and for whom I heard nothing but praise from the soldiers who served under him.

The ILH-KR was also formed in 1943, and for similar reasons, with the amalgamation of the 1st and 2nd battalions to form a motorised battalion functioning as an armoured car reconnaissance unit, under the command of Lieutenant-Colonel Bob Leeves-Moore. The ILH-KR arrived in Italy from Egypt on 21 April 1944, as a unit of the 11th South African Armoured Brigade, commanded by Brigadier J.P.A. Furstenburg, in the 10th Corps of the British 8th Army, with the rest of the division placed in reserve. But on 28 May the 6th SA Armoured Division, including the 11th SA Armoured Brigade, was placed within 1st Canadian Corps.

The division had concentrated near Caserta on 24 May, where its infantry units were augmented by the addition of the British 24th Guards Infantry Brigade, the components of which were the 1st Battalion Scots Guards, the

3rd Battalion Coldstream Guards and the 5th Battalion Grenadier Guards.
This prestigious Guards Brigade remained with the South Africans until
7 January 1945, when it returned to 8th Army command.

By 23 April 1944 South Africans were already in the front line in the
Rapido Valley facing the Gustav Line, beyond Acquafondata and south of
Vallerotonda, from which, in the far distance, they could see the bombed ruins
of the abbey of Cassino. On 5 May they were moved to take part in the fourth
and final battle of Cassino. Following the liberation of Rome on 6 June, an
ILH-KR reconnaissance squadron investigated some burning buildings on
the upper slopes of Monte Soratte, north of the city; these turned out to
be the headquarters of Field Marshal Kesselring. Although much was damaged, the many tunnels had escaped fire, and the ILH-KR recovered valuable
German operational maps, including one showing the position of the yet
unknown 'Gothic Line', and another showing the planned routes of retreat
for the German divisions.

There was bitter fighting for the 11th South African Armoured Brigade
in the thrust towards Mercatale, against very strong rearguard action by the
German 356th Infantry Division supported by Tiger tanks. Then came the
hard slog in the Chianti Mountains, a range of steep, thickly wooded hills
which stretch north-west towards Florence. On 4 August 1944 the 6th South
African Armoured Division, with ILH-KR in the vanguard, was the first Allied
formation to enter and liberate Florence, having had nearly two months of
hard fighting against a determined enemy since passing through Rome.

During September, pressing on north from Florence, the three companies
of the ILH-KR were engaged in close combat on several occasions, which was
a feature of the fierce fighting in the thickly populated mountainous triangle
formed by the old Highway 64 and Route 6620 (with its base between Prato
and Pistoia, and its apex at Praduro, just over 11km south of Bologna). This
entire area, a section of the Gothic Line, was well defended by the German
362nd Infantry Division, with large sections of the front covered in depth with
barbed wire, minefields and elaborate bunkers of both Spandau machine guns
and panzer turrets. On 16 September 1944 the 11th SA Armoured Brigade, in
the toughest battles in this sector, stormed the line of mountains, about 13km
north of Prato, with the ILH-KR engaged in a hostile battle for Monte Porto
del Bagno against stubborn German resistance. And in October, companies
of the ILH-KR were engaged in bitter hand-to-hand fighting with tommy
guns and grenades, flushing out Germans from the village of Cardeda, north
of Monte Vigese.[1]

I have only listed a few of the battles the ILH-KR were engaged in; the ILH-KR's Christmas card for 1944, which was distributed again for Christmas 1945 and given to me and my father, lists thirty-one battles between 6 May and 23 October 1944, and there were more to come in 1945. These were the battle-hardened young men who had rolled into Porto Valtravaglia a year after they had set foot in Italy. In that year, the 6th South African Armoured Division's losses were 711 killed, 2,675 wounded and 157 missing.[2]

21

Another Trip to the Seaside

or my second trip to the Italian Riviera I have to thank General Charles
de Gaulle, the then leader of the Free French. After 8 May 1945 France was
still at war with Italy, in de Gaulle's view, and he maintained that France
was not bound by the September 1943 armistice. The French Resistance and
Italian Partisans had co-operated in 1944 and early 1945, but that came to
an end in April when de Gaulle sent regular French forces and the French
Maquis into the Italian Alpine region of Aosta. On the French border region
Italian Partisans were arrested and offered the choice of either joining the
French Foreign Legion or going to internment camps. De Gaulle's real goal
was to absorb a considerable part of Italian territory into France. This resulted
in clashes between Italian Partisans and the French Resistance, and by late
May 1945 the French were on the Italian Riviera where I had gone to recu-
perate after my operation in 1941. The Americans threatened to cut off all aid
to the French army, and under that pressure they started to withdraw in June
but did not completely leave Italian territory until July.

It is against this background that in the early autumn of 1945, units of the
6th South African Armoured Division were sent to the western side of the
Italian Riviera, near the French border. But just before this, on 3 September,
accompanied by an officer of the 6th SA Armoured Division, my father went
to San Michele for the unveiling of a memorial to Benedetto Isabella, who
was shot by the Germans in November 1943. The ceremony was attended
by a large group of his relatives and friends, and was conducted by Don
Carlo Agazzi Rota. A photograph shows some very young children there,
too young for the long climb to San Michele, so they were either carried on
their fathers' shoulders or, more probably, were taken up in South African

jeeps. This was the very first memorial in Italy to a victim of a Nazi and Republican Fascist outrage.

For the move to Liguria there were busy days of packing, crating and loading, but finally we pulled out from Porto Valtravaglia in a long convoy of half-tracks, trucks, jeeps and dispatch riders. I was in the back of one of the Bedford QL Three-Ton 4x4 troop carrier trucks, while my father travelled in a jeep. We left early in the morning and reached our destination late in the evening; a journey which can be done in about a quarter of that time today. We drove through Milan; the city was devastated after the many air raids, and as we drove past the ruins it seemed odd to see bright bedroom wallpaper, occasionally with a picture still hanging on a wall, and the stairs blown away.

The drive to Milan had been uneventful and, albeit at slow convoy speed, we made good progress. However, as we got nearer to the River Po the roads became more and more cratered, and south of the Po every bridge over the many rivers was either destroyed or badly damaged. There were pontoon and Bailey bridges at all crossings but these often left very steep descents to get to them and a steep ascent on the other side. Several times the truck I was in couldn't cope, even in first gear, and we would crawl up escarpments in reverse at about 2mph or wait our turn for a tracked recovery vehicle to winch us up. The devastation I saw on that seemingly endless journey made me realise how lucky we had been that the war had ended before the front line reached us.

The ILH-KR's officers' mess was located in a modest but very comfortable hotel on Spotorno's seafront, and my father and I had a room on the top floor. And so I found myself less than 10 miles from Loano. The Italian Riviera has extraordinarily clement weather: the temperatures are mild and there are palm trees in abundance, with a wide variety of flowers and exotic plants. It seemed like spring all the year round, and driving around in an open jeep on traffic-free roads was sheer pleasure. The ILH-KR carried out coastal runs in jeeps from Ventimiglia, close to the French border, to beyond Spotorno, but these were purely unarmed symbolic patrols and I was often taken along on the flimsy excuse that they might need an interpreter.

The Italian staff at the officers' mess included Ernesto, a top professional chef from Florence; so in the space of a few months, I went from eating almost anything that moved to some of the finest dishes of continental cuisine. Ernesto would regale me with stories of his work before the war in some of the best hotels in London, Paris and Rome. I used to love watching him cook. He showed me how to use a whisk for stiffening egg whites, or at least he tried to, for he would watch with a pained expression before taking over and finishing it himself in a flurry of lightning-fast whisks. It was there that I first tasted a delicious zabaglione.

One afternoon, two of the officers I knew well hired a fishing boat with tackle for catching octopuses, and we rowed out to a recommended spot off a small island. The gear for catching octopuses was very simple but effective; it consisted of a bucket with a glass bottom and a strong fishing line which ended in a lead weight embedded with lots of hooks and bits of reflective glass. Holding the bucket in the water gave a surprisingly clear view of the bottom. All you did then was lower the lure and jiggle it up and down near rocks. After a few minutes an octopus would come out and pounce on it, at which point you gave the line a sharp tug and brought up the octopus. The first one was fairly large, and as soon as I unhooked it, it started slithering along the boat, causing both officers to jump up in alarm, nearly tipping us over. I had watched local fishermen deal with live octopuses and quickly dispatch them with a quick bite underneath, as they wrapped their tentacles around their faces, so I knew they were perfectly harmless. I took hold of ours but it seemed glued to the boat with its suckers, and I had difficulty in prising it off as it continued to slither along. I drew the line at biting it though; so, having pulled it off the planking, I turned it over and a quick knife thrust proved just as efficient. At the time I found it strange that two brave officers who had fought from El Alamein to the River Po were unnerved by a poor octopus. We caught three this way before I snared the lure on a seabed rock and the line broke as I tried to yank it loose. Ernesto made a very tasty dish with them, but only he, my father and I ate them.

On several occasions I walked past a prison in Spotorno which was full of Fascists awaiting trial. I could only see the top floor above the perimeter wall, but the barred windows were always crowded. Initially prison sentences were quite severe, like the eighteen years that our Milanese neighbour Barbuto had received. But the civil service and judiciary of the Badoglio government, taken over by Ivanoe Bonomi on 9 June 1944, and then by Ferruccio Parri in June 1945, remained un-purged. As a result, sentences got more and more lenient, until finally, on 22 June 1946, there was a general amnesty. Thousands of Fascists awaiting trial were freed, and convicted Fascists, including some of the worst criminals, had their convictions quashed. The amnesty legislation was loosely drafted by the General Secretary of the Italian Communist

Party, Palmiro Togliatti, serving as Minister of Justice in the newly formed De Gasperi government. This legislation was then very liberally interpreted in the courts by judges who had served almost their entire juridical careers under the Fascist regime.

On one momentous evening, on 15 August 1945, I was at another dance arranged by the South Africans. I was quickly told that I would have to interpret an important announcement. I was rushed up on to the stage where the dance band was seated, and an officer went to the microphone with me standing beside him. A sea of faces looked up at us, puzzled as to why the music had stopped in the middle of a dance number. I felt very embarrassed standing in front of them all, even without speaking. I cannot now remember his exact words, but the officer said something like: 'I have an important announcement to make. Following the dropping of atomic bombs by the Americans on Hiroshima and Nagasaki, the Japanese have just announced that they have surrendered!'

I had never heard of an atomic bomb and didn't know what it was in Italian (simple enough, it is *bomba atomica*), nor had I heard of the cities, so I started to say words to the effect that the Americans have dropped a special bomb on … but I got no further. My words were drowned out in a big cheer, and the whole place erupted, as the announcement in English sank in without being translated. At last the war was finally over, although the official surrender wasn't signed until 2 September 1945 and some Japanese units continued fighting on even then.

We spent Christmas and the New Year of 1946 at Spotorno, as there was no way of getting back to Musadino. Trains were running sporadically and the few that did run were overcrowded. If we could have got home, getting back to Spotorno after the holidays would also have been problematic. I cannot now recall what we had for Christmas dinner, only that there was a choice of wonderful dishes from a top menu. Just after Christmas my father told me that one of the officers, I think his name was Captain Peters, had offered to take me back with him to South Africa. My father said I would have a good life and I would be given a good start on his farm; he said it was a really generous offer and that if I wanted to go he would agree to it. It was very tempting, but by the next day I had decided not to accept. The officer who had made this offer was one of the two I had gone fishing with. Two years later, the National Party won the election; apartheid became law and South Africa was changed forever, so I never regretted not going.

22

HOME AGAIN, AND ON TO VARESE

It was around mid-January 1946 when the ILH-KR left the Italian Riviera. The officers' mess was unbelievably generous to us: two South Africans took us back to Musadino in a 15cwt truck absolutely laden with tinned food of every description, packets of tea, coffee, cartons of 200 cigarettes and many tins of 50, and about 2 gallons or more of South African brandy. It took far less time to get to Lake Maggiore than it had taken us to get to Spotorno in convoy, and it was quite an emotional farewell as our friends drove away. When researching this book, I mentioned the South Africans to my childhood friend Roberto Rivolta of Musadino. He told me he remembered my return very well because my father had gone to the *osteria* in Musadino with dozens of cartons of cigarettes and distributed them free to everyone. Like everything else, tobacco was rationed during the war: thirty cigarettes a week or 30g of pipe tobacco, or six *toscani* (Italian cigars). But even this meagre ration was seldom available in 1944 and smokers bartered on the black market or hunted for cigarette butts the Germans or Fascist militia had thrown away – to be replaced later by those of the Allied forces. By 1945 cigarettes had almost replaced money and were a valuable means of exchange, and no doubt those free cigarettes my father distributed were greatly appreciated.

My father decided that he would now stay at home in Musadino with my mother and my sister Gloria, and he returned to work in Porto Valtravaglia at the Boltri factory. We both had been given excellent references by the ILH-KR, and I went to Varese where a South African artillery unit was stationed and applied for a job as interpreter. At the guardroom I was told that I first had to get clearance from the Allied Commission, but on the strength of the glowing reference and a short interview I was allowed to start immediately as batman to two officers, pending official clearance by the Commission.

In due course I was called to the Allied Commission for my clearance interview with an NCO of the Intelligence Corps. Almost immediately it got off to a bad start. As soon as I went into the interview room I saw that he was wearing black army boots (all units of the South African army wore brown boots), so I asked him, being the first British soldier I had seen: 'Are you an English soldier?'

I remember he looked at me rather oddly and said something like 'Yes, of course I am'. Then he asked me where I had learnt to speak English and I told him that it was my mother-tongue, and that I had been born in Leeds and was British, and so was my mother. He looked at my identity card, which had not yet been replaced, and he said: 'It says here that you were born in Musadino, now why would it say that?'

Things seemed to go from bad to worse. I told him the card was a forgery, but he took it away and came back and said it was genuine and matched the records in Varese. This got me confused and I ended up agreeing with him that I was born in Musadino. Then he asked me if my father had served in the army, and if so where. But I didn't fully understand what he meant and, thinking he was talking about the Fascist militia after 1943, I said he hadn't. When he said that this was most unusual, it gradually dawned on me that he was asking about service in the Italian forces prior to 1943, but having just said that he hadn't been in the army I stuck to that. I could have said he was in a reserve occupation and that would have been the end of it, but I didn't. All this was done in his bad Italian, which he insisted on speaking.

A few days later I was told I could continue working as a batman, but there was no mention of being an interpreter. I was slightly annoyed but, looking on the bright side, my work was incredibly easy. I was batman to two officers, a captain and a lieutenant, and my entire workload consisted of rolling up their field sleeping bags in the morning and cleaning two pairs of shoes in the evening; plus, once a week, taking their washing to the camp laundry where it was hand-washed by Italian women. We were in a large building, but the two officers were quartered in an unfurnished room, hence the sleeping bags. In the late afternoon I would unroll their sleeping bags and that was it; my entire working day amounted to little more than an hour. I slept in a similar sleeping bag on the ground floor, along with two other locally employed batmen, both around my age and both from Varese; they had just a smattering of English and their officers found it easier to tell me if they wanted anything out of the ordinary, so I ended up being an unofficial interpreter between the officers and their batmen. Not quite the job I had envisaged, but gradually the knowledge that I was bilingual spread and, as they had done in the ILH–KR, small groups of soldiers took me along with them, much as they had in Spotorno.

In the 1940s it was most unusual for a man not to smoke; so one night I decided that I would start smoking. I already knew that the first one or two cigarettes made you dizzy, so I decided to begin smoking in style. I got into my sleeping bag, turned on my bedside lamp and opened one of the free army issue round tins of fifty Player's. You did this by taking off the lid and sliding a pointed bit of metal over, which acted as a cutter, then replacing the lid and turning it around to cut the tin's sealed top off. I lit my first cigarette and started reading *Lorna Doone* from my captain's small stock of books. I must have chain-smoked about thirty cigarettes, drawing on them deeply to get through them faster, lighting one after the other. I neither enjoyed the cigarettes nor the book; both for me were a big disappointment. It would be nice to say that I never smoked again, but I did try sporadically from time to time – cigarettes, cigars and pipes – but I never really enjoyed it and I finally gave it up for good in the 1950s.

One lovely sunny afternoon I learnt that a group of soldiers were going over to Lake Maggiore, to the lido at Luino, for a swim. I mentioned that I knew Luino well, but that I had never been swimming there, so they invited me to go along with them. I didn't have a swimming costume, but the cook, a brawny Afrikaner with little English, told me I could borrow his. His swimming trunks were far too big for me and I kept them up with some string. There was a very high diving tower on Luino's beach and, although it had wheels for repositioning, it had been located at the same spot for years; it had a slight tilt and looked unsteady. It had three diving levels, but perhaps because of the tilt few dived off the very top.

The soldiers I was with were daring each other to go to the top and dive off, and eventually one of them did so. At this I got up and climbed to the top level, more than half regretting it when I got up there. Suddenly the two on the beach looked very far away and tiny, and the diving tower felt unstable. I felt, however, that there was no going back, so I dived off and nearly knocked myself out in a spectacular belly flop. My stomach felt red-raw and I kept underwater as long as possible to avoid any guffaws from spectators. When I surfaced I discovered that the cook's swimming trunks and I had parted company, and, despite repeated searches, I couldn't find them. The two soldiers thought this was hilarious.

When I got back in the late afternoon, having gone to the kitchen to explain what had happened, the cook, who had been drinking, was furious. He flatly disbelieved what I told him; he kept saying that his swimming trunks weren't made of lead and would have floated, and that I had either stolen or sold them. He went berserk and in his drunken state picked up a meat cleaver from his chopping board and chased me. Fortunately I was fleeter of foot than he was, but I stayed away from his kitchen for several days.

On another occasion, a sergeant who I had come to know quite well mentioned that he was driving over to Lake Maggiore to dispose of some hand grenades. Other lakes were closer, Lake Como and Lake Varese, for example, but they didn't have sheer drops to the water from the road as the spectacular Laveno–Luino road had. I told him I knew that road very well and in particular Caldé, the location he was looking at on the map, so he let me go along with them. Three of us went in a 15cwt truck loaded with four wooden boxes of grenades. As I found out when we got there, each box contained twelve Mills 36M Mk I grenades, together with a tin container of twelve grenade igniters and a special key for fitting the igniters. The grenades had a lever which you held tight as you withdrew a safety pin attached to a ring; as long as you held the lever to the grenade you were safe for as long as you wished, but once released it exploded in four and a half seconds. The bombs were thrown two at a time; some reaching the water, others exploding on the rocks. As soon as they were thrown we ducked behind the road parapet in case shrapnel or rock chips came hurtling up. At first I just watched, but on the second box I fitted the igniters and tightened up the base plugs while they threw them. The noise was deafening, but it was all very exhilarating.

Getting rid of these grenades was just a small part of a huge shedding of equipment before the South Africans finally left Italy. Only small arms were taken back, but all medium and heavy equipment, such as tanks, was left behind. There was a gigantic pile of discarded equipment and I was told I could take whatever I wanted from it. I took a pair of skis, a leather football, a large compass (about 9 inches in diameter), mosquito nets and several other items, almost filling the truck that brought me back to Musadino. I never got to use the skis, and the football had a very short life. I went to the churchyard of San Pietro's, the Musadino village church, to kick it around with Roberto, Riccardo and Flavio, but after a few kicks it was impaled on an iron spike on the perimeter wall and punctured beyond repair.

Around this time, many people in Europe were succumbing to and dying of diseases their bodies could not resist after years of malnutrition. My close friend Dino had died of typhoid and, after a very short illness, Amatore's sister Anita died of meningitis on 17 April 1946. She was 17. She was an intelligent and vivacious girl and her death was as painful to me as it was unexpected. Three days after her death I went to Prè to see Amatore and to offer my condolences. We went for a long walk, ending up in Porto by the lake, and as we were returning we passed the cinema. Amatore said how much Anita had loved films. It was a Saturday afternoon and the cinema was open, so I suggested that we go inside in her memory. When it came to changing the film reels the lights went up and someone we knew, unbeknown to us, spotted us. News of where we had been preceded our return; this caused quite a scandal in the village and poor Amatore caught it in the neck. I tried to take the blame, but I needn't have bothered as I was in trouble myself, and trying to explain that we had done it in memory of Anita didn't wash.

Surprisingly, the cinema in Porto Valtravaglia stayed open throughout the war, even in the darkest days of 1944, and the tickets remained cheap. The only difference, as time went on, was that fewer and fewer men went, particularly young men liable for military service, and like all public places the cinema closed at 8.30 p.m., half an hour before curfew. No doubt one of the reasons that cinemas were kept open was to spread German propaganda. During the German occupation Italian films had vanished to be replaced by German ones, particularly after Rome fell to the Allies, and with it Cine Città. Gradually, the light escapist Italian films featuring the comic Maccario, or entertaining films like *Mamma* starring Beniamino Gigli, were replaced by Nazi propaganda in such films as *Ohm Krüger* (*Uncle Kruger*), an anti-British film about the Boer war, with Queen Victoria portrayed as a cunning old whisky-sodden harridan and Churchill as the fat brutal commandant of a British concentration camp. Another German film shown in Porto was *Jüd Suss* (*Jew Suss*), a period film of quite shockingly virulent anti-Semitism.

Italian newsreels, also, were replaced by German ones; these, on the whole, were factual but much more brutal than Italian or British newsreels. For example, it was first brought home to me how bad conditions were during the Russian winter when I saw footage in early 1944 of a German sentry standing rigidly at his post; he was covered in frost, holding his rifle, and filmed as he was pushed over to demonstrate that he was dead and totally frozen stiff. Apparently the point of this macabre scene was to encourage Germans to give freely to the winter appeal for warm clothing.

23

THE LONG JOURNEY BACK TO LEEDS

After returning from Varese, and after I had received a copy of my birth certificate from Leeds, I went with my father to Milan to get an emergency
travel document, in lieu of a passport, from the British Consulate General.
I then had to get French and Swiss transit visas from their consulates. This meant
endless waiting at all three consulates, but finally everything was in order. All
this was in preparation for my return to Leeds, accompanied by my great-aunt,
Esther Maturi, who had come over from Leeds to visit her relatives at Altipiano.

Once again I had collected many books, plus a stamp collection, but my
father said I could only take one suitcase. So, just as it had been in 1940,
I only had room for three books. I took Manzoni's *I promessi sposi*, Hugo's *Les
Misérables* and a book given to me by the South African captain I was batman
to in Varese: William McDougall's *An Introduction to Social Psychology*, twenty-
third edition, printed in 1936, which I still have. It has the booksellers' sticker,
'J.L.Van Schank Ltd, Pretoria', still in it. One day I was sitting in the captain's
room reading it when he came in, and as I put it down and got up to leave, he
said to me: 'Keep it Peter, I've had that book with me since North Africa but
never quite got round to studying it.' I haven't either, but it is of great senti-
mental value to me when I think of all the battles it has been carried through
and survived, and its slow journey up the length of Italy. Sadly, the captain's
name is not inscribed in it and I have now forgotten it.

My parents assured me that they would bring over the rest of my books, but
as I suspected might be the case, they were all left behind in Italy. No one
could blame them; they had other more important things on their mind.

On the day of my departure I said goodbye to my friends; Roberto gave
me his photograph, wished me luck, and said 'Don't forget us, Peter'. I still

have his photo, although it was almost sixty years before we got in touch again. I said goodbye to my mother and Gloria in Musadino, and my father took me and Great-Aunt Esther down to Porto Valtravaglia to see us off on the train to Bellinzona. I remember the wooden seats in the carriages and passing the spot where my father had traded wood for fish when we were hungry. Then we passed Maccagno, beyond Luino, where the ferry had called on the excursion to Cannóbio. And within a few minutes we were at Zenna, the Italo-Swiss border post. First *Guardia di Finanza* (the Italian passport and customs officers) came on board and there was a very lengthy examination as many Fascists were now trying to flee the country. Then the train moved a few yards and the Swiss frontier guards came on; and they spent an equally long time examining us. All my documents were in perfect order, but I remember feeling very scared in case I was taken off the train because of some minor irregularity.

Our route on the first stage of our journey across Switzerland was Luino–Bellinzona–St Gotthard–Lucerne–Basel, though I cannot now remember whether we changed trains at Bellinzona or whether we stayed on the same train all the way to Zurich. I do, however, remember that at Zenna, while frontier guards were on the train checking our passports, the Italian engine was taken off and a Swiss Federal Railways engine was coupled to our train. It was quite a spectacular journey to Lucerne. From Bellinzona the line goes along the Valle Levantina, via Biasca, Chronico and Faido, crossing and re-crossing the Ticino and through two long spiral tunnels, the Travi and Piantondo tunnels. Just before we started to climb up to the St Gotthard Pass we had a second engine put on our train to cope with the steep gradients. This is one of the finest railway journeys in the world and I enjoyed every minute of it. In all, the St Gotthard Pass railway, in 1946, had 80 tunnels and 324 bridges, with four great spiral tunnels on the south side and three on the north face. We, of course, went through the old tunnel from Airolo to Göschenen, built in 1890 – 15km long; the highest point was mid-tunnel at 1,106m. Looking out of the window fascinated me as we criss-crossed back and forth, often looking down on a section of rail we had traversed, or up to another bridge we would shortly cross. For centuries this great Alpine massif acted as a language barrier; from Airolo and to the south only Italian is spoken, and from Göschenen to the north, only German.

We arrived at Basel, on the River Rhine – the meeting point of France, Germany and Switzerland – just as night was falling. The city was brilliantly lit up; the last time I had seen a city lit up like that was in 1940 when we were in Lisbon, and Basel to me in 1946 looked like a fairytale city. We had a few hours to spare and the shops were still open so, after we had dropped off our luggage at the French station, Esther took me round the city centre. I couldn't believe the sight that met my eyes: shop windows were a blaze of light with luxury goods of every description on display. Esther wanted to buy some Swiss chocolates to take back to England, and my jaw dropped as we walked into a veritable Aladdin's Cave of mouth-watering chocolate.

As soon as we crossed the border into France, on the train to Paris, the scene changed completely and we were plunged back into the nightmare of post Second World War Europe. The journey took the best part of three days with detours and shunting back and forth. Esther had forewarned me of this; nearly every bridge was down and the train had to slow to a crawl across the temporary structures and Bailey bridges. What she hadn't foreseen was how crowded the return journey would be, with many hundreds of Allied soldiers being either demobbed or going on leave. At a couple of stations we had extra carriages attached, forming a very long and overcrowded train. At night we even had soldiers sleeping in the luggage racks. We just slept and ate as best we could where we were sitting, all the way to Paris.

I don't recall seeing any war damage in Paris in the short distance we walked from the Gare de l'Est to the Gare du Nord, where we caught our train to London. The train from Paris was the *Golden Arrow*, which had only resumed running in April 1946. The whole train went on to the cross-Channel Calais to Dover ferry, where you stayed in your seats on the train. Immigration and customs control was at Dover, and for this we had to get off the train. But at last, after I had handed over my emergency travel document to a Special Branch officer, we were back on our way to Waterloo station. At Waterloo I don't recall seeing a single civilian – the entire station was buzzing with serv- icemen and women. The station itself was standing but most of the glass roof had been blown off during the Blitz. From Waterloo we travelled by Tube to Kings Cross to get the train to Leeds, but before doing so I had a quick look round the city centre and saw the extensive damage caused by the Blitz and the 1944 V1s and V2s.

We arrived late at night at Leeds City station, the same station at which, six years earlier, I had stood as a 10-year-old waiting for the sealed diplomatic train to pull in. Uncle Peter was there with his car to meet us and sometime after midnight he drove me to my grandmother's house in Holbeck. There she and my Uncle Louis, who had recently been demobbed from the army, were wait- ing to greet me; my Uncle John was still at sea in the Merchant Navy.

Louis had been called up in 1940; he was British born but, being the son of an enemy alien, had been placed in the Pioneer Corps, along with many other sons of Italians and volunteer German refugee Jews. He had served in Italy and north-east Europe. In Italy he had taken part in Operation Avalanche, the Allied landing at Salerno on 9 September 1943, clearing mines from the beachhead under fire. In early 1944 he was moved back to Britain and subsequently was in one of the twenty-six Pioneer companies that landed on the beaches of Normandy on D-Day.

As soon as I had an identity card issued I was allocated a ration card and clothing coupons, and my Uncle Louis took me into town to buy a complete outfit of clothing: shoes, socks, flannel trousers, tweed sports jacket, a raincoat and an overcoat, shirts and underwear; all my old clothing was thrown out. About a week after this my grandmother had her tailor come to the house with his samples of cloth and he measured me up for a suit.

A few days after my return, while I was waiting for clothing coupons, I went to the yard where I had watched my grandad make ice cream in the 1930s, just as my Uncle Louis was doing in 1946. I had forgotten that salt was used in the freezer surrounding the tub of ice cream. There was a mountain of it piled up on a large wooden tray and it was put into the icy water in the freezer with a shovel as if it were mere dirt. I just stared at what appeared to me to be vast wealth, and I thought that my grandmother must be very rich to have so much salt. In the bitter winter of 1946–47 I was astounded to see cartloads of salt being spread almost daily on the roads; it took me quite a while to grasp that salt had little monetary value and was available in abundance.

According to the Met Office records for that winter, intensely cold conditions affected much of England and Wales in the final week of January; on the morning of the 30th, the temperature at a place in Essex was −20°C and between January and March that year, snow fell every day somewhere in the country for fifty-five days straight. Easterly winds persisted throughout February, with only brief breaks in the cold snowy weather. On no day did the temperature at Kew Observatory top 5°C, and only twice in the month was the night minimum temperature above freezing. In some parts snow fell for twenty-six consecutive days; it was often light and powdery so it was easily whipped up into deep drifts that affected the roads and railway network. At Kew, Nottingham and Edgbaston there was no sun on twenty-two days, and at Kew there was none at all from 2 to 22 February. When skies were clear, night-time temperatures plunged, and if February hadn't been bad enough,

March proved to be even worse. In the first half of the month there were more gales and heavy snowstorms. On 4 and 5 March heavy snow fell over most of England and Wales, with severe drifting. On 6 March drifts were 5m deep in the Pennines and 3m in the Chilterns. In some places, glazed frost occurred. On 10 and 11 March southern Scotland had its heaviest snowfall of the winter, and on the 12th the Scottish Highlands reported drifts more than 7m deep.[1] The odd thing was that I thought this was normal winter weather, as I had been used to Italian mountain weather; I thought that a lot of fuss was being made over nothing, particularly as everyone had such warm clothing and coal fires.

My uncle tried to get me enrolled in a college, but in those days it wasn't so easy and, although I was fluent in both English and Italian, on paper I had only attended primary school and had not even completed that. Having had no formal education or passed any examinations, college was out of the question. Next he tried to get me an apprenticeship, first with an optical firm, and then with Waddingtons the printers. Printing was then an important industry in Leeds, and Waddingtons was a leading producer of playing cards, card games, and printers of many foreign currencies. But it was not to be; no certificates of education, no apprenticeship. So I had to settle for working in a printing shop without an apprenticeship. The result was an enjoyable few months working for Mr Mann, who had a small printing press opposite my grandmother's shop. He specialised in printing wine bottle labels and I was soon operating a manual platen and learning printing from the ground up.

Shortly after I returned to Leeds, I thought I would go back to Longroyd Street, to the house I first remember. I wondered if my childhood friend Peter still lived there. As I walked up Dewsbury Road and across Hunslet Moor, memories came flooding back. There was the *Blooming Rose*, the pub my dad used to go to, and here at last was Longroyd Street, with the primary school at the top, where I had been held down by some of the pupils and made to inhale those pungent smelling salts. Our old house still had the rustic archway over the front gate that my father had made, and the crazy paving he had laid in 1936. I walked on and found my friend's house easily and knocked. Peter's mother came to the door and looked at me enquiringly.

'I'm Peter,' I said. 'Peter Ghiringhelli. We used to live four doors down.'

With a welcoming smile, she said, 'Peter! Peter, do come in, where have you been?'

'Italy,' I said.

Looking back on my time as a boy in Fascist Italy, the good memories outweigh the bad, and I shall never forget the kindness of the people of Musadino in particular, and of the Valtravaglia in general. And perhaps I was lucky, after all, to have spent the war in Italy. On the night of 14 March 1941 Leeds had been bombed and many fires started; 52 people had been killed and nearly 2,000 rendered homeless – and that was just a minor raid compared to what London, Coventry, Liverpool and many other major cities suffered.

Unable to settle in 'civvy street', I joined the Royal Artillery in August 1948, for five years with the colours and seven on reserve, serving in Germany and the Far East. In February 1949, after finishing a training course with the 2nd Battalion Grenadier Guards in Verden, I travelled to Hamburg by train where I was to be picked up by jeep and taken to my unit, the 3rd Regiment Royal Horse Artillery. I got out of the train at what was supposed to be Hamburg station, except that there was no station, just the railway platforms isolated amidst ruins as far as the eye could see.

As for the fate of some of the people I have mentioned, Marshal Rodolfo Graziani managed to stave off being tried until October 1948, and even then it was only for collaboration and not for any war crimes. Sentenced to nineteen years' imprisonment, he served only a few months before being set free on 3 May 1950. His trial represented the final defeat of the Partisans. The courts and regular Royal Army were full of ex-Fascists underlining the *continuità dello stato* (the continuity of the state), and in March 1953 Graziani became the honorary president of the *Movimento sociale italiano*, Italy's postwar neo-fascist party. He died in Rome in January 1955.

At the war's end Renato Ricci, who had headed the Republican Fascist militia, avoided arrest until 28 June 1945. Twice sentenced to thirty years' imprisonment at two trials, he was finally released in 1950 under a general amnesty. In 1955 he became a founder member and vice-president of the neo-fascist Association of Servicemen of the RSI. He died in 1956.

Theodor Emil Saevecke, the sadistic Gestapo chief in Milan, also led a charmed life. He surrendered to the Americans but was released in 1948 and recruited by the American Central Intelligence Agency (CIA), serving as an intelligence agent in Berlin, under the code name 'Cabanio'. He joined the German police in 1952 and rose through the ranks to become the deputy head of the intelligence services of West Germany. Italy made several attempts to extradite him, starting in 1962, but all were unsuccessful. Finally, in July 1999, an Italian court sentenced him in absentia to life imprisonment, but he was not extradited to stand trial or serve his sentence and he died peacefully in his bed in 2004.

As for Bastianini, in early 1944 he took to the mountains – a wanted man both by the Germans and Republican Fascists. At the Verona trial of Ciano and others in 1944, he was condemned to death in absentia but managed to cross the mountain border to safety in Switzerland, where he found refuge. In 1947, having returned to Italy, he was discovered living incognito in Calabria; he was arrested and put on trial in Rome for his Fascist past, but was absolved and acquitted. He died in Milan in 1961. In 2003 he was honoured, along with other Italian Fascist diplomats and military personnel, in the Israeli documentary *Righteous Enemy*, screened at the United Nations, for his part in saving over 40,000 Jews in Yugoslavia while he was governor of Dalmatia, by issuing false documents and helping them get to Switzerland. He himself had said he helped about 2,000.

In 1959 the old rogue had published his memoirs; candid but still blind to the damage that Mussolini had inflicted on Italy, he remained a Fascist of the old school, of the 1920s and '30s, to the end. But he was a modest man and in his memoirs he makes no mention whatever of the good he did as governor of Dalmatia.

My mother and my sister Gloria returned to Leeds in March 1947, and my father in November that year; in the intervening time my sister Christine was born in May. But we were still split up as there wasn't room for us all at my grandmother's house. My mother and Gloria stayed there with Christine, while my father and I shared a furnished room in Chapletown, let to us by one of my parents' friends. In 1953 my father visited his parents, his two brothers and three sisters in France, who he had not seen since he left them as a young lad in 1920. He then went on to Musadino. He returned to Leeds after a month on the continent. It was his last visit; in July 1966 he died of a heart attack, aged 62.

The church of San Martino was rebuilt and re-consecrated; it opened to the public on 24 August 1958. In October 1963, just below the church, a 12m-high monument was erected to the Partisans who had died in the battle of San Martino. Facing it is a crypt, built into the hillside, which contains the bones of the Partisans who had fallen or were executed. The dedicatory plaque says, inter alia, that it is in remembrance of the fallen in 'The first battle of the resistance to the German invader and the fascist usurpers which showed the nation the bloodstained road to independence and freedom'.[2] That small band of Partisans had grown, in round figures, to 200,000 by 1945, of which some 100,000 were actively operative. Casualties had been extremely high, with 45,000 Partisans killed and about 10,000 civilians executed in reprisals. There were some 35,000 female Partisans, young women mainly acting as couriers; of those caught, 2,750 were deported to German concentration camps and 2,812 were shot or hanged in Italy.[3] It had indeed been a long and bloody road.

In 1967 I returned to Musadino for a short visit, but my mother and sister Gloria never went back; much as they loved the people, the memories were still fresh and painful. Much had changed. The cobbled streets were tarmacked, and the roads were full of Lambrettas and Vespa scooters. Many villagers were now working in Milan or Varese, commuting daily. Virginia, Lidia and Fiorito, our next-door neighbours, had emigrated to Argentina. Nearly everyone now spoke formal Italian, and Lombard dialect was almost non-existent. The oxen too had disappeared, a forgotten memory. The family house now had running water and a flushing lavatory. When I mentioned the latrine, and that the contents of the cesspits were used as fertiliser, there were gasps of incredulous disgust.

Our house, with its 'mod cons', was used as a summer vacation home by my French relatives for a number of years, but it has since been sold. The villages were completely transformed in that all houses had running water, most with hot and cold. Sewer and storm drains had been laid with guttering and drain pipes from roofs. Street signs and telephone lines were everywhere, with all the common street furniture that we are now so accustomed to, including signs on ancient buildings explaining what they were and providing the usual architectural details for tourists. The fountain tap opposite the shrine of the Pietà, outside our courtyard door, was still there, a disconnected relic, and many were amazed when I told them that it had been our sole source of water for five years. Many of the old people I had known had since died, and the war seemed a world away. Even the Germans had returned, but now as welcome tourists.

NOTES

1. Pre-war Days in Leeds

1. Giuseppe Bastianini (1899–1961) was a *Fascista della prim'ora* (Fascist of the first hour) and a prominent *Squadrista* leader; he organised the fascist movement in Umbria. In 1921 he was General Vice-Secretary of the PNF (Partito Nazionale Fascista), and from 1923–26 First Secretary of the *Fasci all'estero*. He served in the Diplomatic Service from 1928; Italian Ambassador to Greece: 1929–32; Ambassador to Poland: 1932–36; Under-Secretary for Foreign Affairs, together with Ciano: 1936–39; Ambassador to the UK: 1939–40. Subsequently he was governor of Italian-occupied Dalmatia. He then succeeded Ciano as Foreign Secretary. In July 1943 he voted for the Grandi motion which led to Mussolini's fall.

2. Dino Grandi (1895–1986) was one of the most important leaders of Italian Fascism and a senior member of the national directorate of the movement. He was a major figure in the formulation of Italian Fascist policy. He was Italian Foreign Minister from 1929–32. He was appointed Italian Ambassador to Britain in 1932, a post he held until July 1939. He played an important role in the period 1936 to the 1938 Munich crisis and was behind Chamberlain's request that Mussolini use his influence with Hitler to resolve the Czech crisis of 1938. For this reason, Grandi was held in high esteem in British conservative circles and it also explains the hostility towards him of the Nazis and pro-German Italian Fascists. The invasion of Greece by Italy in October 1940 was a decisive moment for Grandi and from then on, until he succeeded in July 1943, he sought to bring the Fascist dictatorship to an end. At the Verona Trials in 1944 Grandi was condemned to death in absentia by the Nazi-controlled Italian Social Republic.

3. Quoted in Tracy Koon, *Believe, Obey, Fight: Political Socialization of Youth in Fascist Italy*, p. 235; and in D.A. Binchy, *Church and State in Fascist Italy*, p. 651.

4. Quotation from Avro Manhattan, *The Vatican in World Politics*, Chapter 9: 'Italy, the Vatican and Fascism', at www.cephas-library.com/catholic/catholic_vatican_in_world_politics_chpt_9.html.

5. Less than a year later, on 3 May 1937, the *Hindenburg* was destroyed by fire in seconds as it was mooring at Lakehurst, New Jersey. The incident was filmed

and is widely remembered as one of the most dramatic accidents of modern times.

6. See Hansard: H.C. Deb 08 July 1936, vol. 314 cc1183-7, http://hansard.millbank-systems.com/commons/1936/jul/08/german-airship-hindenburg.

2. The Phoney War

1. Amy Johnson, born in Hull in 1903, was everyone's heroine. She was continually breaking long-distance flying records, flying from England to Australia in 1930; to Japan in 1931; and to Cape Town in 1932. She became a pilot in the Air Transport Auxiliary and was drowned in 1941 after bailing out over the Thames estuary.

2. See Clay Blair's *Hitler's U-Boat War*, vol. 1, pp. 66–8. Remarkably for a German submarine, *U-30* survived the war and was scuttled in Flensberger Förd on 5 May 1945.

3. Lord Haw-Haw was the nickname of William Joyce (1902–46). He fled to Germany in 1939 and broadcast from Radio Hamburg until 1945. A dedicated admirer of Hitler and a virulent anti-Semite, he had taken German citizenship but was brought back to England, tried and hanged as a traitor.

3. Italy Declares War

1. For fuller accounts, see Lucio Sponza, *Divided Loyalties*, Chapter 4; and Peter and Leni Gillman, *Collar the Lot!* Chapter 14.

2. Mass Observation, *File Reports*, 184, p. 1, quoted by Sponza, ibid., p. 85.

3. Count Galeazzo Ciano (1903–44) was Mussolini's son-in-law, having married his eldest daughter Edda in 1930. On 9 June 1936 Ciano, then only 33, became Minister for Foreign Affairs and a major power in the Fascist regime. His late entry into the Fascist Party, rapid ascent and strong ambition was resented by the fascist hierarchs and 'Fascists of the First Hour'. He was, however, like many Italian Fascists, strongly anti-German and increasingly his path diverged from Mussolini on that issue and he did his best to forestall the *Patto d'acciao* (the basis of the Axis). At the 24–25 July Grand Council meeting he voted for the Grandi motion which deposed Mussolini. Captured by the Germans, he was put on trial at Verona (8–10 January 1944), and along with other hierarchs who had voted for the Grandi motion, was found guilty and executed. His wife Edda smuggled his diaries out to Switzerland.

4. Egidio Ortona (1910–96), Italian diplomat. Following graduation in law, he entered the diplomatic service in 1932. In 1937 he was posted to the Italian Embassy in London and worked with both Grandi and Bastianini. From 1940–43 he worked in Bastianini's office in Zadar, and in Rome when Bastianini was Foreign Secretary. In November 1944 he was part of the Italian delegation from the southern liberated zone to the United States, and he remained in Washington with the Italian Embassy until 1958. He was the Italian Ambassador to the United Nations from 1958–61.

Ortona returned to Italy in 1961, becoming Director General of Economic Affairs at the Ministry of Foreign Affairs and then Secretary General of the Ministry. In 1967 he was appointed Italian Ambassador in Washington, a post which he held for the next eight years. He retired from the diplomatic service in 1975, subsequently becoming president of the *Istituto per gli Studi di Politica Internazionale* (Institute for International Policy Studies) and published several volumes of his diaries which together cover the years 1937–75.

5. See *l'esodo da Londra del Ambasciata italiana nel 1940*, Ortona, *Storia contemporanea*, 21/1, February 1990, pp. 173–82.
6. Sources: Sponza, *Divided Loyalties: Italians in Britain during the Second World War*, pp. 95–102; the quote regarding the War Office appears in P. and L. Gillman, *Collar the Lot*, p. 153.

4. *Monarch of Bermuda*

1. I remember the title of this atlas, Odham's *The New Pictorial Atlas of the World*, because in 1995 I found and bought a copy of it in a second-hand bookshop in Otley. It would be nice to think that this was my confiscated copy, but mine was probably pulped.
2. Source: Giuseppe Bastianini, *Volevo fermare Mussolini: memorie di un diplomatico fascista*, Preface, p. xiii.

5. *Conte Rosso*

1. See James R. Ross, *Escape to Shanghai: a Jewish Community in Shanghai*, The Free Press, 1994; and Ernest G. Heppner, *Shanghai Refuge: a Memoir of the World War II Jewish Ghetto*, University of Nebraska Press, 1993.
2. See B.J. Crabb, *The Forgotten Tragedy: The Story of the Sinking of HMT Lancastria*, Appendix 9, p. 235; and J. Rohwer, *Chronology of the War at Sea 1939–1945*, entry for 22–25 May 1941.
3. See M. Arthur, *Symbol of Courage: a History of the Victoria Cross*, p. 407.
4. For example, the misreported 'mutiny' on the *Duchess of York*, which was transporting 6,000 German internees (many of them Jews) and POWs. See P. and L. Gillman, *Collar the Lot*, pp. 170–1.
5. Telephone interview with Mr Algerio Cavalli on 24 July 2009.
6. Hansard: Loss of 'Arandora Star', HC Deb 09 July 1940, vol. 362 cc1074-6.
7. P. and L. Gillman, op. cit., Chapter 17: 'The Last Torpedo', pp. 185–201; www. bluestarline.org/arandora.html8.P. and L. Gillman, op. cit., pp. 181, 196.

6. *Arrival in Italy*

1. On 28 October 1922 fascist columns converged on Rome threatening to seize power by force. They could have easily been dispersed by the army, loyal to the king, but the Prime Minister, Luigi Facta, failed to act decisively and King Emmanuel III, fearing an escalation into civil war, decided to revoke a decree of martial law and, after a consultation with those running the country, invited Mussolini to form a government. Mussolini arrived from Milan the next day by train. However, fascist propaganda portrayed this as a heroic event with Mussolini entering Rome on foot at the head of his fascist columns to cheering Romans greeting him as a liberator.

7. *Musadino*
1.   Data from Tracy Koon, *Believe, Obey, Fight*, p. 105.

8. *An Interlude at the Seaside*
1.   J. Rohwer, *Chronology of the War at Sea 1939–1945*.
2.   Venè, *Mille Lire al Mese*, p. 85.

9. *Return to Musadino*
1.   See P. Morgan, *The Fall of Mussolini*, pp. 46–50. Morgan states: 'In 1940, there were, apparently, 230 anti-aircraft batteries in existence, defending ports and airfields but not the cities.'
2.   Karl Clodius was head of the economic section of the German Foreign Ministry. He was arrested in Romania by the Russians in September 1944.

11. *My Father's Return Home*
1.   Venè, *Mille lire al mese*, Chapter V: '*L'Italia va al lavoro*'.

12. *Fall and Rise of Il Duce*
1.   Adelchi Serena (1895–1970). Made Fascist Party Secretary in October 1940, he was dismissed in December 1941. He relinquished fascism in 1943 and as a consequence was sought by both Fascists and the Germans. He successfully stayed in hiding in Rome; after the war he abandoned politics.
2.   Giuseppe Bottai (1895–1959) was a Fascist journalist and minister. He was Minister for Education 1936–43. He voted for the Grandi motion. A warrant for his arrest was issued by the Republican Fascists and he was condemned to death in absentia at the Verona trials in 1944. He escaped to North Africa that same year where he joined the French Foreign Legion under the name 'Bataille'. He served in France and Germany in the last year of the war and in North Africa from 1945 to 1947. He returned to Italy in 1948 under a general amnesty and resumed his journalistic activities in Rome, where he founded the periodical *abc* in 1953. Nevertheless, he remained an unrepentant Fascist to the end.
3.   Marshal Pietro Badoglio (1871–1956) was Chief of the General Staff from November 1939 to December 1940. He was the Italian premier after the fall of Mussolini. After the capture of Rome by the Allies he resigned, returned to private life, and was little more heard of.
4.   I was, of course, unaware of this background and detail until well after the war. Nor had I heard of Colonel Croce and his exploits. The source for much of this is from Daniele Santucci (ed.), *Luoghi e gente di Valtravaglia*; and Francesco Scomazzon, *Maledetti figli di Giuda, vi prenderemo!* p. 23.
5.   *Cinque Giornate* (Five Days) is a reference to the five days of rebellion on 26 March 1848, when the city of Milan rose up against the harsh rule of the occupying Austrians under General Josef Radetzsky, forcing him out of the city for five days. Radetzsky is regarded in Austria as a hero and Strauss composed music in his honour (*The Radetzsky March*). In Italy he is regarded

as the symbol of the long Austrian occupation; he was governor of Milan from 1818 to his death in 1858.

6. The best account is still that given in Deakin, *The Brutal Friendship*, pp. 538–54.
7. Letter dated 4 October 1943. Quoted in Deakin, ibid., p. 588.
8. Theodor Emil Saevecke (1911–2004). In Tunisia, as deputy head of the SD *Einsatzkommando* 'Tunis', he helped perfect gassing vans for Jews.

13. German Occupation and the Battle of San Martino

1. Alessandro Pavolini (1903–45) was a journalist and Fascist of the first hour. He helped draft the Verona Manifesto calling for the execution of all who had voted for the Grandi motion which toppled Mussolini.
2. Translated by the author. Original text: *Al fornaio di Musadino- Consegnerete al latore nostro incaricato, 6 quintali di derrate alimentari (riso) che trovansi giacenti presso di voi e che sono di proprietà dell'Esercito Italiano. A consegna avvenuta saranno segnati a penna i quantitativi sul presente foglio che avrà valore di regolare buono di prelevamenti. Comunicherete verbalmente il totale delle giacenze esistenti presso di voi. Il comandante: t. col. Giustizia- W l'Italia Libera nel mondo liberato.* Source: www.isisluino.it/resistenza/BLOCCO1.html.
3. WO 204/11496. Quoted in R. Lamb, *War in Italy 1943–1945*, p. 316.
4. Source: *Nazi Conspiracy and Aggression*, vol. VIII. USGPO, Washington, 1946, pp. 572–82.

14. Race Laws and Persecution of the Jews

1. See P. Morgan, *The Fall of Mussolini*, p. 127.
2. SS-Obergruppenführer (Major-General) Odilo Globocnik (1904–45). He was in charge of Operation Reinhard, the plan to exterminate all Polish Jews. In 1943 he was transferred to Trieste where he was made Higher SS and Police Chief for the Adriatic region. At the end of the war he evaded arrest but was eventually tracked down in Austria by British troops of the 4th Queens Hussars on 31 May 1945. He committed suicide while being arrested.
3. Translated by the author. Original text and source: *Triangolo Rosso – Journal of the National Association of Political Deportees*, New Series – Year XX, No 2, April 2000.
4. Giovanni Preziosi (1881–1945) was a Catholic priest who was defrocked and excommunicated in 1914. A minor figure on the fringes of the party before 1938, he was considered to be one of the few trustworthy Fascist leaders by Hitler and Nazi officials.
5. R. De Felice, *The Jews in Fascist Italy*, pp. 65–6, 696.
6. Ibid., p. 236.
7. The best account of how the 1938 racial laws affected Italian Jews in the period leading up to the war is that given by Giorgio Bassani in his historical novel *The Garden of the Finzi-Continis*, which is based on the experiences of people he knew.
8. Italo Balbo (1896–1940). One of the most powerful and popular leaders of Italian fascism, he ranked second only to Ciano as Mussolini's possible successor. He had a reputation as a dissident and *frondeur*. Balbo was shot down

over Tobruk by an Italian battery which mistook his aircraft for an enemy intruder.

9. Roberto Farinacci (1892–1945) was an intransigent Blackshirt leader and Fascist hierarch, and an acknowledged leader of the anti-Semitic crusade. He veered more to the right, by 1943 fully supporting German Nazism and all it stood for. Captured by Partisans in April 1945, he was executed by firing squad after a summary trial.

10. De Felice, *The Jews in Fascist Italy*, p. 440.

11. OSCAR: *Operazione Soccorso Cattolico Aiuto Ricercati* (Catholic Assistance Organisation to Help Wanted Persons).

12. Translated by the author. Quoted in Giannantoni, *Maladetti Figli di Giuda, Vi Prenderemo!* p. 109.

13. De Felice, *The Jews in Fascist Italy*, footnote 1182.

15. *The Republic of Salò Slides into Civil War*

1. Marshal Rodolfo Graziani (1882–1955) Viceroy of Ethiopia 1936–37. Commander of the Italian army in Libya 1940–41, he was then dismissed by Mussolini for inefficiency; he resurfaced in July 1943 to become Minister for Defence and Chief of Staff of the RSI armed forces.

2. Renato Ricci (1896–1956) had a reputation as a violent Fascist from 1921. He had links with Himmler through the Fascist militia before July 1943. With Nazi support, he created the GNR, along with Pavolini, and commanded it.

3. J. Holland, *Italy's Sorrow*, Prologue, p. xlv.

4. See Mimmo Franzinelli, *Le stragi nascoste*, p. 362; and http://rete-eco.it/it/documenti/35-riflessioni/6187-onna-e-le-altre-le-stragi-naziste-sulla-linea-gustav.html.

5. WO 235/509, quoted in R. Lamb, *War in Italy*, p. 68.

17. *Death and Destruction from Lake Maggiore to Santa Maria del Taro*

1. The witness was Emilio Ligouri, a lawyer, who after the war became president of the Judicial Court of Verbania.

2. Ferruccio, *S. Maria del Taro e il Monte Penna*, pp. 143–69.

18. *A New Job*

1. Pancrazio De Micheli made a full recovery after several operations. I am indebted to him for providing me with many of the photographs in this book.

2. Quoted in Holland, *Italy's Sorrow*, p. 445.

3. Ian Mitchell, *The Cost of a Reputation*, p. 5.

4. P. Morgan, *The Fall of Mussolini*, p. 129.

5. Graham and Bidwell, *Tug of War – The Battle for Italy: 1943–45*, p. 394.

6. The National Archives, WO 204/7283.

7. General Sir William Jackson, *History of the Second World War – United Kingdom Military Series. The Mediterranean and Middle East*, vol. VI 'Victory in the Mediterranean Part II – June to October 1944', p. 283.

19. The War Ends in Italy

1. Nicola Bombacci (1879–1945) was a founder member of the Italian Communist Party, a member of its Central Committee and the editor of two Communist newspapers. In 1927 he was expelled from the party for 'opportunism'. Isolated from the Communist Party, he slowly moved to support the Fascist regime. He was personally grateful to Mussolini who had helped his son. In 1943 he fled north and became one of Mussolini's advisors. Captured by the Partisans, he was executed at Dongo.

2. Francesco Maria Barracu (1895–1945). He was under-secretary to the Council of Ministers in the Salò Republic. His extreme Fascism led him to accuse Pavolini and other ultra-Fascists of moderation.

3. Achille Starace (1889–1945). Fascist Party Secretary 1931–39, he made himself a public laughing stock and figure of ridicule by issuing a stream of orders, almost daily, such as banning the hand shake in favour of the Fascist salute, and banning foreign words such as 'hotel'. Mounting criticism by the other *gerarchi* finally resulted in his dismissal.

4. P. Morgan, *The Fall of Mussolini*, p. 226.

5. Quoted in Mosley, *The Last Days of Mussolini*, p. 333.

6. No exact figure is known, which has allowed neo-Fascist groups to claim that some 300,000 were killed in a bloodbath. For the estimate of 9,000 and later claims, see Morgan, *The Fall of Mussolini*, p. 218.

7. General Sir William Jackson, *History of the Second World War – United Kingdom Military Series. The Mediterranean and Middle East*, vol. VI 'Victory in the Mediterranean Part III – November 1944 to May 1945', p. 322.

8. Franzinelli, *Le stragi nascoste*, pp. 182–4. There are no sources in English that I know of for these sad events but they are all well documented in Italian and all locations have memorials.

9. WO 204/2190, cited in R. Lamb, *War in Italy 1943–1945*, Appendix L, but wrongly dated 2 May 1944.

20. My Time with the ILH-KR

1. Sources: N. Orpen, *Victory in Italy*; General Sir William Jackson, *History of the Second World War: United Kingdom Military Series*; Linklater, *The Campaign in Italy*.

2. Orpen, op. cit., p. 309.

23. The Long Journey Back to Leeds

1. Source: Met Office at www.metoffice.gov.uk/corporate/pressoffice/anniversary/winter1946-47.html.

2. The full dedication reads:

> From Mount San Martino
> at Italy's furthest frontier
> the first battle of the resistance
> to the German invaders and the Fascist usurpers

showed the nation
the bloodstained road to independence and freedom.

Varese witness and participant
of courageous actions and unspeakable torments
on the twentieth anniversary of the battle
remembers her fallen sons
with pride and gratitude
from the five glorious days of San Martino
to the triumphant day of liberty.

3.   *Alcune cifre sulla Resistenza*: http://it.wikipedia.org/wiki/Resistenza_italiana.

Bibliography

Arthur, Max, *Symbol of Courage: a History of the Victoria Cross*, Sidgwick & Jackson, 2004
Bastianini, Giuseppe, *Volevo fermare Mussolini: Memorie di un diplomatico fascista*, Rizzoli, 2005
Cannistraro, Philip V. (ed.), *Historical Dictionary of Fascist Italy*, Greenwood Press, 1982
De Felice, Roberto, *The Jews in Fascist Italy: a History*, New York, Enigma Books, 2001
Ferrari, Ferrucio (ed.), *S. Maria del Taro e il Monte Penna*, supplement to *L'Eco di Tornolo*, Parma, G. Ferrari & Figli, 1964
Franzinelli, Mimmo, *Delatori – Spie e confidenti anonimi: l'arma segreta del regime fascista*, Mondadori, 2001
Koon, Tracy H., *Believe, Obey, Fight: Political Socialization of Youth in Fascist Italy, 1922–1943*, University of North Carolina Press, 1985
Mitchell, Ian, *The Cost of a Reputation*, Canongate, 1998
Ortona, Efidio, 'L'esoda da Londra dell'Ambasciata italiana nel 1940', *Storia contemporanea*, 21/1, February 1990, pp. 173–82
Rohwer, Jurgen, *Chronology of the War at Sea 1939–1945: the Naval History of World War Two*, Chattam Publishing, revised edition 2005
Santucci, Daniele, *Luoghi e gente della Valtravaglia*, Germignaga, Nastro & Nastro, 2004
Scomazzon, Francesco, *Maledetti figli di Giuda vi prenderemo: La caccia nazifascista agli ebrei in una terra di confine Varese 1943–1945*, Varese, Edizioni Arterigere, 2005
Sponza, Lucio, *Divided Loyalties: Italians in Britain during the Second World War*, Peter Lang, 2000
Venè, Gian Franco, *Mille lire al mese: Vita quotidiana della famiglia nell'Italia fascista*, Mondadori, 1988

INDEX